Sybex's

Study Guid

for Snowflal

SnowPro Core

Certification

Sybex's Study Guide for Snowflake SnowPro Core Certification

COF-C02 EXAM

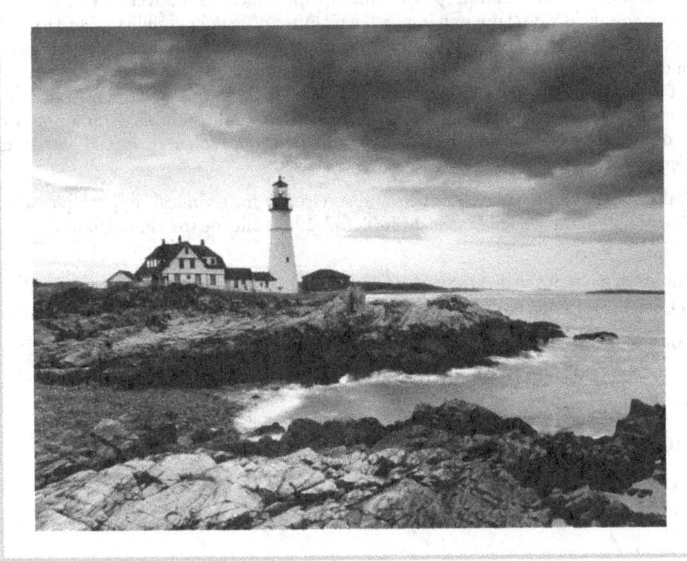

Hamid Mahmood Qureshi

Published by John Wiley & Sons, Inc., Hoboken, New Jersey.

Published simultaneously in Canada.

978-1-119-82444-2
978-1-119-82445-9 (ebk.)
978-1-119-82446-6 (ebk.)

For general information on our other products and services or for technical support, please contact our Customer Care Department within the United States at (800) 762-2974, outside the United States at (317) 572-3993 or fax (317) 572-4002.

Wiley also publishes its books in a variety of electronic formats. Some content that appears in print may not be available in electronic formats. For more information about Wiley products, visit our web site at www.wiley.com.

Library of Congress Control Number: 2022939912

Cover image: © Jeremy Woodhouse/Getty Images
Cover design: Wiley

SKY10038210_110922

To my wife and my children, who have provided support and encouragement throughout the strenuous process of writing this book.

Acknowledgments

Although this book lists my name as author, it would not be in its current form without the absolutely amazing team that contributed to its creation. Acquisitions Editor Devon Cajas got the wheels rolling on this book. Janet Wehner served as project manager, supported by Managing Editor Pete Gaughan and Saravanan Dakshinamurthy, content refinement specialist. Special thanks to the technical editor, Hassaan Sajid, who reviewed each chapter for content, structure, and technical correctness; Nancy Carrasco, who proofread and corrected many of my writing shortcomings; and Christopher Marland, who reviewed the book technically for correctness. Special thanks to all the other people who contributed to this book.

About the Author

Hamid Mahmood Qureshi is a Senior Cloud and Datawarehouse Professional with two decades of experience architecting, designing, and leading the deployment of many data warehouses and business intelligence solutions. He has substantial experience and qualifications with various data analytics systems, including Teradata, Oracle, Hadoop, and modern cloud-based tools like Snowflake. Having worked extensively with traditional technologies. combined with his knowledge of modern platforms, he has accumulated substantial practical expertise in data warehousing and analytics, which he has captured in his publications.

About the Technical Editor

Hassaan Sajid has 13 years of experience in data warehousing and business intelligence (BI/DW) in the retail, telecommunications, banking, insurance, and government sectors. He is currently working at Coles Australia, where his role as a senior technical analyst enables the business to understand the power and value of data. In the past, he has worked with various clients in Australia, UAE, Pakistan, Saudi Arabia, and the United States in multiple BI/DW roles including BI architect, BI developer, ETL developer, data modeler, operations analyst, data analyst, and technical trainer. He holds a master's degree in business intelligence and is a Professional Scrum Master. He is also certified in Snowflake, MicroStrategy, Tableau, Power BI, and Teradata. His hobbies include reading, traveling, and photography.

Contents at a Glance

Contents

Table of Exercises

Introduction

Why should you learn Snowflake? Over the last few years, Snowflake has become increasingly popular with data-led organizations and data enthusiasts. Snowflake is a data warehousing and data analysis platform built for the cloud and has been built from scratch to take full advantage of cloud features. It provides several novel features that changes how you work with data platforms.

With its increasing popularity, learning Snowflake means you increase your standing in the job market. Even if you are already knowledgeable in one or more data warehousing platforms, understanding Snowflake will give you an edge when searching for a new job or aiming for a promotion. Snowflake does not have a steep learning curve because of its simplicity and its use of SQL as the primary language. Once you have grasped the foundations of Snowflake architecture, the rest of the learning naturally flows.

Snowflake has a range of certifications available. SnowPro Core certification is at the foundation level, while other role-specific advanced certifications are also available for focused areas such as data engineering, administration, or data science on the Snowflake platform. The SnowPro Core certification is a prerequisite for the advanced certifications; therefore, it's a good way to kick-start your Snowflake journey.

This book aims to help you pass the SnowPro Core exam. This exam covers all the foundational concepts, such as Snowflake architecture, virtual warehouses, storage, security, Time Travel, cloning, data sharing, and data loading. These topics are emphasized in this book to help you prepare for the exam. Even after you pass the SnowPro Core exam, this book should remain a useful reference for you.

What Is Snowflake?

Snowflake is a relatively new cloud-optimized database, designed primarily for data warehousing solutions on the cloud. Snowflake Inc. was founded in 2012 by three data warehousing experts: Benoit Dageville, Thierry Cruanes, and Marcin Zukowski. Snowflake was designed from the ground up as a cloud-only data warehouse platform.

A significant advantage of the Snowflake platform compared to other data warehouses is its differentiated architecture. Snowflake takes full advantage of the underlying cloud platform's novel features. The outcome is a hybrid architecture in which the computation or processing layer can be scaled independently of the storage layer. Snowflake's hybrid architecture also brings out a unique array of features not seen in many other databases, introducing concepts such as zero-copy cloning, Time Travel, and secure data sharing.

Why Become SnowPro Core Certified?

There are several good reasons to get your SnowPro Core certification:

Professional Development Certifications are an easy pathway for continuous professional development and adding to your skillset. Because the SnowPro Core certification exam tests all the foundational concepts of Snowflake, even preparing for the exam will give you enough technical skills to develop Snowflake-based solutions.

Increases Your Marketability SnowPro Core certification increases your marketability to prospective employers. SnowPro Core certified candidates may negotiate a better starting salary because hiring businesses don't need to spend on training and upskilling such candidates.

Takes You a Step Closer to Advanced Certifications The SnowPro Core exam is a steppingstone to several advanced Snowflake certifications, such as SnowPro Advanced Data Engineer. Gaining the SnowPro Core certification will allow you to undertake any of the advanced Snowflake certifications suited to your line of work.

Provides Proof of Professional Achievement Organizations recognize the importance and benefits of certifications such as SnowPro Core and are increasingly encouraging their employees to obtain certification. As a result, a growing number of individuals add the SnowPro Core certifications to their professional profiles every day.

Raises Employer Confidence Management is more confident to take on significant initiatives and work for new clients when they have faith in the team's skills. Certifications are a great way to instill the skills in your team and gain management's confidence. If you can prove you have the necessary skills, they are more likely to undertake new initiatives and likely to put you in charge with confidence in your skills.

How to Become SnowPro Core Certified

The SnowPro Core certification is available to anyone who wishes to take the exam. There are no prerequisites; however, it is recommended that you develop an understanding and experience of the Snowflake platform with self-study and by performing hands-on exercises and experimentation with the Snowflake platform.

Snowflake's SnowPro Certification exam is administered by Pearson Vue, and you can take it in any of the 1,000+ testing centers worldwide or at home with a virtual proctor.

To register for the exam with Pearson Vue, visit `https://home.pearsonvue.com/snowflake`. You will need to register for a new account. Once you do, you can schedule your SnowPro Core exam.

Finally, Snowflake exam policies are subject to change. Please be sure to check `www.snowflake.com/certifications` for the current policies before you register and take the exam.

Like all exams, the SnowPro Core certification from Snowflake is updated periodically and may eventually be retired or replaced. At some point after Snowflake is no longer offering this exam, the old editions of our books and online tools will be retired. If you have purchased this book after the exam was retired, or are attempting to register in the Sybex online learning environment after the exam was retired, please know that we make no guarantees that this exam's online Sybex tools will be available once the exam is no longer available.

Who Should Buy This Book

This book is useful for anyone who wishes to pass the SnowPro Core certification exam. If you're new to Snowflake, this book provides the basics you'll need to learn Snowflake from scratch. The book also provides in-depth information you need to complete the exam.

How This Book Is Organized

This book consists of 10 chapters plus supplementary information, including a glossary and an assessment test, which follows this introduction. The chapters are organized as follows:

Chapter 1, "Introduction and Overview," covers the history of Snowflake and discusses the various Snowflake certifications with a focus on the SnowPro Core certification.

Chapter 2, "Snowflake Architecture," provides a detailed understanding of the unique Snowflake architecture, how the storage is decoupled from the compute, how data is stored in the form of micro-partitions, and the advantages of this unique architecture. The chapter also covers the critical architectural layers in Snowflake.

Chapter 3, "Interfaces and Connectivity," talks about various interfaces, focusing on Snowflake web interfaces and SnowSQL, through which a user can interact with a Snowflake instance. The chapter also describes various connectors and drivers that can be used to connect to Snowflake. Finally, the chapter discusses the partner ecosystem in Snowflake.

Chapter 4, "Loading Data," discusses the variety of methods provided by Snowflake for loading data, including bulk data loading and processing data in a continuous manner. This chapter walks you through the concept of staging in Snowflake, describing the internal and external stage types. The chapter also discusses loading semi-structured data, basic data transformations, and exporting data from Snowflake.

Chapter 5, "Data Pipelines," discusses Snowflake's capability to schedule SQL statements and stored procedures through the concept of tasks. The chapter also touches on streams, which is Snowflake's method of providing change data capture.

Chapter 6, "Continuous Data Protection," covers the components of continuous data protection and explores Time Travel, Fail-Safe, and the undrop functionality, which are Snowflake features that help protect and recover data in the event of human error. The chapter also covers the concept of transient and temporary tables.

Chapter 7, "Cloning and Data Sharing," describes zero-copy cloning and how it works behind the scenes. The chapter then explores data sharing and the three approaches to data sharing in Snowflake.

Chapter 8, "Performance," focuses on the performance optimization features and techniques that you can use to improve query performance and, at times, reduce costs. The chapter covers scaling up and down a virtual warehouse and autoscaling a virtual warehouse to accommodate increased concurrency. This chapter also touches on data clustering and materialized views, which can be used to optimize query execution.

Chapter 9, "Security," explains several Snowflake features that enable security at various levels in the Snowflake software stack. The chapter discusses security implementation starting from the data storage layer to other levels such as authentication control, data access control or authorization, and network-level controls to manage access to your Snowflake instance.

Chapter 10, "Account and Resource Management," covers the prebuilt views and table functions that enable Snowflake customers to keep track of their Snowflake credit and storage usage. The chapter also discusses resource monitors used for tracking and managing credit usage. Finally, the chapter discusses Snowflake's release management processes.

Chapter Features

Each chapter begins with a list of the SnowPro Core exam objectives that are covered in that chapter. The book doesn't cover the objectives in order, so you shouldn't be alarmed at some of the odd ordering of the objectives within the book.

Each chapter has exercises that apply the newly taught material. At the conclusion of each chapter, you will find two exam preparation tools:

Exam Essentials This section provides a summary of the key information presented in the chapter. You should have a complete grasp of the information summarized in this section.

Review Questions Each chapter concludes with a set of review questions. You should answer these questions and compare your response against the provided answers. If you are unable to correctly answer at least 80 percent of these questions, you should revisit the chapter or at least the areas that you do not fully understand.

The review questions, assessment test, and other testing elements in this book are not derived from the SnowPro Core exam questions; therefore, you should not memorize the answers and assume that doing so would enable you to pass the exam. You should study the fundamentals and understand the concepts, which will enable you to answer the exam questions and pass the SnowPro Core exam. Learning the underlying topics is also the approach that will serve you best in the workplace—the ultimate goal of certification exams.

Bonus Digital Contents

This book is accompanied by an online learning environment that provides several additional elements. Items available among these companion files include the following:

Practice Tests All of the questions in this book appear in our proprietary digital test engine—including the 30-question assessment test at the end of this introduction and the questions that make up the review question sections at the end of each chapter. In addition, there is a 100-question practice exam.

Electronic "Flashcards" The digital companion files include 170 questions in flashcard format (a question followed by a single correct answer). You can use these to review your knowledge of the SnowPro Core exam objectives.

Glossary The key terms from this book, and their definitions, are available as a fully searchable PDF.

Interactive Online Learning Environment and Test Bank

You can access all these resources at `www.wiley.com/go/sybextestprep`.

Conventions Used in This Book

This book uses certain typographic styles in order to help you quickly identify important information and to avoid confusion over the meaning of words such as on-screen prompts. In particular, look for the following styles:

- *Italicized text* indicates key terms that are described at length for the first time in a chapter. (Italics are also used for emphasis.)
- `A monospaced font` indicates SQL code, contents of files, filenames, and Internet URLs.

In addition to these text conventions, which can apply to individual words or entire paragraphs, a few conventions highlight segments of text:

A note indicates information that's useful or interesting but that's somewhat peripheral to the main text.

A tip provides information that can save you time or frustration and that may not be entirely obvious. A tip might describe how to get around a limitation or how to use a feature to perform an unusual task.

Sidebars

A sidebar is like a note but longer. The information in a sidebar is useful, but it doesn't fit into the main flow of the text.

Real World Scenario

Real-World Scenario

A real-world scenario is a type of sidebar that describes a task or example that's particularly grounded in the real world. This may be a situation I or somebody I know has encountered, or it may be advice on how to work around problems that are common in real, working Snowflake environments.

EXERCISES

An exercise is a procedure you should try on your own to help you learn about the material in the chapter. Don't limit yourself to the procedures described in the exercises, though! Tinker with different Snowflake features to really learn about Snowflake.

SnowPro Study Guide Exam Objectives

Sybex's Study Guide for Snowflake SnowPro Core Certification has been written to cover every SnowPro exam objective at a level appropriate to its exam weighting. The following table provides a breakdown of this book's exam coverage, showing you the weight of each section and the chapter where each objective or subobjective is covered:

Subject Area	% of Exam
Snowflake Cloud Data Platform Features and Architecture	20–25%
Account Access and Security	20–25%
Performance Concepts	10–15%
Data Loading and Unloading	5–10%
Data Transformations	20–25%
Data Protection and Data Sharing	5–10%

Domain 1.0: Snowflake Cloud Data Platform Features and Architecture

Exam Objective	Chapter(s)
1.1 Outline key features of the Snowflake Cloud Data Platform	1, 2, 3, 7
▪ Elastic Storage	1, 2
▪ Elastic Compute	1, 2
▪ Snowflake's three distinct layers	2
▪ Data Cloud/Data Exchange/Partner Network	3, 7
▪ Cloud partner categories	3
1.2 Outline key Snowflake tools and user interfaces	3
▪ Snowflake User Interfaces (UI)	3
▪ Snowsight	3
▪ Snowflake connectors	3
▪ Snowflake drivers	3
▪ SQL scripting	3
▪ Snowpark	3
1.3 Outline Snowflake's catalog and objects	3, 4, 5, 6, 7, 8, 9
▪ Databases	4
▪ Schemas	4
▪ Tables Types	6
▪ View Types	8, 9
▪ Data types	4

Exam Objective	Chapter(s)
▪ User-Defined Functions (UDFs) and User Defined Table Functions (UDTFs)	3
▪ Stored Procedures	3
▪ Streams	5
▪ Tasks	5
▪ Pipes	4
▪ Shares	7
▪ Sequences	4
1.4 Outline Snowflake storage concepts	**2, 8, 10**
▪ Micro partitions	2
▪ Types of column metadata clustering	2, 8
▪ Data Storage Monitoring	10
▪ Search Optimization Service	8

Domain 2.0: Account Access and Security

Exam Objective	Chapter(s)
2.1 Outline compute principles	**9**
▪ Network security and policies	9
▪ Multi-Factor Authentication (MFA)	9
▪ Federated authentication	9
▪ Single Sign-On (SSO)	9
2.2 Define the entities and roles that are used in Snowflake	**9**
▪ Outline how privileges can be granted and revoked	9
▪ Explain role hierarchy and privilege inheritance	9

Exam Objective	Chapter(s)
2.3 Outline data governance capabilities in Snowflake	**7, 9, 10**
▪ Accounts	9
▪ Organizations	9
▪ Databases	9
▪ Secure views	7, 9
▪ Information schemas	10
▪ Access history and read support	10

Domain 3.0: Performance Concepts

Exam Objective	Chapter(s)
3.1 Explain the use of the Query Profile	**8**
▪ Explain plans	8
▪ Data spilling	8
▪ Use of the data cache	8
▪ Micro-partition pruning	8
▪ Query history	8
3.2. Explain virtual warehouse configurations	**2, 8**
▪ Multi-clustering	8
▪ Warehouse sizing	2, 8
▪ Warehouse settings and access	2, 8
3.3 Outline virtual warehouse performance tools	**8, 10**
▪ Monitoring warehouse loads	8
▪ Query performance	8
▪ Scaling up compared to scaling out	8
▪ Resource monitors	10

Exam Objective	Chapter(s)
3.4 Optimize query performance	8
▪ Describe the use of materialized views	8
▪ Use of specific SELECT commands	8

Domain 4.0: Data Loading and Unloading

Exam Objective	Chapter(s)
4.1 Define concepts and best practices that should be considered when loading data	4
▪ Stages and stage types	4
▪ File size	4
▪ File formats	4
▪ Folder structures	4
▪ Adhoc/bulk loading using the Snowflake UI	4
4.2 Outline different commands used to load data and when they should be used	4, 5
▪ CREATE PIPE	4
▪ COPY INTO	4
▪ GET	4
▪ INSERT/INSERT OVERWRITE	4
▪ PUT	4
▪ STREAM	5
▪ TASK	5
▪ VALIDATE	4
4.3 Define concepts and best practices that should be considered when unloading data	4
▪ File formats	4
▪ Empty strings and NULL values	4

Exam Objective	Chapter(s)
▪ Unloading to a single file	4
▪ Unloading relational tables	4
4.4 Outline the different commands used to unload data and when they should be used	4
▪ LIST	4
▪ COPY INTO	4
▪ CREATE FILE FORMAT	4
▪ CREATE FILE FORMAT . . . CLONE	4
▪ ALTER FILE FORMAT	4
▪ DROP FILE FORMAT	4
▪ DESCRIBE FILE FORMAT	4
▪ SHOW FILE FORMAT	4

Domain 5.0: Data Transformation

Exam Objective	Chapter(s)
5.1 Explain how to work with standard data	3, 4
▪ Estimating functions	4
▪ Sampling	4
▪ Supported function types	4
▪ User-Defined Functions (UDFs) and stored procedures	3
5.2 Explain how to work with semi-structured data	4
▪ Supported file formats, data types, and sizes	4
▪ VARIANT column	4
▪ Flattening the nested structure	4
5.3 Explain how to work with unstructured data	4
▪ Define and use directory tables	4
▪ SQL file functions	4
▪ Outline the purpose of User-Defined Functions (UDFs) for data analysis	4

Domain 6.0: Data Protection and Data Sharing

Exam Objective	Chapter(s)
6.1 Outline Continuous Data Protection with Snowflake	6, 7
▪ Time Travel	6
▪ Fail-safe	6
▪ Data Encryption	6
▪ Cloning	7
▪ Replication	6, 7
6.2 Outline Snowflake data sharing capabilities	7
▪ Account types	7
▪ Data Marketplace and Data Exchange	7
▪ Private data exchange	7
▪ Access control options	7
▪ Shares	7

How to Contact the Publisher

If you believe you have found a mistake in this book, please bring it to our attention. At John Wiley & Sons, we understand how important it is to provide our customers with accurate content, but even with our best efforts an error may occur.

In order to submit your possible errata, please email it to our Customer Service Team at `wileysupport@wiley.com` with the subject line "Possible Book Errata Submission."

Assessment Test

1. Which is the term used for Snowflake's architecture composed of shared storage and multiple compute engines?

   A. Multi-cluster shared data

   B. Hybrid architecture

   C. Multicompute architecture

   D. Shared Storage, multicompute

2. Which of the following are layers in Snowflake architecture? (Select all that apply.)

   A. On-Premises layer

   B. Database Storage

   C. Query Processing

   D. Cloud Services

3. Which of the following is true regarding micro-partitions? (Select all that apply.)

   A. Each micro-partition contains 50 MB to 500 MB of uncompressed data.

   B. Micro-partitions are immutable.

   C. Snowflake automatically compresses data in a micro-partition.

   D. Each micro-partition contains 1 MB to 5 MB of uncompressed data.

4. Which of the following is true regarding data clustering in Snowflake? (Select all that apply.)

   A. Data in a Snowflake table cannot be reclustered.

   B. Snowflake automatically clusters data in a table.

   C. If required, clustering keys can be defined to recluster the data.

   D. Snowflake does not automatically cluster data in a table.

5. Which of the following are Snowflake's Data Integration partners? (Select all that apply.)

   A. Collibra

   B. Matillion

   C. Informatica

   D. Power BI

6. What is the command-line tool for connecting to Snowflake?

   A. Snowpipe

   B. SnowSQL

   C. SnowCD

   D. Snow Mobile

7. You are required to load data from a named internal stage into a Snowflake table. Which command should you use?

   A. `GET`

   B. `VALIDATE`

   C. `COPY`

   D. `PUT`

8. You need to upload data from an on-premises system to a named internal stage. Which command should you use?

   A. `GET`

   B. `PUT`

   C. `COPY`

   D. `VALIDATE`

9. Which of the following can be used to load streaming or real-time data in Snowflake?

   A. `GET`

   B. Snowpipe

   C. `COPY`

   D. `PUT`

10. Snowflake supports which semi-structured file formats? (Select all that apply.)

    A. DOM

    B. Avro

    C. ORC

    D. XML

11. True or False: Data in an internal stage contributes to overall storage costs.

    A. False

    B. True

12. True or False: The `VARIANT` data type can store any type of data.

    A. False

    B. True

13. True or False: Snowpipe can load data from an internal or an external stage.

    A. True

    B. False

14. Snowflake tasks can execute which of the following? (Select all that apply.)

    A. A single SQL statement

    B. Snowpipe

    C. A call to a stored procedure

    D. Automatic clustering

15. Which of the following correctly describes streams in Snowflake? (Select all that apply.)
    - **A.** They are used to track data changes made to a table, including inserts, updates, and deletes.
    - **B.** They are used as a queuing mechanism for user queries.
    - **C.** They are used for change data capture (CDC).
    - **D.** They are used to load data in a real-time manner.
16. What is the minimum Snowflake edition that allows up to 90 days of Time Travel?
    - **A.** Standard Edition
    - **B.** Virtual Private Snowflake
    - **C.** Enterprise Edition
    - **D.** Business Critical Edition
17. Which of the following commands will let you recover dropped tables, schemas, and databases?
    - **A.** `UNDROP`
    - **B.** `RECOVER`
    - **C.** `CREATE`
    - **D.** `TIME TRAVEL`
18. True or False: Cloning and Time Travel can be combined to create clones of data that exist at a certain time.
    - **A.** False
    - **B.** True
19. Which layer in Snowflake architecture is responsible for data sharing?
    - **A.** Query Processing
    - **B.** Data Sharing
    - **C.** Cloud Services
    - **D.** Cloud Storage
20. True or False: The compute charges are billed to the data consumer when sharing data with another Snowflake account.
    - **A.** True
    - **B.** False
21. True or False: Data Exchange is your own private data sharing hub where you can share data with an invite-only group of people.
    - **A.** True
    - **B.** False

22. Which scaling policy ensures maximum performance?
    - A. Standard
    - B. Economy
    - C. Performance
    - D. Maximum

23. True or False: If a query has been run before and the underlying data hasn't changed, the query result cache is used to fulfill results for a semantically similar query.
    - A. True
    - B. False

24. What is the name of the service responsible for redistributing data according to the clustering key?
    - A. Redistribution Engine
    - B. Snowflake Optimizer
    - C. Automatic Clustering
    - D. Clustering Engine

25. True or False: All data at rest in Snowflake is encrypted using AES 256-bit encryption.
    - A. True
    - B. False

26. What of the following roles are built into Snowflake roles? (Select all that apply.)
    - A. SECURITYADMIN
    - B. PUBLIC
    - C. SYSADMIN
    - D. SNOWFLAKEADMIN

27. True or False: Network policies can be used to allow or deny access to specific IP addresses.
    - A. True
    - B. False

28. Which of the following is true regarding resource monitors?
    - A. They help manage user workload on the system.
    - B. They help manage costs and avoid unexpected credit usage by virtual warehouses.
    - C. They help manage costs and avoid unexpected storage usage.
    - D. They are used to allow or deny users access to Snowflake.

29. Which of the following statements are correct regarding data retention and latency for the ACCOUNT_USAGE schema? (Select all that apply.)
    - A. It has no latency.
    - B. It has 365 days of retention.
    - C. It has 45 minutes to 3 hours of latency.
    - D. It has 30 days of retention.

30. How often does Snowflake release new software?
    - A. Fortnightly
    - B. Yearly
    - C. Weekly
    - D. Monthly

Answers to Assessment Test

1. A. Snowflake uses a hybrid architecture approach in which the data is stored on a shared-data storage layer, but multiple compute clusters can simultaneously perform processing on that data. The architecture is often referred to as multi-cluster, shared-data architecture. For more information, see Chapter 2.

2. B, C, D. Snowflake's architecture comprises of database storage layer, query processing layer and cloud services layer. For more information, see Chapter 2.

3. A, B, C. Micro-partitions in Snowflake are immutable and contain 50 to 500 MB of uncompressed data. However, Snowflake compresses the data before storing it in a micro-partition. For more information, see Chapter 2.

4. B, C. Snowflake automatically clusters data in a table; however, clustering keys can be defined to change the clustering behavior if needed. For more information, see Chapter 2.

5. B, C. Snowflake has several integration partners, Matillion and Informatica being two examples. For more information, see Chapter 3.

6. B. SnowSQL is the command-line tool through which you can connect to your Snowflake instance and run queries. For more information, see Chapter 3.

7. C. The `COPY` command loads data from internal and external stages into a Snowflake table. The `COPY` command is also used to export data from a table. For more information, see Chapter 4.

8. B. You will need to use the `PUT` command through SnowSQL or a similar client. `PUT` transfers data from an on-premises system to a Snowflake internal stage. Similarly, `GET` is used to download data from a Snowflake internal stage to an on-premises system. For more information, see Chapter 4.

9. B. Snowpipe is the Snowflake service used for loading near-realtime data into Snowflake. For more information, see Chapter 4.

10. B, C, D. Snowflake supports several semi-structured file formats. Avro, ORC & XML are some of the examples of the supported file formats. For more information, see Chapter 4.

11. B. Data in an internal stage is stored and managed by Snowflake, therefore contributing to the overall storage costs. For more information, see Chapter 4.

12. B. That is true. VARIANT is a versatile data type that can store any data. The VARIANT data type is used often for processing semi-structured. For more information, see Chapter 4.

13. A. That is correct. Snowpipe can load near real-time data from an internal or external stage. For more information, see Chapter 4.

14. A, C. Tasks in Snowflake can be used to execute a single SQL statement, call a stored procedure or procedural logic using Snowflake Scripting. For more information, see Chapter 5.

15. A, C. Streams are used to track data changes made to a table and can be used for CDC. For more information, see Chapter 5.

16. C. 90 days of Time Travel is supported from the Enterprise edition and above. For more information, see Chapter 6.

17. A. The `UNDROP` command is used to recover tables, schemas, and databases that have been dropped. For more information, see Chapter 6.

18. B. Cloning and Time Travel can be combined to produce clones of tables, schemas, and databases as they existed at a point in time. For more information, see Chapter 7.

19. C. Data sharing is a metadata-only operation; therefore, the cloud services layer is responsible for data sharing. For more information, see Chapter 7.

20. A. That is correct. When data is shared with another Snowflake account, the data consumer pays for the compute costs; however, the storage costs are billed to the data provider. For more information, see Chapter 7.

21. A. Data Exchange is one of the ways data sharing can be achieved. Data Exchange provides private sharing capabilities. For more information, see Chapter 7.

22. A. Of the two scaling policies, Standard and Economy, Standard ensures maximum performance. For more information, see Chapter 8.

23. A. The query result cache returns results of queries if the underlying data hasn't changed and the query matches another query that has been executed before. For more information, see Chapter 8.

24. C. Automatic clustering takes care of clustering behind the scenes. For more information, see Chapter 8.

25. A. That is correct. All data at rest in Snowflake is encrypted using AES 256-bit encryption. For more information, see Chapter 9.

26. A, B, C. Snowflake has several built-in roles, including PUBLIC, SYSADMIN, and SECURTYADMIN. For more information, see Chapter 9.

27. A. That is correct. Network policies can be used to restrict or allow access to IP addresses. For more information, see Chapter 9.

28. B. Resource monitors track and manage costs and help avoid unexpected costs. For more information, see Chapter 10.

29. B, C. The views in ACCOUNT_USAGE schema have 365 days of data retention; however, they have 45 to 3 hours of latency, depending on the view being used. For more information, see Chapter 10.

30. C. Snowflake releases new features, updates, and fixes every week. For more information, see Chapter 10.

Introduction and Overview

THE SNOWPRO CORE EXAM TOPICS COVERED IN THIS CHAPTER INCLUDE THE FOLLOWING:

✓ **Domain 1.0: Snowflake Data Platform Features and Architecture**

- 1.1 Outline key features of the Snowflake Cloud Data platform.
  - Elastic Storage
  - Elastic Compute

In this chapter, you learn the history of Snowflake and an overview of the Snowflake journey so far. We also discuss the various Snowflake certifications and focus on the SnowPro Core certification.

Introducing Snowflake

Snowflake is a relatively new database that has been built specifically for the cloud and is geared primarily toward data warehousing solutions. Snowflake has been built from scratch as a cloud-only data warehousing platform. A significant advantage of the Snowflake platform compared to other data warehouses is its differentiated architecture. Unlike several other database engines designed to work on the cloud, Snowflake takes full advantage of the cloud platform's novel features. The result is a hybrid architecture in which the compute or the processing layer can be scaled up and down independently of the scaling of storage. This powerful and cost-effective capability allows customers to acquire additional processing power when they need it. Once the required workloads are processed, customers can return to a lower processing state to conserve costs.

The hybrid architecture of Snowflake also brings out a unique array of features not seen in other databases, introducing concepts such as the following:

Time Travel Snowflake enables users to retrieve data as it existed at a point in time or before a data modification query was run. The Snowflake Time Travel feature allows some fascinating use cases, such as the ability to recover data corrupted due to incorrect queries or the ability to track how data changed over time. Combining Time Travel with cloning provides a compelling feature that can be used for debugging or standing up development or testing environments based on the historical point of view of data.

Zero-Copy Cloning Zero-copy cloning enables users to make complete copies of tables or even databases without making a physical copy. Zero-copy cloning is a metadata operation that points cloned tables to the existing table storage, thus reducing additional storage requirements. Snowflake manages the original table and the cloned table independently, so data changes to either table can be made without affecting the other table. Zero-copy cloning can be combined with Time Travel to allow cloning of tables as they existed at a point in time.

Secure Data Sharing Snowflake provides data sharing capability without actually moving the data. The result is that shared data is always up-to-date. Any changes made by the data provider are automatically and instantaneously available to the consumer of the shared data. Several sharing methods are available, including direct data sharing, Snowflake Data Marketplace, and private data exchange.

Snowflake Journey

Snowflake Inc. was founded in 2012 by three data warehousing experts: Benoit Dageville, Thierry Cruanes, and Marcin Zukowski. Dageville and Cruanes previously worked as data architects at Oracle Corporation; Zukowski was a co-founder of Vectorwise. The company's name was chosen as a tribute to the founders' love of snow sports. Snowflake came out of stealth mode in October 2014 and became generally available (GA) in June 2015, with about 80 customers. Snowflake was listed as No. 2 on *Forbes* magazine's Cloud 100 list and was ranked No. 1 on LinkedIn's 2019 U.S. list of Top Startups. In May 2019, Frank Slootman joined Snowflake as its new CEO, and in September 2020, Snowflake went public and saw a massive uptake of its stock, essentially doubling in value immediately on IPO. Tycoons like Warren Buffett invested as part of the IPO, and Snowflake's IPO was the highest valued software IPO ever. At the start of 2022, Snowflake had 5,900 active customers and it has a constantly expanding customer base.

Snowflake Certifications

Snowflake offers a variety of certifications (Figure 1.1). As you can see, these certifications range from the fundamental SnowPro Core certification to the more advanced role-specific certifications.

SnowPro Core certification is the foundational certification. As of this writing, this certification was a prerequisite for all advanced certifications. The SnowPro Core certification exam evaluates the candidate's fundamental abilities of understanding and implementing a Snowflake-based solution. A certified individual demonstrates a comprehensive understanding of the Snowflake architecture and its working as a cloud data warehouse and has the skills to design, develop, and manage a Snowflake solution.

At a high level, concepts for the following subject areas are tested in the SnowPro Core exam:

Snowflake Overview and Architecture This subject area, among the most critical aspects of the exam, deals with the basics of the Snowflake architecture, including the

FIGURE 1.1 Snowflake certification map

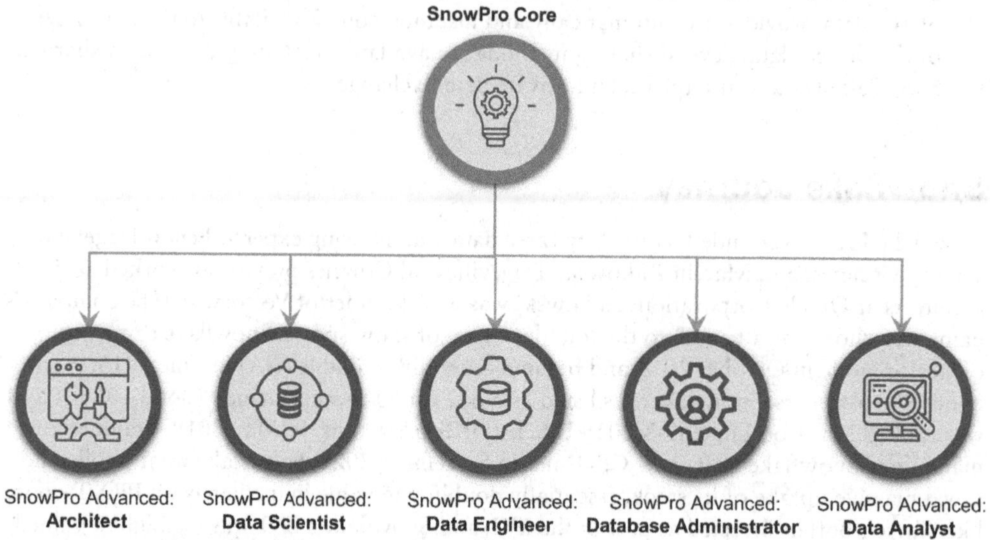

hybrid architecture approach, the concept of decoupled compute and storage, the three primary layers in the Snowflake architecture, data storage in Snowflake using micro-partitions, and the basics of how virtual warehouses or the compute layer works. The overview also elaborates on Snowflake pricing, the Snowflake support model, Snowflake partners, the update process, and other concepts such as the interfaces to Snowflake.

Virtual Warehouses An equally important area is a detailed understanding of the virtual warehouse concept in Snowflake. The exam tests the candidate's ability to understand multi-cluster virtual warehouses, scaling up, scaling down, scaling across virtual warehouses, pausing or resuming existing virtual warehouses, and creating as many virtual warehouses as required. The concepts around the pricing and consumption through Snowflake credits and the understanding of the impact of the virtual warehouse size on the credit consumption are also evaluated.

Snowflake Storage and Protection This subject area deals with understanding how Snowflake stores its data using the novel micro-partitioning strategy, using columnar storage and compression. Snowflake also employs concepts such as Time Travel, fail-safe, cloning, and sharing related to micro-partitioning-based storage. A candidate undertaking the SnowPro Core certification is expected to understand these concepts thoroughly.

Data Loading and Unloading The SnowPro Core exam also evaluates the candidate's ability to load data into Snowflake using the bulk copy method and streaming data loading using Snowpipe. Also tested is the ability to extract or unload data from a Snowflake-based system and the data pipeline concept through Snowflake tasks and streams.

Semi-Structured and Unstructured Data This subject area relates to Snowflake's native capability to load and process semi-structured data such as JavaScript Object Notation (JSON) and Apache Parquet. The FLATTEN function and the VARIANT data type used to process and transform semi-structured data are of particular significance. It also covers how unstructured data is handled in Snowflake using URLs, directory tables, and UDFs.

Snowflake Account and Security The account's security and management, including resource management, are also essential concepts evaluated in the SnowPro Core exam. Concepts evaluated include fundamentals of role-based access management (RBAC), permissions, multifactor authentication, and cost management through resource monitors.

Snowflake Performance and Tuning The SnowPro Core exam also touches on basic performance optimization techniques, including optimizing data ingestion jobs by splitting files into the most efficient sizes, making changes to table cluster keys to enable better partition pruning, and scaling up/down/across virtual warehouses to improve performance and response times.

Signing Up for a Snowflake Trial

The concepts in this book are explained in a hands-on manner, so the expectation is that students attempt the exercises in each chapter. The first step to ensure that you can attempt the upcoming exercise is to sign up for a Snowflake trial instance. As of this book's writing, Snowflake offered trial instances with $400 of credit to use within that trial instance with a 30-day expiry. The trial does not require credit card information; however, after 30 days, you must add credit card information to continue using the instance.

Snowflake is available on three cloud platforms: Amazon Web Services (AWS), Microsoft Azure, and Google Cloud Platform. Your choice of cloud platform depends on your requirements and where the rest of your cloud infrastructure is placed. Ideally, you should choose the cloud platform on which all or most of your cloud infrastructure is hosted. This is, of course, generic advice, and your organization's circumstances, where its data is, and your future cloud strategy will influence your choice.

The Snowflake platform is available in four different editions, each with different pricing and a slightly different feature set. You can find the latest information on the Snowflake editions here:

`www.snowflake.com/pricing`

Standard The Standard edition of Snowflake provides all the basics of a cloud-based data warehousing solution. These include complete SQL data warehouse capabilities, data sharing, data encryption in transit and at rest, access to the Snowflake Data Marketplace, and the ability to create your own data exchange. However, the Standard edition doesn't provide multi-cluster virtual warehouses, dynamic data masking, or external data tokenization. Also, one of the vital Snowflake features, Time Travel, is limited to only one day. Choose the Standard edition if you want to keep your costs down, especially for development or proof-of-concept environments that don't necessarily need all the bells and whistles.

Enterprise The Enterprise edition provides all the capabilities of the Standard edition but adds 90 days of Time Travel, multi-cluster virtual warehouses, materialized views, dynamic data masking, and external data tokenization. Many enterprise customers are likely to choose the Enterprise version, given its rich feature set and the price point.

Business Critical The Business Critical edition adds several security features to the Enterprise edition, including customer-managed keys, payment card industry (PCI) compliance, private connectivity support, and failover, to name a few.

Virtual Private Snowflake The Virtual Private Snowflake (VPS) edition provides the same capabilities as Business Critical. Additionally, it provides a customer-dedicated metadata store and a customer-dedicated pool of compute resources that are not shared with other customers.

Table 1.1 lists critical Snowflake features and the Snowflake editions in which they are available. The easiest way to recall the information in this table is to remember that most base features are available in all Snowflake editions. In addition, the Enterprise edition adds a variety of features such as materialized views, column-level and row-level access control, and 90 days of Time Travel. The Business Critical edition supports additional standards, failover, and failback. And finally, VPS provides dedicated and isolated metadata and compute.

You can access the complete and up-to-date Snowflake editions and supported features here:

`https://docs.snowflake.com/en/user-guide/intro-editions.html`

TABLE 1.1 Snowflake feature matrix

Feature or service	Standard	Enterprise	Business Critical	VPS
Standard Time Travel support (up to one day)	√	√	√	√
Up to 90 days of Time Travel		√	√	√
Fail-safe storage	√	√	√	√
Share data as a data provider and consume shared data as a data consumer	√	√	√	
Share data across regions and cloud via replication	√	√	√	
Snowflake Data Marketplace access	√	√	√	
Data exchange capabilities	√	√	√	
Virtual warehouses for compute	√	√	√	√
Multi-cluster virtual warehouses		√	√	√
Multifactor authentication support	√	√	√	√
Federated authentication and SSO	√	√	√	√
OAuth support	√	√	√	√
Automatic encryption of all data	√	√	√	√
Object-level access control	√	√	√	√
Column-level security for masking		√	√	√
Row-level access policies		√	√	√
Support from semi-structured data types, i.e., JSON, Parquet, Avro, ORC, and XML	√	√	√	√
User-defined functions (UDFs) support in SQL, JavaScript, and Java language	√	√	√	√
Support for external functions	√	√	√	√
Snowpipe support	√	√	√	√

TABLE 1.1 Snowflake feature matrix *(continued)*

Feature or service	Standard	Enterprise	Business Critical	VPS
Streams support for tracking table changes	√	√	√	√
Tasks for scheduled execution of SQL	√	√	√	√
Clustering support	√	√	√	√
Search optimization service		√	√	√
Materialized views		√	√	√
Resource monitors for monitoring credit use	√	√	√	√
24 hours early access to weekly new releases		√	√	√
Private connectivity to Snowflake via AWS PrivateLink, Azure Private Link, or Google Cloud's Private Service Connect			√	√
Dedicated metadata store and dedicated compute resources				√

Exercise 1.1 outlines the steps for creating a new Snowflake trial.

EXERCISE 1.1

Signing Up for a Snowflake Instance

1. Open your browser and navigate to `www.snowflake.com`. You will see a Start For Free button at the top-right corner of the screen. Click this button to begin the signup process.
2. You will be presented with a screen like the one shown here. Fill in your information and click Continue.

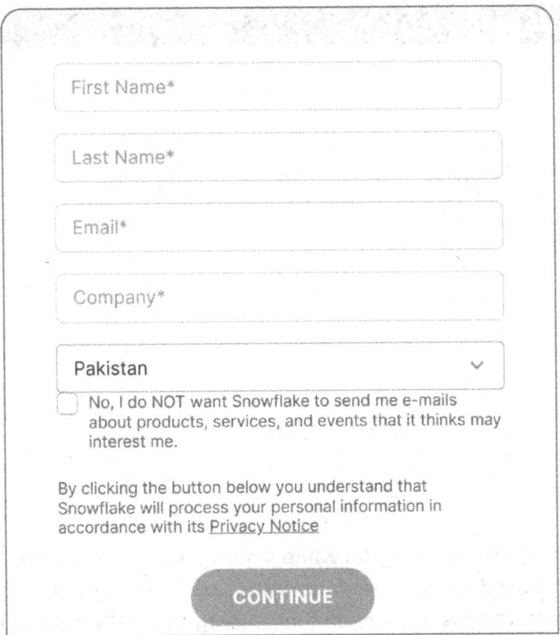

3. The next screen will ask you to select the Snowflake edition. Our recommendation is to choose the Enterprise edition because it provides all the Snowflake capabilities tested in the SnowPro Core certification exam.

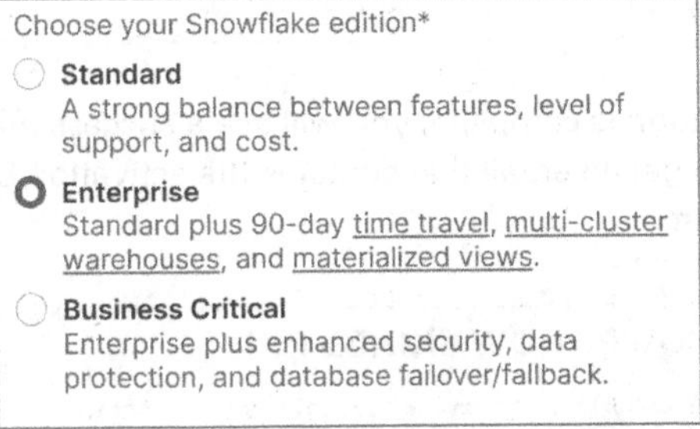

4. Next, choose your preferred cloud provider. The choice of the optimal cloud platform depends on various factors, including your currently preferred cloud platform and the future direction of cloud adoption for your organization. To prepare for your SnowPro Core certification exam, choose the platform with which you are most comfortable. Once you have selected a cloud platform, you will be required to select a region.

EXERCISE 1.1 *(continued)*

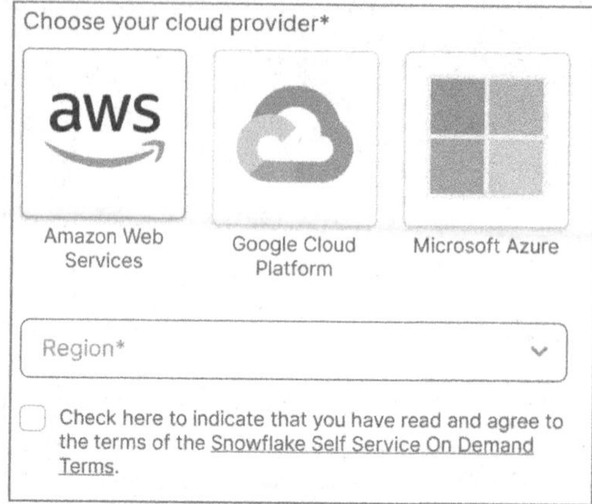

5. Selecting the most appropriate region while signing up is quite critical. It would be best to choose a region based on your organization's cloud configuration. To prepare for the SnowPro Core exam, choose any region that is geographically near to your location. Once you have selected the region, click the Get Started button. If all goes well, you will be taken to the following screen, indicating that your account is being set up.

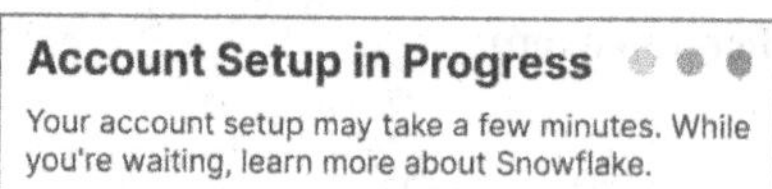

6. When the account creation is complete, you will see a success message similar to the following. You will also get an email that contains the activation URL and the link to your Snowflake account.

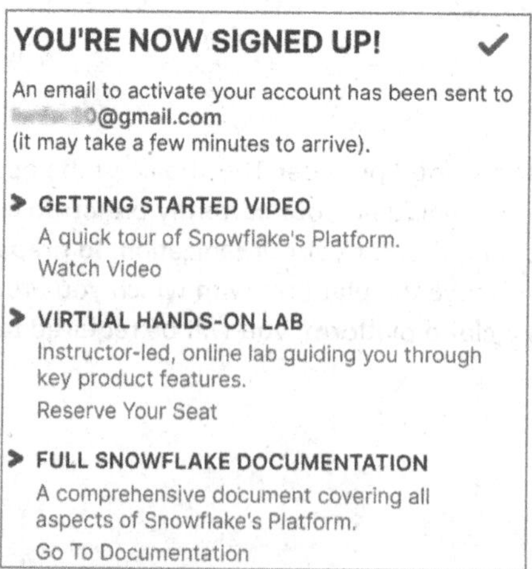

7. At this point, check your email for the activation URL and the link to your Snowflake account. The email looks similar to the sample shown here. Make a note of the URL in the email, as that is the permanent link to your Snowflake account. Click the Click To Activate button to activate your account and set up the login and password.

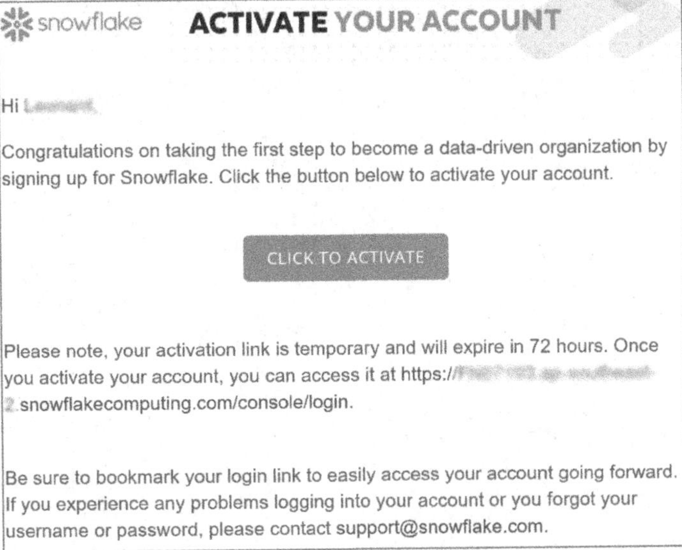

8. Upon clicking the Activate button, you will be taken to a welcome screen, where you will be asked to set up a username and password. Please note that the username that you choose here is the account administrator username for your Snowflake account. Make sure you record the username and the password.

EXERCISE 1.1 ***(continued)***

Welcome to Snowflake!

, please choose a username and password to get started

Username

Username can contain only letters and numbers.

Password

Your password must be at least 8 characters long and contain a number, uppercase, and lowercase letters.

Confirm password

Get started

9. Once you have selected a username and password and have clicked Get Started, you will be logged into your Snowflake account.
10. Once logged in, you will be able to view the Snowflake web user interface (UI). We will be using the new Snowflake web UI as our primary tool for interacting with Snowflake. Chapter 3, "Interfaces and Connectivity," discusses the classic Snowflake web UI and the new Snowflake web UI in more depth.

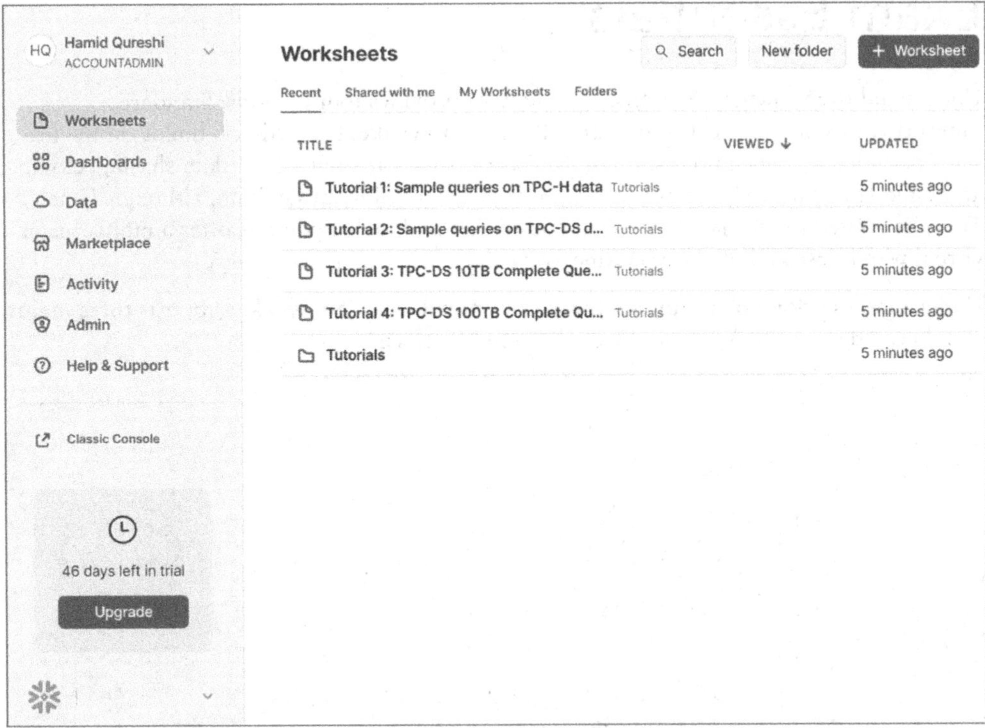

Summary

We have covered the introduction to the Snowflake data platform in this chapter, how Snowflake was founded, and a brief history of the platform. We also reviewed the Snowflake certification track and the process of signing up for a Snowflake trial instance. Snowflake is supported on the three major cloud platforms—AWS, Azure, and Google Cloud—and provides four different editions: Standard, Enterprise, Business Critical, and Virtual Private Snowflake, with each edition featuring more capabilities than the previous edition.

Exam Essentials

Understand the Snowflake editions. Snowflake provides four editions: Standard, Enterprise, Business Critical, and Virtual Private Snowflake. Each edition builds on the features provided by the edition before it. Key aspects to note are that the data sharing, cloning, and Time Travel features are available starting with the Standard edition, although Time Travel is limited to one day. The Enterprise edition and higher editions offer a multi-cluster virtual warehouse and 90 days of Time Travel.

Understand the cloud platforms supported by Snowflake. Snowflake supports three major cloud providers: AWS, Azure, and Google Cloud Platform.

Review Questions

1. Which of the following are Snowflake editions? (Select all that apply.)
   - A. Standard
   - B. Enterprise
   - C. Basic
   - D. Advanced
   - E. Business Critical
2. What is the minimum edition of Snowflake that supports multi-cluster virtual warehouse capability?
   - A. Standard
   - B. Enterprise
   - C. Business Critical
   - D. Virtual Private Snowflake
3. The Standard edition of Snowflake provides how many days of Time Travel?
   - A. 90
   - B. 1
   - C. 45
   - D. 30
4. What is the minimum Snowflake edition required for applying masking policies on columns?
   - A. Standard
   - B. Enterprise
   - C. Business Critical
   - D. Virtual Private Snowflake
5. What is the minimum Snowflake edition required for sharing data?
   - A. Standard
   - B. Enterprise
   - C. Business Critical
   - D. Virtual Private Snowflake
6. Snowflake is supported on which of the following cloud platforms? (Select all that apply.)
   - A. Amazon Web Services
   - B. Oracle Cloud
   - C. Microsoft Azure
   - D. Google Cloud Platform
   - E. IBM Cloud Services

7. What minimum Snowflake edition supports database replication between Snowflake accounts (within an organization)?
   - **A.** Standard
   - **B.** Enterprise
   - **C.** Business Critical
   - **D.** Virtual Private Snowflake

8. What is the minimum Snowflake edition required to utilize the search optimization feature for point lookup queries?
   - **A.** Standard
   - **B.** Enterprise
   - **C.** Business Critical
   - **D.** Virtual Private Snowflake

Snowflake Architecture

THE SNOWPRO CORE EXAM TOPICS COVERED IN THIS CHAPTER INCLUDE THE FOLLOWING:

✓ **Domain 1.0: Snowflake Data Platform Features and Architecture**

- 1.1 Outline key features of the Snowflake Cloud Data platform.
  - Elastic Storage
  - Elastic Compute
  - Snowflake's three distinct layers
- 1.4 Outline Snowflake storage concepts.
  - Micro-partitions
  - Types of column metadata clustering

✓ **Domain 3.0: Performance Concepts**

- 3.2. Explain virtual warehouse configurations.
  - Warehouse sizing
  - Warehouse settings and access

Snowflake employs a hybrid architecture to solve the massively parallel processing problem, and in this chapter, you learn about that unique architecture approach. As you'll see, the architecture uses a shared-disk approach for storage but uses multiple independent compute clusters to process the data.

Traditional Database Architectures

Historically, two architecture approaches have been used for database systems. The most common is the shared-disk architecture used by most online transaction processing (OLTP)-oriented database systems. In this architecture, the database system consists of a single physical computing system where the data for the database resides on a shared disk. A CPU (or multiple CPUs) performs the data processing within the same physical computing system, sharing the same memory and the storage disk. To make it easier to understand this architecture, think of a standard database server, such as SQL Server, MySQL, or Oracle, installed on your laptop. The data is on a single disk in your laptop, shared by the CPUs, and the memory is also shared. One obvious problem with this architecture is scaling up. Since a single physical system is typically used in shared-disk architecture, in order to scale up, the system's specification must be improved, which means increasing the memory, the type and size of the disk, and the number of CPUs in the system. However, the reality is that you can only get to a specific number when increasing memory, CPU, and storage within a single system, beyond which you *cannot* scale any further. That's where the *shared-nothing* architecture comes in.

As described in Figure 2.1, each node has its own processing power and its own allocated slice of data in the shared-nothing architecture. Each node is concerned with processing only its specific slice of data. An advantage of this approach is the massive parallelism it provides, since the data and the processing is distributed efficiently and evenly across all the nodes. Such systems are often referred to as massively parallel processing (MPP) systems.

Although shared-nothing architecture based systems can efficiently process large amounts of data, increasing such a system's processing and storage capacity is not straightforward. Any increase in the storage must be accompanied by a corresponding increase in the processing power to ensure that the scaled-up system can handle larger amounts of data with the same efficiency as before. The critical challenge to note here is that you cannot scale storage and the compute independently—they must be scaled in relation to each other because the storage and the compute are tightly coupled.

FIGURE 2.1 Shared-disk and shared-nothing architectures

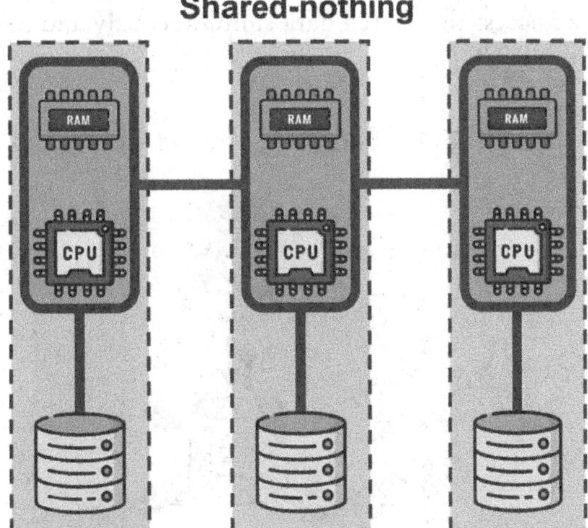

When an shared-nothing architecture based system is scaled up, the data must be redistributed so that it resides in the correct allocated node. For example, consider the shared-nothing system depicted in Figure 2.1; it consists of three nodes, each with its own compute and storage. If we were to increase this system's size, we would likely need to take the system offline while additional nodes are added. Once the nodes are added to the system, the data must be redistributed so that the new nodes get their share of data to take advantage of the additional processing.

In most cases, organizations need to scale up their system because either they have run out of storage space or they do not have enough computing power. But when using technology based on shared-nothing architecture, they cannot scale storage or compute independently, since doing so requires scaling storage and compute relative to each other.

Snowflake's Hybrid Architecture

The shared-disk architecture can only scale in a limited manner, and the shared-nothing architecture requires that storage and compute must be scaled together. Unfortunately, neither of these approaches fully addresses the scalability and agility requirements in the modern world of data warehousing and analytics on the cloud. This is where Snowflake's unique architecture comes in.

Snowflake implements a new hybrid architecture that combines the best features of shared-disk and shared-nothing architectures. Snowflake stores data in a shared and centralized manner, like how data is stored in shared-disk architecture. But it also provides the capability to run one or more compute engines, each with its independent memory and processing power, which is how shared-nothing architecture works. Each compute engine can access the shared data simultaneously and perform processing on that data, as shown in Figure 2.2.

FIGURE 2.2 Snowflake's hybrid architecture

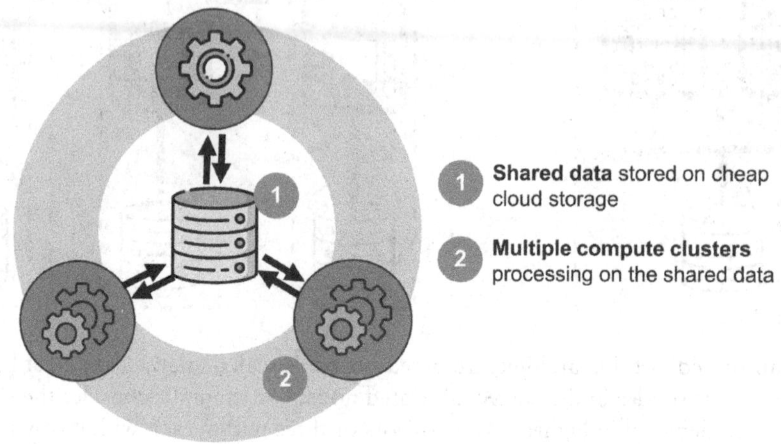
1
2
1 Shared data stored on cheap cloud storage
2 Multiple compute clusters processing on the shared data

This approach offers several advantages, the most crucial being that you can scale your storage and compute independently of each other. So, at any given time, if you need additional processing power available to your queries, you can increase the size of your compute engines or add additional compute engines. These compute engines are called virtual warehouses, and they are used for query processing and data loading jobs. Data in Snowflake is stored on inexpensive cloud storage and can be scaled independently, and since it is using cloud storage, it can be scaled almost infinitely. The data is stored in a Snowflake proprietary format utilizing a concept called micro-partitions.

The Three Layers of Snowflake Architecture

The preceding hybrid architecture discussion is a high-level view of the architecture used by Snowflake. At a slightly more detailed level, Snowflake architecture has three distinct layers:

Database Storage Cheap cloud storage on AWS, Azure, or Google Cloud

Query Processing Primarily composed of virtual warehouses

Cloud Services The brain of the whole operation

Let's take a closer look at each of these layers.

The Database Storage Layer

The shared storage layer in Snowflake resides on inexpensive object cloud storage. Currently, Snowflake supports AWS S3 storage, Azure Blob Storage, or Google Cloud Storage to store its data. Since Snowflake stores data on object storage on the cloud platform, the storage can scale indefinitely and independently of compute. The cloud platform is responsible for providing the durability for these stored files; therefore, Snowflake can take advantage of the underlying cloud platform's disaster recovery and fault tolerance.

Data loaded into Snowflake is stored as files on the cloud-based object storage. It is worth mentioning here that files stored on cloud-based object storage are immutable, which means stored data cannot be updated once written but can only be appended. If updates to a file written to an object store are required, you must remove the complete file, perform an update, and write the new file. The immutability of files on object stores presents an interesting challenge that Snowflake solves through its unique micro-partitioning approach. We will be looking into more details regarding micro-partitions later in this chapter. These micro-partitions also form the architectural basis of many exciting Snowflake features such as Time Travel, secure data sharing, and cloning.

The Query Processing Layer

The query processing layer is the compute layer through which queries and data processing jobs are executed on the stored data. For a given Snowflake instance, the compute layer can have multiple compute clusters running simultaneously. The compute engines in Snowflake are referred to as *virtual warehouses*. This name can be confusing when you come from a data warehousing background and think it refers to the virtualization-based data solution. Whenever we use the term virtual warehouse, it refers to a compute cluster in the Snowflake context.

Virtual warehouses are entirely independent of storage. You can have as many or as few of them running simultaneously; however, each virtual warehouse accesses the same shared data. Multiple virtual warehouses can be active simultaneously, and they can be of a different configuration and dedicated for a specific purpose or group of users. They can be started up and shut down as per requirements, therefore incurring costs only when active. They can even be resized from a smaller size to a large size so that you can process a more complex query more quickly and then return to a smaller size when additional power is not required.

The capability to create as many virtual warehouses of the desired configuration provides MPP capability to Snowflake while still accessing a single shared data. Hence the architecture for Snowflake is often referred to as multi-cluster, shared-data architecture.

The Cloud Services Layer

The cloud services layer is the brain of the Snowflake system. It is a highly available, fault-tolerant, always-on service. All access to a Snowflake account is through the cloud services layer. Requests for any user connecting to Snowflake, whether via the Snowflake web UI or SnowSQL, go through the cloud services layer. This layer contains and manages a variety of metadata, including details regarding how the data is stored, information on the micro-partitions, metadata regarding the databases and tables in your system, the users, roles and security, and so forth (Figure 2.3).

FIGURE 2.3 Cloud services layer

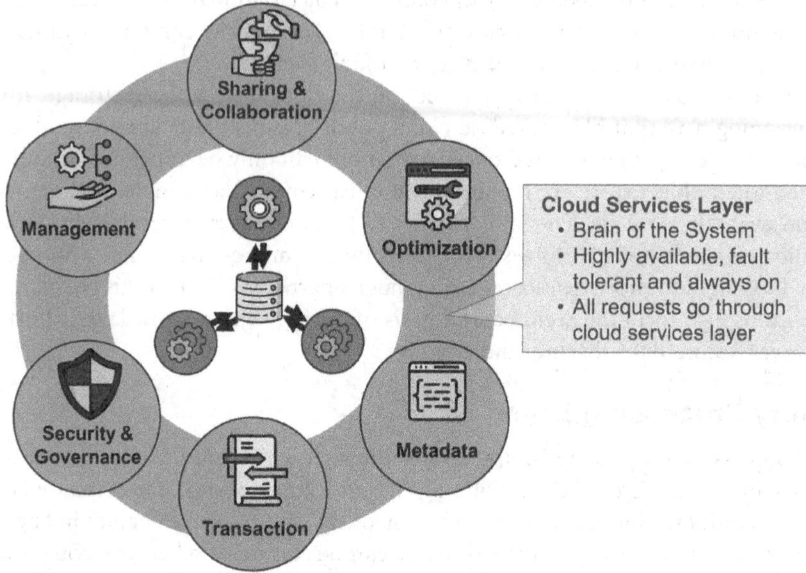

The cloud services layer also controls the authentication and authorization or, in other words, the system's security and governance. For example, when a user attempts to log in, the user's credentials are validated by the cloud services layer. After a user is connected to their Snowflake instance, any queries they execute are parsed by the cloud services layer, optimized for execution, and dispatched for execution.

Additionally, the cloud services layer provides transaction control, or ACID compliance. ACID stands for atomicity, consistency, isolation, and durability. At a high level, ACID refers to the fact that a database system must allow multiple transactions to execute in isolation, and commit or roll back a transaction as a single unit, ensuring a consistent system state.

The data sharing, cloning, and data exchange features provided by Snowflake are all managed through the cloud services layer, which can achieve data sharing and cloning through metadata operations without moving the data.

The Database Storage Layer: Micro-Partitions and Clustering

As discussed earlier, Snowflake stores data in a proprietary format on cloud object storage, such as AWS S3, Azure Blob Storage, or Google Cloud Storage. As described in Figure 2.4, the data stored on cloud object storage is transparent to the users—that is, they cannot see the actual files, look at how the data is stored, or access the file directly. When a table is created in Snowflake and loaded with data, the table's metadata in the cloud services layer stores the location of the underlying files that constitute the table. When a user queries a table, the query processing components in the cloud services layer are responsible for accessing the correct underlying files that correspond to the table.

FIGURE 2.4 Micro-partitions are transparent.

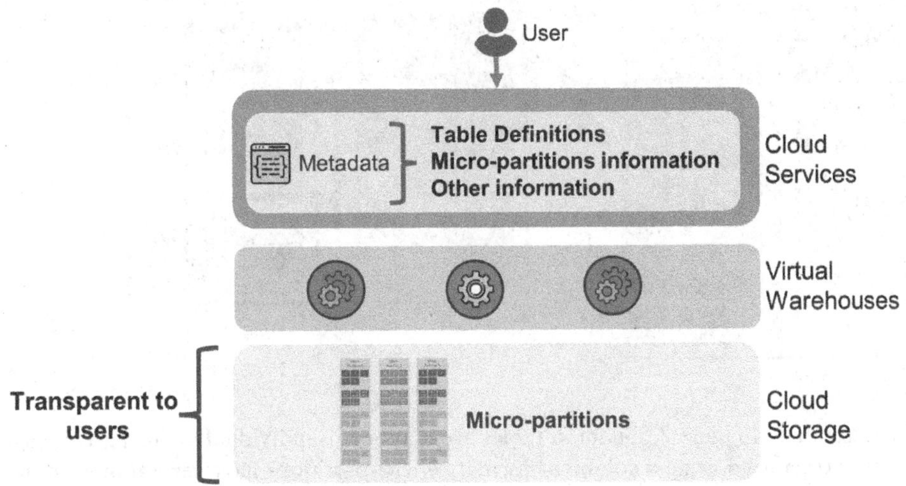

Since cloud storage is virtually infinite, the storage in Snowflake can also scale in an unlimited manner. However, storing the data on object storage brings with it some challenges. For example, data stored on an object store is immutable—it cannot be modified once written. But data in a database is constantly being inserted, updated, and deleted; therefore, the storage needs to be modified constantly. For typical databases like Postgres or MySQL, the data is in files on a filesystem, and the database engine can update any part of the file when processing updates, deletes, or inserts. In the case of Snowflake, due to the immutability of data stored on object storage, files cannot be updated, and an alternate approach is required to manage changes in data.

To overcome this challenge, Snowflake uses a concept called micro-partitioning to store the data. Data in Snowflake is automatically organized into small partitions, known as micro-partitions (Figure 2.5).

FIGURE 2.5 Micro-partitioning in Snowflake

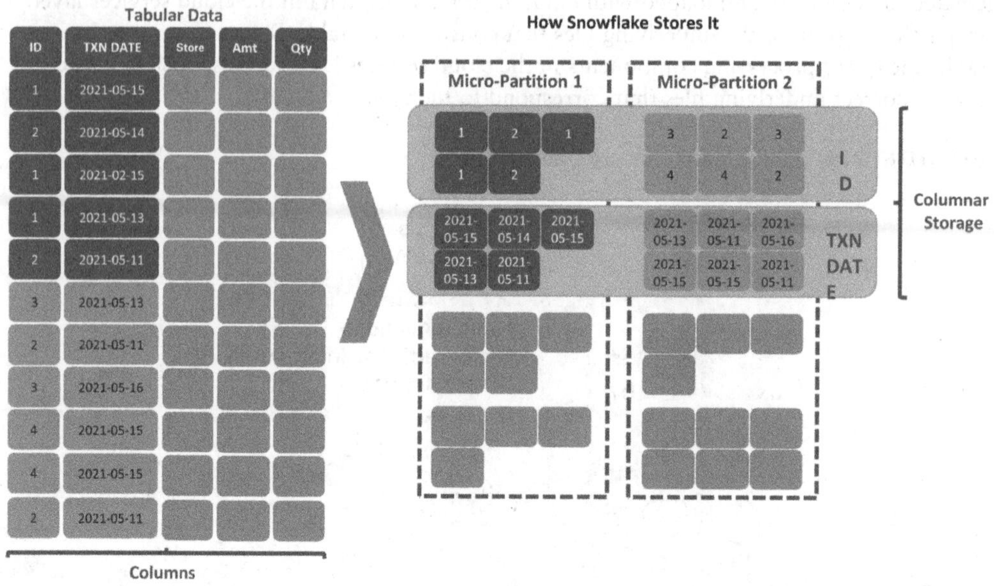

As illustrated in Figure 2.5, data in tables are mapped to individual micro-partitions and are further organized using a columnar format. Micro-partitions have several interesting characteristics:

Micro-partitions are immutable. Snowflake partitions are immutable, which means they cannot be changed once created. Therefore, loading new data or updating existing data for a table results in new micro-partitions.

Micro-Partitions are compressed and relatively small. As the name suggests, micro-partitions are relatively small, and each micro-partition generally contains 50 MB to 500 MB of uncompressed data. However, it is worth noting that the actual size of the stored data is smaller since Snowflake always compresses data before writing it to the storage. Individual micro-partitions also enable Snowflake to eliminate partitions while executing queries, resulting in efficient and cost-effective queries. We explore partition elimination or partition pruning in more depth while discussing data clustering in Chapter 8, "Performance."

The number of micro-partitions can grow very large. The number of micro-partitions for a given table depends mainly on the amount of data in that table. For a very large table, the number of micro-partitions can run into millions or hundreds of millions of micro-partitions.

Each column is stored in columnar format. Within each micro-partition, Snowflake stores each column in a columnar storage format. Storing data in a columnar format enables Snowflake to optimize the queries by retrieving only the referenced columns. Each column in a micro-partition is compressed individually as well, in addition to the micro-partition level compression. Snowflake determines the best and most efficient compression algorithm for each column in each partition.

Partition values can overlap. Because micro-partitions are immutable, and any data updates or new data must be added into a new micro-partition, similar values will not always be in the same physical partition. Figure 2.5 shows data from the table on the left stored in two micro-partitions. Notice that the values in the two micro-partitions overlap between the partitions. There are two partitions for the same column values and overlaps between partitions for different column values. The micro-partition distribution approach taken by Snowflake helps prevent partition skew, which is commonly observed in other static partitioning techniques. The skew is avoided because each micro-partition is of a standard size. Similar clustering keys don't have to be in the same micro-partition, and partition values can overlap.

Micro-partitions are added in the order of data arrival. Micro-partitions are added to a table in the order of how the data arrived in the table. When additional data is added to a table, another micro-partition or possibly multiple micro-partitions (depending on the data size) are created to accommodate that data. Since the micro-partitions are added in the order of data arrival, identical data values for a given column may be stored in different physical partitions.

Metadata is maintained for each micro-partition. Because the column values are spread across multiple partitions, Snowflake must keep track of what range of data is in which partitions to use that information for efficient query processing. As shown in Figure 2.6, Snowflake maintains several types of metadata for a given table.

FIGURE 2.6 Metadata at the micro-partition level

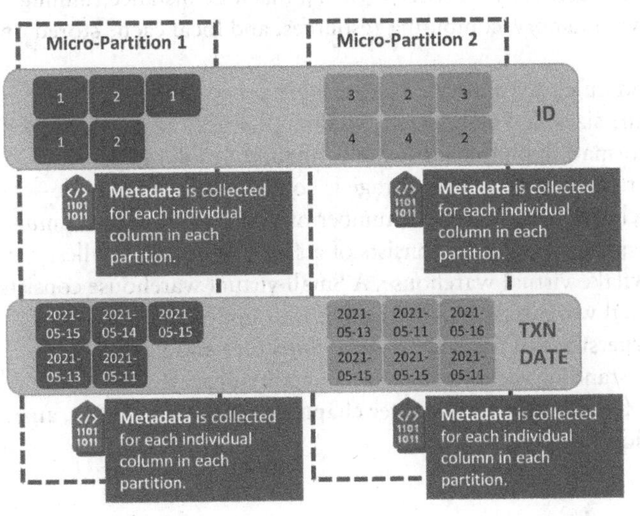

What is collected in Metadata?

- Range of values including Max, Min & Count
- Number of distinct values
- Other optimization metadata

Snowflake stores the range of column values in its metadata: the maximum and the minimum value for each column in each micro-partition. Snowflake can intelligently decide which partitions to read when processing a query using this metadata. Additionally, Snowflake stores the count of distinct values for each column in each partition in the metadata and certain other information to assist in query optimization.

This metadata is stored in the cloud services layer and can be used by Snowflake to optimize query processing. Snowflake is intelligent enough to answer some of the queries directly from the metadata; for example, a count(*) of a table does not scan the whole table but instead returns the result from the metadata.

Data is automatically clustered. Intricately linked with micro-partitioning is the concept of automatic clustering. Snowflake automatically clusters the data as it is inserted into a table.

In the case of exceptionally large tables with a lot of data inserted over time, the query performance can degrade since the WHERE predicates in the SQL cannot effectively eliminate partitions. In such cases, it is advisable to manually specify a clustering key, which then redistributes the data according to the clustering key. In Chapter 8, "Performance," we will be looking into clustering keys and how they can improve performance.

The Query Processing Layer: The Concept of a Virtual Warehouse

A virtual warehouse in Snowflake is basically a multinode compute cluster used to process queries and data loading processes. A virtual warehouse provides resources such as CPU, memory, and temporary storage to process queries and run data load jobs. Each node in a virtual warehouse compute cluster is generally a low-cost virtual machine instance running in the cloud. Each node has its own memory, computing resources, and local cache stored on a solid-state disk (Figure 2.7).

Snowflake has made it easy and quick for a user to choose a virtual warehouse by labeling the configuration in T-shirt sizes: X-Small, Small, Medium, Large, and so on. Snowflake doesn't publicly provide information on the hardware configuration of a node—it is not known how much memory or CPU or local disk storage is configured for each node—but what *is* known is that as the cluster size grows, the number of nodes in that cluster multiplies. For example, an X-Small virtual warehouse consists of a single node, the smallest possible configuration for a Snowflake virtual warehouse. A Small virtual warehouse consists of two nodes, and a Medium virtual warehouse is composed of four nodes.

Virtual warehouses are the cornerstone of the Snowflake architecture and have several distinct features essential to understanding the Snowflake architecture properly. We will be going through several of these features in-depth in later chapters; for the time being, an introduction to these features follows:

FIGURE 2.7 A single node in a virtual warehouse cluster

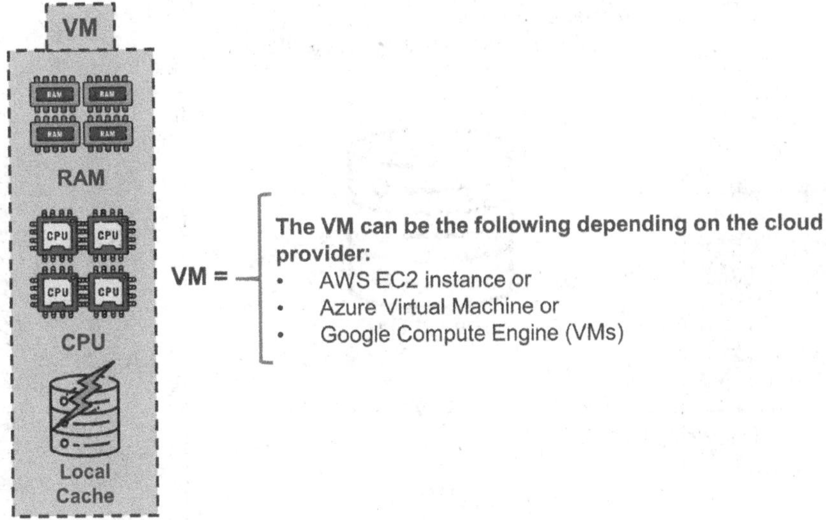

Virtual Warehouse Size A virtual warehouse can be created in any of the available sizes—X-Small (1 node), Small (2 nodes), up to 6X-Large (a staggering 512 nodes). Multiple virtual warehouses can be created for a given Snowflake account, but it is worth noting that they access the same shared data, hence the term multi-cluster, shared data (Figure 2.8).

You can resize a virtual warehouse at any time, even when they are running. When a virtual warehouse is resized while in a suspended state, there are no nodes to decommission or provision; therefore, the updated size takes effect only when the virtual warehouse is resumed. Snowflake adds or removes nodes as per the new size when a running virtual warehouse is resized. The removal of nodes takes place only when all active queries on those nodes have finished. When a virtual warehouse is resized, any currently executing queries are not impacted—only new queries are affected by the new size.

Billing Snowflake credits are used to pay for the processing time used by the virtual warehouses. The amount of Snowflake credits consumed depends on the size of the virtual warehouse, the length of their running state, and how many virtual warehouses you have created. As the size of a virtual warehouse increases, the number of credits consumed per hour also increases.

Snowflake credits are billed on a per-second basis; however, a minimum of 60 seconds billing applies. If a virtual warehouse were provisioned or resumed and suspended or deleted within the first 60 seconds, a minimum of 60 seconds of credit usage would apply.

FIGURE 2.8 Multiple virtual warehouses of varying sizes

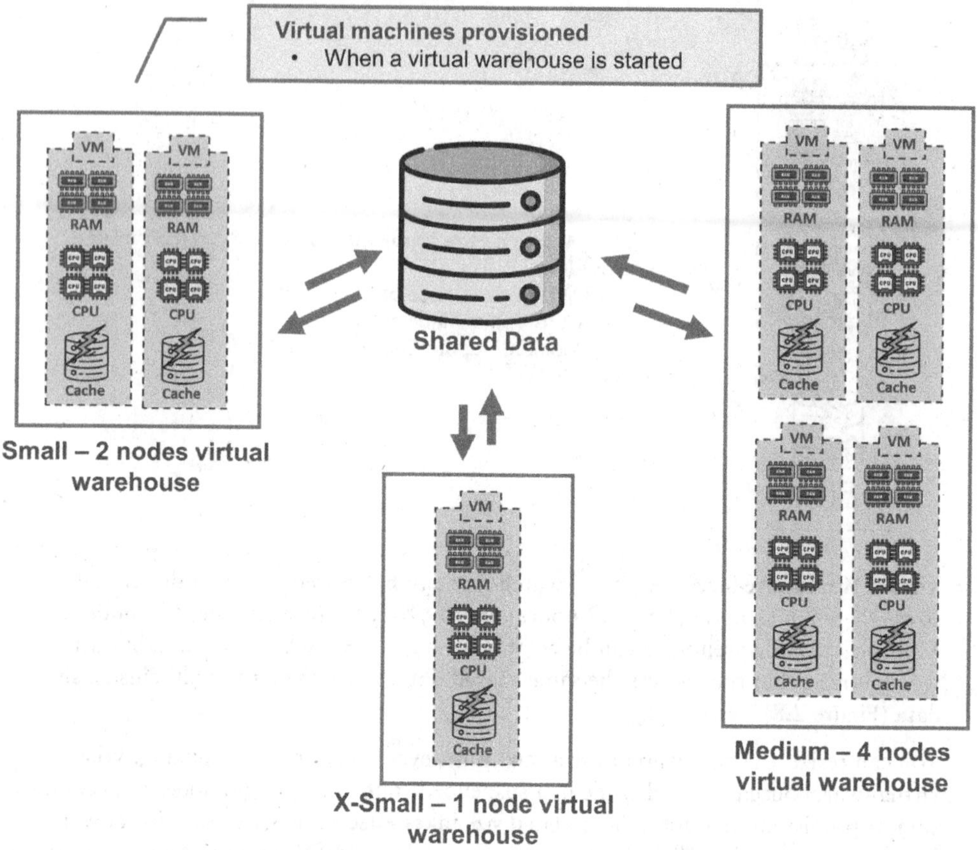

Scale Up A customer can resize a virtual warehouse to match the needs of changing workloads. As an example, let's say the customer started with a small virtual warehouse. In that instance, it is possible that the complexity of the query workload has expanded dramatically over time and a small virtual warehouse is no longer sufficient to meet the demand. The virtual warehouse's size can be increased to accommodate the increasing task complexity in such instances; this is called scaling up. Additional nodes are provisioned and added to the virtual warehouse compute cluster when a virtual warehouse is expanded to a bigger size.

When a virtual warehouse is scaled up, the charge for the new size is not incurred until all the new nodes in the increased size virtual warehouse are provisioned. Only new queries can take advantage of the increased size; all queries already running on the virtual warehouse are not impacted.

Scale Down Scaling down a virtual warehouse is typically done in reaction to reduced query complexity, where a smaller virtual warehouse can still perform queries efficiently and on time. Keeping a larger virtual warehouse when the queries can be executed efficiently and quickly on a smaller virtual warehouse wastes resources and incurs additional costs. In such instances, reducing the virtual warehouse size, called scaling down, is a viable alternative.

When a virtual warehouse is scaled down, nodes are removed from the virtual warehouse only when they are no longer running a query.

Multi-cluster Virtual Warehouse Also referred to as scaling out or autoscaling, multi-cluster virtual warehouses allow you to add and remove multi-cluster virtual warehouses in an automated manner. Multi-cluster virtual warehouses are typically used for scenarios where concurrent users increase beyond a single virtual warehouse capability. Additional queries start queuing when the concurrent workload increases beyond the maximum for a given virtual warehouse. Multi-cluster virtual warehouses address this issue by dynamically adding more clusters based on the demand. Once the demand reduces, the additional clusters are removed.

A minimum of Enterprise edition of Snowflake is required to use the multi-cluster virtual warehouse capability.

Real World Scenario

Autoscaling to Adapt to Changing User Demands

A large retail organization uses Snowflake as its data warehouse and analytics solution. Using the data in Snowflake, several reports are refreshed daily. Business users also perform ad hoc analyses on the data stored in Snowflake. In addition, the business users may connect and perform their analysis at any time during the day. Because several business users perform analysis simultaneously, their queries can be delayed.

The data warehouse team is tasked with providing a solution to ensure that queries never get delayed, even if approximately 50 business users are simultaneously performing ad hoc analyses. As a solution, the data warehouse team configured multi-cluster virtual warehouses, which can scale out automatically as the number of simultaneous users increases, thus catering for simultaneous ad hoc querying by many users. Once the number of simultaneous users reduces, the multi-cluster virtual warehouse automatically scales back, thus avoiding unnecessary costs.

Suspend, Resume, Auto Suspend, and Auto Resume A virtual warehouse may be suspended when it is not being used to save costs and resumed when required. A suspended virtual warehouse does not consume any credits and therefore does not cost the customer. A customer may resume a suspended virtual warehouse as required so that it can start processing queries. It is also possible to set a virtual warehouse to Auto Resume. As soon as a new query tries to execute on a suspended virtual warehouse, the virtual warehouse automatically enters the resumed state and starts processing the query. Similarly, a virtual warehouse may be set to Auto Suspend so that after a defined period of inactivity, it enters the suspended state automatically.

When a virtual warehouse is requested to be suspended, it does not enter a suspended state until all active queries using that virtual warehouse have been completed.

Configuring a Virtual Warehouse

Virtual warehouses are designed to be dynamic. They can be created or deleted as per demand, suspended, and resumed based on the query workload and resized according to the changing complexity of queries. As with most Snowflake objects, a virtual warehouse can be managed using SQL or the Snowflake web UI.

Exercise 2.1 outlines the steps for creating a new virtual warehouse using the UI.

EXERCISE 2.1

Creating a New Virtual Warehouse Using the UI

1. Open your browser and navigate to the URL for your Snowflake instance. Log in to your Snowflake instance using the account administrator you created in Exercise 1.1. As a result of this step, you are logged in to the Snowflake web UI.

2. Click the Warehouses button on the top bar, which opens the Warehouses view as shown here:

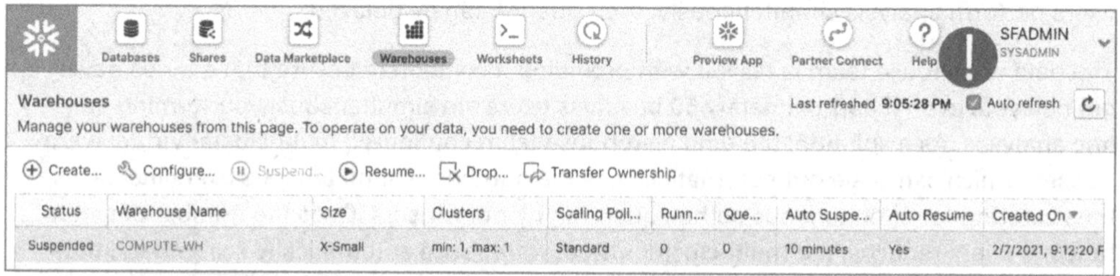

3. Click the Create button to initiate the process of creating a new virtual warehouse. You will be presented with the following screen.

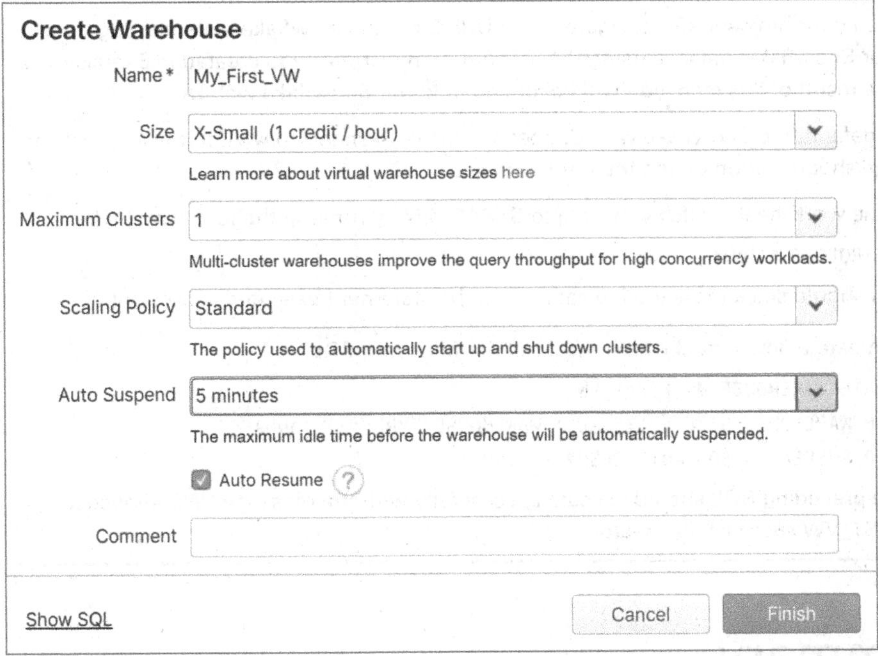

4. Provide a name for the virtual warehouse, select X-Small from the Size drop-down list, and set Maximum Clusters to 1 and Auto Suspend to 5 minutes. Leave Scaling Policy as Standard and leave Auto Resume selected. Click Finish.

5. There may be a brief delay while the virtual warehouse is created. Once the virtual warehouse is created, you will see the new warehouse appear in the list. By default, it will be in a running state, but if you don't run any query on this virtual warehouse, it enters the suspended state after 5 minutes.

Please make sure that you have set your role to SYSADMIN at the top-right corner; otherwise, you may not have the privilege of seeing existing virtual warehouses or creating new ones.

Exercise 2.2 outlines the steps for creating a new virtual warehouse using SQL.

EXERCISE 2.2

Creating a New Virtual Warehouse Using SQL

1. Open your browser and navigate to the URL for your Snowflake instance. Log in to your Snowflake instance using the account administrator you created in Exercise 1.1. As a result of this step, you will be logged in to the Snowflake web UI.

2. By default, the Snowflake web UI opens in the Worksheets view. If it doesn't, click the Worksheets button on the top bar to open it.

3. In the worksheet, switch your role to SYSADMIN by running the following SQL:

   ```
   USE ROLE SYSADMIN;
   ```

   You should see a message indicating that the statement executed successfully.

4. To create a new virtual warehouse, run the following SQL:

   ```
   CREATE WAREHOUSE My_First_VW
   WITH WAREHOUSE_SIZE = 'XSMALL' WAREHOUSE_TYPE = 'STANDARD'
   AUTO_SUSPEND = 300 AUTO_RESUME = TRUE;
   ```

   The preceding SQL should execute successfully with the message "Warehouse MY_FIRST_VW successfully created."

Summary

We have covered the foundational and architectural basics in this chapter, building an understanding of each of the three layers that constitute Snowflake's architecture. Snowflake uses a hybrid architecture approach: multi-cluster compute and shared data. Snowflake uses inexpensive cloud storage to store data in a shared manner and allows multiple compute clusters to operate on the shared data simultaneously. The approach is also referred to as multi-cluster, shared-data architecture. Data is stored using Snowflake propriety format and is organized in multiple micro-partitions using columnar storage. The compute layer consists of one or more compute clusters, also known as virtual warehouses. Virtual warehouses can be of various sizes and can be stopped, restarted, or deleted. In addition to the shared data and multiple compute layer, Snowflake has a cloud services layer that provides various functions such as security, transaction control, data sharing, metadata management, and query optimization services. In the coming chapters, we expand on the architectural basics you learned in this chapter and show how the micro-partitioning approach plays a role in cloning, Time Travel, and data sharing and how data clustering can improve query performance.

Exam Essentials

Understand the Snowflake hybrid architecture. Snowflake uses a hybrid architecture approach, a combination of shared-disk and shared-nothing architectures. Like shared-disk architecture, Snowflake stores data in a shared location, but it performs processing on that data using multiple compute clusters, also known as virtual warehouses.

Know the three layers of Snowflake architecture. Snowflake architecture consists of three primary layers: the shared storage layer, the compute layer, and the cloud services layer. The cloud services layer is the brain of the whole operation. It is the entry point to a Snowflake system and provides security, login and user management, transaction control, query planning and optimization, and metadata management.

Understand micro-partitioning and how Snowflake stores data. Snowflake stores data in a shared manner using inexpensive cloud storage. The data is organized in micro-partitions, where each micro-partition can store 50–500 MB of uncompressed data. The data is stored in a columnar format, and each column within each partition is compressed individually, using algorithms determined by Snowflake. Micro-partitions are immutable—that is, they cannot be changed once written; therefore, inserts, updates, and deletes require the creation of new micro-partitions.

Be able to describe the purpose of virtual warehouses. Virtual warehouses are compute clusters that can be spun up on-demand to process queries and run data loading jobs. When running, each virtual warehouse accesses the same shared data. Virtual warehouses come in various sizes, ranging from a single-node X-Small instance to the 512 nodes 6X-Large cluster. Virtual warehouses can be paused to save costs and resumed when a query workload is available. A virtual warehouse can be increased or decreased in size, also called scaling up or down. Multi-cluster virtual warehouses enable autoscaling of virtual warehouses based on changes in workload demand.

Review Questions

1. Which of the following terms best describes the architecture of Snowflake?
   - **A.** Shared-nothing architecture
   - **B.** Shared-disk architecture
   - **C.** Hybrid architecture (a mix of shared-nothing compute and shared-disk)
   - **D.** Three-tier architecture
2. Which of the following is true regarding Snowflake data storage?
   - **A.** A Snowflake-based data warehouse can store only up to 100 TB of data.
   - **B.** The capacity of a Snowflake-based data warehouse is nearly unlimited because it is backed by cloud-based storage, which itself is nearly unlimited in nature.
   - **C.** Snowflake running on an on-premises server can store only 50 TB of data.
   - **D.** A Snowflake-based data warehouse can store only up to 1 PB of data.
3. Which of the following statements are true regarding virtual warehouses in Snowflake? (Select all that apply.)
   - **A.** The term *virtual warehouse* refers to compute clusters in Snowflake.
   - **B.** Only one virtual warehouse can be started at a time.
   - **C.** Virtual warehouses can be suspended, resumed, and deleted altogether as per the workload requirement.
   - **D.** Virtual warehouses can be resized to a smaller or larger size, whether in a running state or a suspended state.
4. A virtual warehouse is resumed from a suspended state and then suspended again within 30 seconds. What is the minimum amount of credits that a virtual warehouse will consume?
   - **A.** No Snowflake credits will be consumed.
   - **B.** One minute's worth of Snowflake credits.
   - **C.** 30 seconds' worth of Snowflake credits.
   - **D.** One hour's worth of Snowflake credits.
5. Which of the following best describes the Snowflake architecture?
   - **A.** Multi-cluster distributed data
   - **B.** Single-cluster distributed data
   - **C.** Multi-cluster, shared-data
   - **D.** Multi-cluster, replicated data

6. True or False: As the size of a virtual warehouse increases, the amount of Snowflake credit used increases proportionately.
   - **A.** True
   - **B.** False
7. True or False: A large table in Snowflake may contain millions or hundreds of millions of micro-partitions.
   - **A.** True
   - **B.** False
8. True or False: If you create multiple virtual warehouses in a Snowflake-based solution, the virtual warehouses share the memory and CPU resources.
   - **A.** True
   - **B.** False
9. Snowflake stores which of the following metadata about rows in a micro-partition? (Select all that apply.)
   - **A.** The range of values for each of the columns in the micro-partition
   - **B.** The count of distinct values
   - **C.** Additional properties for optimization and efficient processing
   - **D.** List of users who have access to each row
10. True or False: Snowflake automatically determines the most efficient technique for compressing columns in micro-partitions.
    - **A.** True
    - **B.** False
11. Which of the following statements correctly describes a virtual warehouse in Snowflake?
    - **A.** The virtual warehouse is a concept through which two or more physical tables are linked together.
    - **B.** Reporting views are called virtual warehouses.
    - **C.** Virtual warehouses are the compute cluster(s) that Snowflake uses to execute queries and data load/unload jobs.
    - **D.** Virtual warehouse provide virtualization capabilities.
12. True or False: At any point in time, a virtual warehouse can be suspended or resumed as needed.
    - **A.** True
    - **B.** False

13. True or False: When a virtual warehouse is provisioned, terminating it inside the first 60 seconds has no significance because that period has already been billed.

    A. True

    B. False

14. When a virtual warehouse cluster is resized to a smaller size or scaled down, extra nodes are removed from the virtual warehouse cluster. Which of the following correctly describes when the extra nodes are removed?

    A. Immediately, whether or not a query is using those extra nodes

    B. Immediately, but only if no query is running on the extra nodes

    C. After a delay of one minute

    D. When the cluster is suspended or stopped

15. True or False: A virtual warehouse may be resized at any moment, whether it's in a suspended state or running queries.

    A. True

    B. False

16. True or False: When a request is made for a virtual warehouse to suspend, it enters the suspended state once all active queries on the virtual warehouse have completed execution.

    A. True

    B. False

17. Data in Snowflake tables is divided into micro-partitions and stored in a compressed format. What is the size of uncompressed data stored in each micro-partition?

    A. 10 MB to 20 MB

    B. 20 MB to 50 MB

    C. 50 MB to 500 MB

    D. 1 GB to 2 GB

18. Data in Snowflake tables is divided into micro-partitions and stored in a compressed format. Which one of the following is a characteristic of micro-partitions?

    A. Micro-partitions are immutable; once written, they cannot be changed.

    B. A user can control how many micro-partitions are created for a table.

    C. A user can specify the size of a micro-partition.

    D. The storage format of a micro-partition can be controlled through configuration.

19. Which one of the following statements correctly describes data clustering in Snowflake?

    A. Snowflake does not cluster any data, and the data is stored in an unclustered form.

    B. Snowflake automatically clusters the data as it is inserted into a table.

    C. If a clustering key is not defined, Snowflake does not cluster the data.

    D. Snowflake clusters the data only when the CLUSTER command is executed.

20. Which of the following are layers of Snowflake architecture? (Select all that apply.)

A. Cloud services layer

B. Database storage layer

C. Data sharing layer

D. Query processing layer

E. AWS layer

21. How are columns stored within a Snowflake micro-partition?

A. In a row format, with complete rows stored in each micro-partition

B. In a columnar format, with each column compressed and stored individually

C. In a CSV format, in a comma-separated manner

D. In Parquet format

22. At a minimum, which Snowflake edition is required to create multi-cluster data virtual warehouses?

A. Standard

B. Enterprise

C. Business Critical

D. Virtual Private Snowflake

Chapter 3

Interfaces and Connectivity

THE SNOWPRO CORE EXAM TOPICS COVERED IN THIS CHAPTER INCLUDE THE FOLLOWING:

✓ **Domain 1.0: Snowflake Data Platform Features and Architecture**

- **1.1 Outline key features of the Snowflake Cloud Data platform.**
  - Data Cloud/Data Exchange/Partner Network
  - Cloud partner categories
- **1.2 Outline key Snowflake tools and user interfaces.**
  - Snowflake user interfaces (UIs)
  - Snowsight
  - Snowflake connectors
  - Snowflake drivers
  - SQL scripting
  - Snowpark
- **1.3 Outline Snowflake's catalog and objects.**
  - User-defined functions (UDFs) and user-defined table functions (UDTFs)
  - Stored procedures

✓ **Domain 5.0: Data Transformation**

- **5.1 Explain how to work with standard data.**
  - User-defined functions (UDFs) and stored procedures

This chapter talks about various interfaces through which a user can interact with a Snowflake instance. We discuss Snowflake web interfaces and SnowSQL, two primary ways of interacting with Snowflake. The chapter also describes various connectors and drivers that can be used to connect to Snowflake. The chapter also describes methods to extend Snowflake's functionality.

Snowflake Web UI

The primary way of interacting with your Snowflake account is through the Snowflake web UI, also referred to as the classic web interface for Snowflake. It is an easy-to-use and powerful web portal that allows users to connect to their Snowflake instance and perform various functions, including querying, creating new objects such as databases and tables, and even loading data into a table. A user with administrative privileges can also use the Snowflake web UI to perform administrative functions such as creating new users, changing security configuration, creating and managing virtual warehouses, and performing other account management functions. The classic Snowflake web UI is available for most common browsers, including Chrome, Safari, Firefox, Opera, and Edge; however, Snowflake recommends using Chrome because the interface has been tested most extensively on Chrome.

While the Snowflake web UI remains the primary web-based tool, Snowflake has developed a brand-new web interface using modern web architecture methodologies. You have already logged into the classic web interface as part of the introductory chapter's sign-up process. We will now go through some more details regarding the Snowflake web UI to get acquainted with the various sections of the user interface. Figure 3.1 illustrates the Snowflake web UI at a high level.

The interface can be broken down into the following two sections:

Navigation Bar The navigation bar is at the top of the classic web interface and is used to navigate various screens. The navigation bar has several buttons corresponding to different functionalities. It is important to note that the buttons displayed on the navigation bar change based on the selected role. For example, a user with the account administrator role sees many more buttons than an ordinary user would.

Content Based on the screen you have navigated to, the content on the main screen changes to show elements specific to the navigated screen. By default, the Snowflake web interface opens in the Worksheets view.

FIGURE 3.1 Snowflake web UI

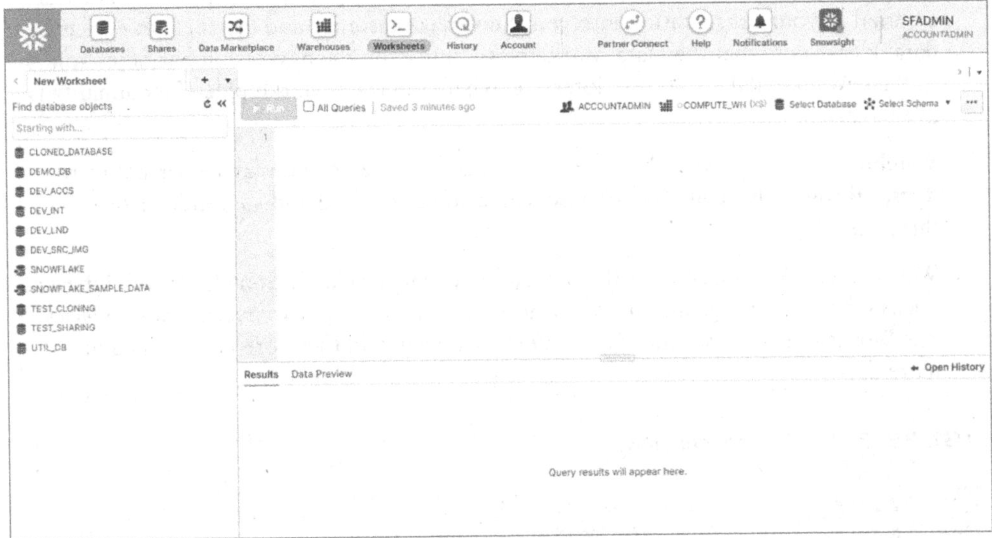

Web Interface Components

Figure 3.2 shows the various user interface components available in the Snowflake web UI. Let's explore each component in detail:

FIGURE 3.2 Navigation Bar

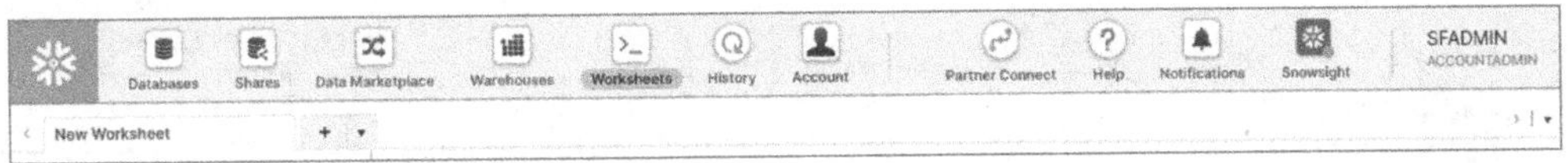

Databases The Databases page shows a list of existing databases in the system. This includes databases that have been created on top of data shared by other Snowflake accounts. A user with the correct privileges can create new databases and manage existing databases through this page.

Shares The Shares page shows information related to data that has been shared by or shared with the Snowflake account. These are often referred to as outbound shares or inbound shares, respectively. A user with the correct privileges can create or manage shares through this page. You learn how data sharing works in Snowflake later in this book.

Data Marketplace Snowflake Data Marketplace is an online store that allows you to buy and sell datasets. Using the Snowflake Data Marketplace, you can bring datasets external to your organization into your Snowflake instance and use them to enrich your data. Please note that the Data Marketplace button on the navigation bar takes you to the new Snowflake web user interface, where the Data Marketplace functionality is available.

Warehouses Users with the correct privileges can create and manage virtual warehouses through this page. Warehouses can also be resumed and suspended from this page.

Worksheets Worksheets are the default view that the classic Snowflake web interface opens when a user logs in. The Worksheet page allows a user to execute SQL queries. The Worksheet page is arguably the most used view and therefore is explained in more detail.

FIGURE 3.3 Worksheets view

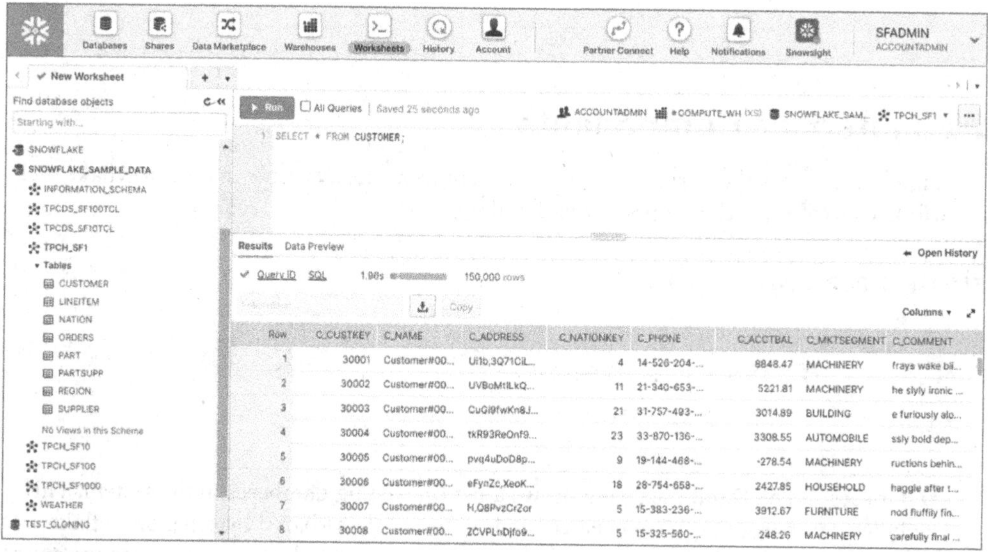

The selected role, virtual warehouse, database and schema are referred to as Context. These settings control the context under which a query executes:

Selected Role The role that is used when a query is executed.

Selected Virtual Warehouse Indicates the virtual warehouse that is used when a query is executed.

Selected Database Shows the database that applies to queries in the worksheet. The advantage of specifying the database is that you don't need to prefix the tables in the queries. However, do note that you can use tables from different databases in the same query, in which case you need to prefix tables that are not in the database specified in the context.

Selected Schema The schema that applies to the specified query. This setting's characteristics are like the database setting.

Query Results This section of the Worksheet page shows the results from the execution of queries. This includes the actual result sets and errors if a query fails to complete.

Database Tree This section shows a list of databases, tables, and views available to the role selected in the worksheet context. A user can navigate the database tree to find various objects and preview the data for a table or a view in this section.

New Worksheets A user can click the + button to create as many worksheets as needed, where each worksheet may have a different context and a different query. The worksheets can be renamed to a meaningful name if necessary. The worksheets and their contents are automatically saved, so when users log off and log back in, they can see worksheets from their previous session.

Throughout this book, the Worksheet page is used extensively, and it is expected that your skills in using the Worksheets view will increase as you progress through the various chapters.

History The History page shows the list of previously executed queries, successfully or with errors. The page shows the query's status, the actual query executed, the duration taken by the query, and other vital information for each query. The query history for a query is available for a maximum of 14 days from the execution of the query. Notably, a user can click on a query's ID and view the query profile or the plan for the query.

Account The Account page (Figure 3.4) is one of the essential administrative pages in the classic Snowflake web interface. By default, the Account page is visible only to the built-in ACCOUNTADMIN and SECURITYADMIN roles. Depending on the role selected at the top-right side of the screen, a user may or may not see the Account button in the navigation bar.

The Account page is divided into several tabs that range from usage and billing information, including payment method setup, user and role management, policies and management of sessions, resource monitors, and reader accounts. Later in this book we explore the functionality offered by these tabs.

FIGURE 3.4 Account page

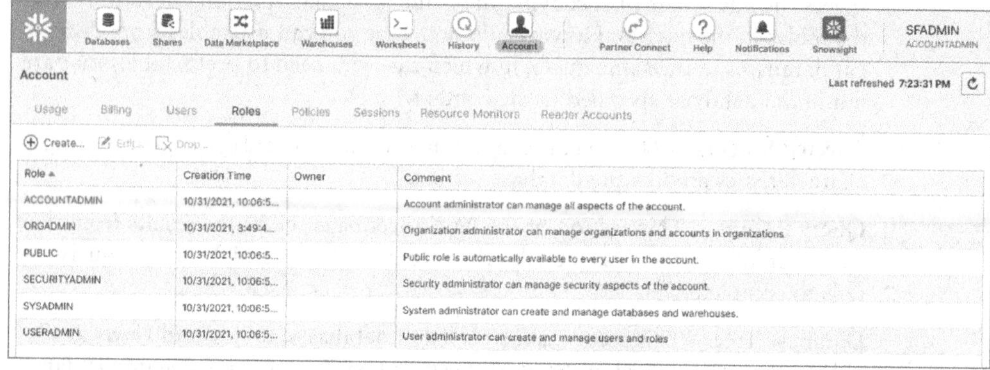

Partner Connect Several organizations have partnered with Snowflake, providing features and additional functionality. Partner Connect allows you to connect and establish trial accounts with Snowflake business partners quickly. The feature allows fast and easy evaluation of third-party tools and utilities. Snowflake partners can be divided into the following categories:

- Data Integration
- Business Intelligence
- Machine Learning and Data Science
- SQL Development and Management
- Security and Governance

The partners' list and categorization can be found here:

`https://docs.snowflake.com/en/user-guide/ecosystem-all.html`

Help The Help button does a bit more than just displaying help content. By clicking this button, a user can navigate to the documentation, open the help panel that appears on the right side, and open the Downloads page, where the user can download various connectors and tools associated with Snowflake. The Downloads page is shown in Figure 3.5.

The SnowPro Core exam can contain questions that test the reader's knowledge of connectors and tools available for download. Therefore, we recommend that you familiarize yourself with the available downloads before attempting the exam.

Notifications The Notifications button and the notification pop-up are available only to the ACCOUNTADMIN role. The notifications capability is not enabled by default and needs to be turned on. Once it's turned on, notifications may be sent via email or shown under the Notifications button, or both.

FIGURE 3.5 Downloads page

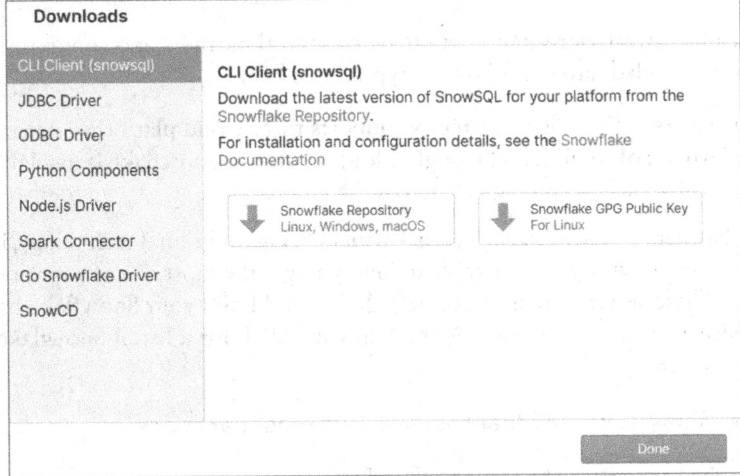

Snowsight This button links to the brand-new web interface that Snowflake has developed. Snowsight is expected to become the primary web interface, and the classic web interface is likely to be completely phased out eventually. This new web interface is lightweight and takes advantage of the features provided by modern browsers. The new web interface also provides a new Worksheets view, which offers querying and interactive analysis capabilities.

User Preferences At the rightmost corner of the navigation bar, the logged-in user is displayed along with a drop-down that provides several options, as shown in Figure 3.6.

Users can change their passwords and set up multifactor authentication (MFA) through these options. A user can also change their active role through one of the options. It is worth noting that the role selected here applies to the whole user interface and influences which buttons on the navigation bar may be available to a user.

FIGURE 3.6 User Preferences drop-down

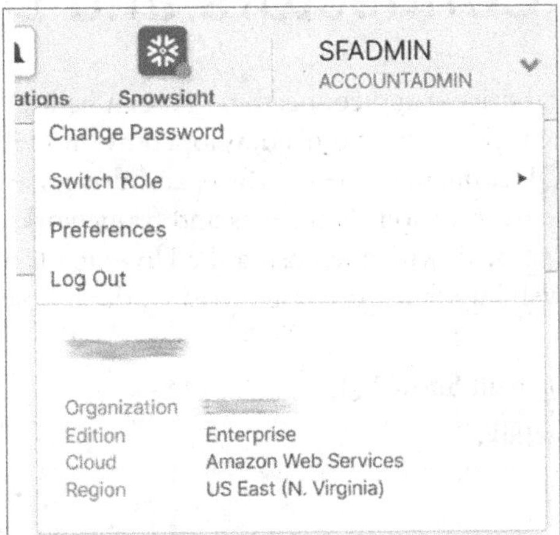

Snowflake Partners

The Snowflake software ecosystem is made up of several partners and connectors. Snowflake partners can be divided into the following types.

Cloud Partners Snowflake currently supports three cloud platforms: Amazon Web Services, Microsoft Azure, and Google Cloud Platform. Snowflake is available on these cloud providers in over 20 regions across the globe.

Service Partners Snowflake Services Partners bring additional technology, industry, and business knowledge to the table to help you get the most out of your Snowflake solution. These service partners can help design and build your Snowflake-based data warehouse environment. Please see the following URL for a list of Snowflake service partners.

```
www.snowflake.com/partners/solutions-partners
```

Technology Partners The Snowflake technology partner ecosystem comprises many partners and connectors and is constantly expanding. Snowflake technology partners have been classified into the following functional categories.

- Data Integration
- Business Intelligence
- Security and Governance
- Machine Learning and Data Science
- SQL Development and Management
- Native Programming Interfaces

Please see the following URL for an updated view of Snowflake technology partners.

```
https://docs.snowflake.com/en/user-guide/ecosystem.html
```

Snowflake Connectors and Drivers

Snowflake provides several drivers and connectors that can be used to connect to your Snowflake instance. These include client tools developed by Snowflake, such as the web interface and the SnowSQL command-line interface, and drivers and connectors that enable connectivity to Snowflake from various languages and frameworks. Most of these tools, drivers, and connectors can be downloaded using the Downloads menu under the Help section through the classic web interface. As of this writing, the following tools, connectors, and drivers were available:

- Command-line (CLI) client SnowSQL
- JDBC driver for Snowflake

- ODBC driver for Snowflake
- .NET driver for Snowflake
- Snowflake driver for the Go language
- Node.js drivers
- PHP PDO drivers
- Snowflake Connector for Python
- Snowflake Connector for Spark
- Snowflake Connector for Kafka
- SnowCD, which is the Snowflake Connectivity Diagnostic Tool

SnowSQL is further covered in more detail in this section since it is the primary tool for interacting with your Snowflake instance, along with the Snowflake web interface.

SnowSQL

SnowSQL is a command-line client used for connecting to Snowflake and running SQL statements. Using SnowSQL, a user can perform operations such as creating, deleting, and managing database objects, commonly referred to as Data Definition Language (DDL) operations, and operations that modify data, commonly referred to as Data Manipulation Language (DML) operations. You can also use SnowSQL to load and unload data from Snowflake. SnowSQL is available for Linux, Windows, and macOS platforms.

Exercise 3.1 outlines the steps for installing and using SnowSQL.

EXERCISE 3.1

Installing and Using SnowSQL

1. Open your browser and navigate to the URL for the Snowflake instance you signed up for in Exercise 1.1.
2. Log into your Snowflake instance, click Help on the navigation bar, and click Download on the resulting menu. As shown in the following screenshot, the page shows a list of software that can be downloaded. These include various drivers, connectors, and client software. Select CLI Client (snowsql) and click the Snowflake Repository link, as highlighted here.

EXERCISE 3.1 *(continued)*

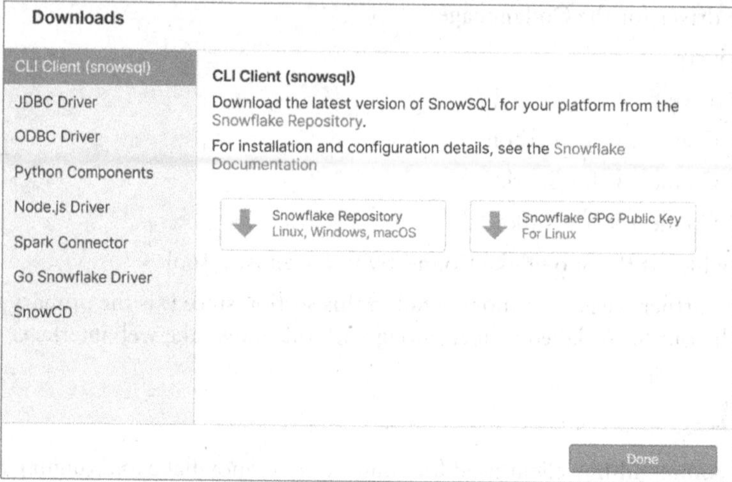

Alternatively, you can directly navigate to the following site, which opens the Snowflake client repository to the same location as step 2:

`https://sfc-repo.snowflakecomputing.com/snowsql/index.html`

3. Navigate the subfolders in the `snowsql` folder until you get to the subfolder, which shows various operating system versions, as shown in the following screenshot. For this exercise, we are using the Windows-based `snowsql` version for installation.

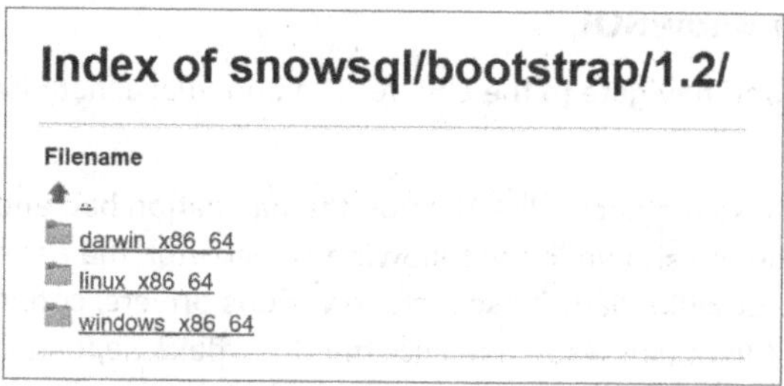

4. Navigate to the `windows_x86_64` folder and download the latest version of the `snowsql` installer. As of this writing, the latest available version was `snowsql-1.2.20-windows_x86_64.msi`.
5. Double-click the installer executable and follow the prompts to install SnowSQL. The detailed instructions are not shown here since the installation is straightforward.
6. Now that `snowsql` is installed successfully, connect to your Snowflake instance and run a few test queries. To do so, open the command prompt and run the following

command, where *<account_name>* is the name of your account and *<login_name>* is the username that you would like to use for the connection:

```
snowsql -a <account_name> -u <login_name>
```

7. One easy method to find the account name is to look at the URL of your Snowflake instance. Generally, the text between `http(s)://` and `snowflakecomputing.com` is your account name. For example, the following figure highlights the account name.

https://fm79999.ap-southeast-2.snowflakecomputing.com

https://ni57541.southeast-asia.azure.snowflakecomputing.com

8. Based on the example URL and assuming a username of SFADMIN, the following two examples show how to connect to your Snowflake instance using `snowsql`.

```
snowsql -a fm79999.ap-southeast-2 -u SFADMIN

snowsql -a ni57541.southeast-asia.azure -u SFADMIN
```

9. After you execute this command, `snowsql` connects to the account using the specified username and prompt for the password. Supply the password for the username and press Enter. If you see an error message such as "failed to initialize log. . .", you can safely ignore the error.
10. If the username, password, and account information are correct, SnowSQL connects to the Snowflake instance. Once a successful connection is made, the following should be shown. Notice that currently, no default database or schema is selected for querying.

```
* SnowSQL * v1.2.18
Type SQL statements or !help
SFADMIN#COMPUTE_WH@(no database).(no schema)>
```

11. Though a database and a schema can be provided when the `snowsql` command is invoked by supplying the `-d` and `-s` parameters to specify the database and schema name, you can also change the database and schema by executing the USE SQL command. Let's do that and then run a sample query to validate that everything works:

```
USE SNOWFLAKE_SAMPLE_DATA;
USE SCHEMA SNOWFLAKE_SAMPLE_DATA.TPCH_SF1;

USE WAREHOUSE COMPUTE_WH;

SELECT * FROM REGION LIMIT 5;
```

12. The results of the query are shown in the following screenshot. We have now successfully connected via SnowSQL and can query the database, create new objects, perform administrative activities, and even load and unload data.

EXERCISE 3.1 *(continued)*

R_REGIONKEY	R_NAME	R_COMMENT
0	AFRICA	lar deposits. blithely final packages cajole. regular waters are final requests. regular accounts are according to
1	AMERICA	hs use ironic, even requests. s
2	ASIA	ges. thinly even pinto beans ca
3	EUROPE	ly final courts cajole furiously final excuse
4	MIDDLE EAST	uickly special accounts cajole carefully blithely close requests. carefully final asymptotes haggle furiousl

SnowSQL can be installed on Windows, Linux, and macOS operating systems.

New Snowflake Web Interface

The classic Snowflake web interface and its various components are described at the start of this chapter. The classic Snowflake web interface has been the primary way of interacting with your Snowflake instance. However, Snowflake has introduced a new web interface using modern architecture and technology. The new web interface can be accessed by clicking the Snowsight button on the navigation bar, as shown in Figure 3.7.

FIGURE 3.7 Link to the new web interface

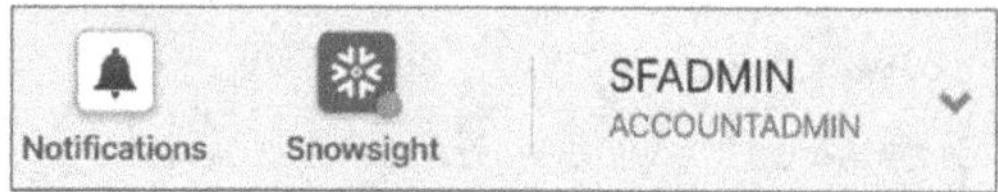

The new Snowflake web UI is available for the following browsers:

- Google Chrome
- Mozilla Firefox
- Apple Safari for macOS

Figure 3.8 shows the navigation bar for the modern Snowflake web interface with brief descriptions for some key screens. Each component is explained in detail further.

A: Profile Profile information for the logged-in user is shown under this drop-down. A user can change their active role through this drop-down, change their password. and also enroll in multifactor authentication on this screen.

B: Worksheets The worksheets in the new web interface have been completely revamped. The new worksheets are designed to provide enhanced features for data analysts, providing interactive analysis, charting, and visualization capabilities using modern web architecture that enables quick slice-and-dice analysis of the data without requiring querying the database again.

FIGURE 3.8 New web interface navigation

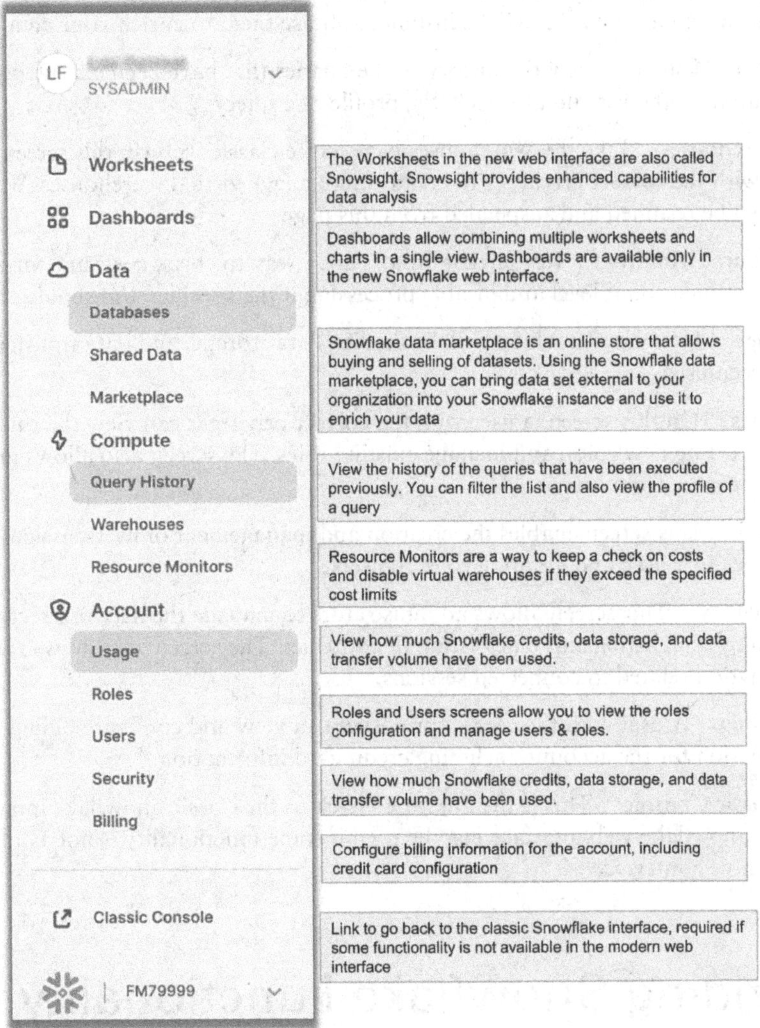

C: Dashboards Multiple worksheets can be combined into a single view through the capabilities offered by the Dashboard view. For example, you can combine tabular and visualization data to create compelling dashboards, all from within the Snowflake interface.

D: Databases This screen enables a privileged user to view, create, and manage databases, schemas, and other child objects within those databases.

E: Shared Data The Shared Data screen shows outbound and inbound shares: data shared by the account or shared with the account. A user with correct privileges can create or manage shares on this page. You'll learn how data sharing works in Snowflake in later chapters.

F: Marketplace Snowflake Data Marketplace is an online store that allows you to buy and sell datasets. Using the Data Marketplace, you can bring datasets external to your organization into your Snowflake instance and use them to enrich your data.

G: Query History View the history of the queries that have been executed previously. You can filter the list and also view the profile of a query.

H: Warehouses Like the Warehouses page in the classic web UI, this screen allows users with the correct privileges to create and manage virtual warehouses. Warehouses can also be resumed and suspended from this page.

I: Resource Monitors Resource monitors are a way to check costs at a virtual warehouse or an account level and disable processing if the specified thresholds are exceeded.

J: Usage View how much Snowflake credits, data storage, and data transfer volume have been used.

K: Roles On this screen, a user with the correct privileges can view the roles in the system, create new roles, and manage existing roles. The screen also allows granting or revoking roles from users.

L: Users This screen enables the creation and management of users, assigning direct privileges to a user, and granting roles to users.

M: Security This screen allows administrators to manage the network security, including whitelisting and blacklisting IP addresses. The screen also shows real-time information related to connected sessions.

N: Billing A user with the correct privileges can view and configure billing information for the account, including credit card information.

O: Classic Console This is the link to go back to the classic Snowflake interface. The classic Snowflake web interface may be used if some functionality is not available in the modern web interface.

Extending Snowflake Functionality

Snowflake provides several methods to add capabilities to your Snowflake instance through concepts such as user-defined functions, stored procedures, Snowflake Scripting, and Snowpark. Here's an overview of these methods:

User-Defined Functions Snowflake provides much built-in functionality and additional capabilities through various partners. However, if there is functionality not supported by Snowflake or its partners, you can extend the system by creating user-defined functions (UDFs). Snowflake UDFs can be written in SQL, Java, JavaScript, and Python. They can be scalar, returning one row for each input row, where each result row has a single column or value. You can also create tabular UDFs that return zero, one, or several rows for each input, and each result row can have multiple columns. User-defined table functions are known as UDTFs.

External Functions It is also possible to create UDFs stored outside Snowflake and executed externally. Known as external functions, these UDFs can access third-party API services outside of Snowflake. An external function does not contain code but calls code stored and executed outside Snowflake. One advantage of creating an external function is that an external function can be written in languages that normal UDFs cannot be. External functions can use functions and libraries that typical user-defined functions cannot access.

Secure UDFs Typically the underlying code used in a UDF can be viewed by ordinary users. Additionally, some internal optimizations can result in data from the tables used in UDFs being exposed to users. Secure UDFs can hide the implementation code from users and ensure that access to underlying data is not available through the UDF.

Stored Procedures Stored procedures in Snowflake enable you to write procedural code that can execute SQL statements. Stored procedures allow if-else logic, looping, and so forth—and these sort of things are not usually allowed in SQL. Using stored procedures, you can dynamically assemble SQL statements and execute them. A stored procedure can return a single value or tabular data; however, it doesn't have to return a value. Using Snowpark, you can write stored procedures in Java, Python, or Scala, or you can use JavaScript or Snowflake Scripting to create stored procedures. While stored procedures and UDFs appear similar, they differ in purpose. The purpose of a UDF is to process input, perform calculations, and return a value, whereas the purpose of a stored procedure is to execute one or more SQL statements. A stored procedure can be run under the caller's or owner's rights: A stored procedure configured to run under the caller's rights runs with the privileges of the caller. A stored procedure configured to run under the owner's right runs with the owner's privileges, thus allowing the stored procedure to access objects and perform actions to which the caller may not have privileges.

Snowflake Scripting Snowflake Scripting is an extension to SQL, which allows procedural logic typically found in programming languages. Snowflake Scripting supports variables, if-else constructs, looping mechanisms, cursors, result set management, and exception handling. Snowflake Scripting is typically used to write stored procedures but can also be used to write procedural code outside of a stored procedure.

Snowpark Snowpark is a library created by Snowflake that provides APIs for querying and processing data using typical application code written in a programming language other than SQL. Snowpark allows developers to use Java, Scala, and Python to create data processing applications using typical programming constructs to process data. The programming constructs that process data are automatically converted to SQL and pushed down to Snowflake for execution. Thus, developers can develop in a language familiar to them but still take full advantage of the scale offered by Snowflake.

Summary

We have covered the Snowflake interfaces and connectivity options in this chapter. Two essential methods of interacting with your Snowflake instance are via the web interface and SnowSQL, the command-line interface, which can be installed on Windows, Linux, and macOS. Snowflake provides a variety of drivers and connectors to enable connectivity with other applications.

Exam Essentials

Understand the Snowflake web interface. One of the primary interaction methods with your Snowflake instance is the Snowflake web interface, also called the Snowflake web UI. In addition to the classic web interface, Snowflake has introduced a new web interface called Snowsight, which, among other things, provides enhanced analytical capabilities.

The classic Snowflake web interface allows all essential capabilities, including database and table creation, querying the existing data, creating security roles and new users, and managing the account and billing.

Understand the connectors and Drivers provided by Snowflake. Snowflake provides a variety of drivers and connectors for different languages and frameworks. The list of available connectors has expanded over time. At present, the following drivers and connectors are available:

- Command-line client (CLI) SnowSQL
- JDBC driver for Snowflake
- ODBC driver for Snowflake
- .NET driver for Snowflake
- Snowflake driver for the Go language
- Node.js drivers
- PHP PDO drivers
- Snowflake Connector for Python
- Snowflake Connector for Spark
- Snowflake Connector for Kafka
- SnowCD, which is the Snowflake Connectivity Diagnostic Tool

Understand methods that can be used to extend Snowflake functionality. User-defined functions, stored procedures, Snowflake Scripting, and Snowpark can be used to extend Snowflake's capabilities:

- UDFs can be written in SQL, Java, JavaScript, and Python.
- External functions can be written in several languages, and their code executes outside Snowflake.
- Secure UDFs can hide implementation details and the underlying tables from users.
- Stored procedures in Snowflake enable writing procedural code that can execute SQL statements.
- Snowflake Scripting adds procedural logic to SQL, such as if-else, looping, cursors, and exception handling.
- Snowpark lets developers create data-processing apps in Java, Scala, and Python that push down SQL to Snowflake.

Review Questions

1. Which of the following connectors and programs can be downloaded from the Downloads section in the Snowflake web UI? (Select all that apply.)
   - **A.** Go Snowflake driver
   - **B.** JDBC driver
   - **C.** Snowpipe connector
   - **D.** OAuth driver
   - **E.** Kerberos driver
2. Consider the Worksheets view on the classic Snowflake web UI. Which of the following can you select for each worksheet? (Select all that apply.)
   - **A.** Database
   - **B.** User
   - **C.** Table
   - **D.** Schema
   - **E.** Virtual Warehouse
3. On the classic Snowflake web UI, which button on the top bar takes you to the screen where you can create new compute clusters?
   - **A.** Databases
   - **B.** Account
   - **C.** Warehouses
   - **D.** Worksheets
4. True or False: You can open only a single worksheet in the Snowflake web UI.
   - **A.** True
   - **B.** False
5. On the classic Snowflake web UI, which of the following are buttons on the top navigation bar? (Select all that apply.)
   - **A.** Worksheets
   - **B.** Warehouses
   - **C.** Databases
   - **D.** Security
6. You have logged into the Snowflake web UI but cannot see the Account button in the top bar. Which one of the following could be the reason?
   - **A.** Snowflake has renamed the Account button to Organization.
   - **B.** The Account button is only available to users with the ACCOUNTADMIN or SECURITYADMIN role. However, your current role is neither of these two roles.
   - **C.** The Account button is shown in only specific browsers.
   - **D.** The Account button is shown only for those Snowflake accounts who have the Enterprise license.

7. What functionality can you access under the Warehouses button? (Select all that apply.)
   A. Review billing and cost information related to virtual warehouses.
   B. Create new virtual warehouses.
   C. Suspend or resume existing virtual warehouses.
   D. See the percentage of space used by each virtual warehouse.

8. True or False: A Snowflake user can configure multifactor authentication (MFA) through the Snowflake Web UI.
   A. True
   B. False

9. You are developing a program in Java. The program needs to connect to a Snowflake instance and run queries. To connect to the Snowflake database, which one of the following drivers will you need?
   A. Go Snowflake driver
   B. JDBC driver
   C. Snowpipe connector
   D. ODBC driver
   E. CLI client (SnowSQL)

10. You plan to use a business intelligence tool to connect to Snowflake to create new reports and dashboards. Which of the following are possible drivers that you can use in the tool to connect to Snowflake? (Select all that apply.)
    A. Python connector
    B. JDBC driver
    C. ODBC driver
    D. Spark connector
    E. CLI client (SnowSQL)

11. Which type of Snowflake partner is Matillion?
    A. Data Integration
    B. Business intelligence
    C. Machine learning and data science
    D. SQL development and management
    E. Security and governance

12. Where does the code for an external function execute?
    A. Inside Snowflake
    B. Outside Snowflake
    C. In a sandbox inside Snowflake
    D. In the web browser

13. True or False: Snowflake Scripting is an extension to SQL, which allows procedural logic.
    A. True
    B. False

Loading Data

THE SNOWPRO CORE EXAM TOPICS COVERED IN THIS CHAPTER INCLUDE THE FOLLOWING:

✓ **Domain 1.0: Snowflake Data Platform Features and Architecture**

- 1.3 Outline Snowflake's catalog and objects.
  - Databases
  - Schemas
  - Data types
  - Pipes
  - Sequences

✓ **Domain 4.0: Data Loading and Unloading**

- 4.1 Define concepts and best practices that should be considered when loading data.
  - Stages and stage types
  - File size
  - File formats
  - Folder structures
  - Ad hoc/bulk loading using the Snowflake UI
- 4.2 Outline different commands used to load data and when they should be used.
  - CREATE PIPE
  - COPY INTO
  - GET
  - INSERT/INSERT OVERWRITE
  - PUT
  - VALIDATE

- 4.3 Define concepts and best practices that should be considered when unloading data.
  - File formats
  - Empty strings and NULL values
  - Unloading to a single file
  - Unloading relational tables
- 4.4 Outline the different commands used to unload data and when they should be used.
  - LIST
  - COPY INTO
  - CREATE FILE FORMAT
  - CREATE FILE FORMAT . . . CLONE
  - ALTER FILE FORMAT
  - DROP FILE FORMAT
  - DESCRIBE FILE FORMAT
  - SHOW FILE FORMAT

✓ **Domain 5.0: Data Transformation**

- 5.1 Explain how to work with standard data.
  - Estimating functions
  - Sampling
  - Supported function types
- 5.2 Explain how to work with semi-structured data.
  - Supported file formats, data types, and sizes
  - VARIANT column
  - Flattening the nested structure
- 5.3 Explain how to work with unstructured data.
  - Define and use directory tables
  - SQL file functions
  - Outline the purpose of user-defined functions (UDFs) for data analysis

Data loading and processing is a crucial activity for a data analytics system. Snowflake provides a variety of methods for loading data, including bulk data loading and processing data in a continuous manner. This chapter walks you through the concept of staging in Snowflake, describing the internal and external stage types. We cover data loading using the COPY command and continuously through Snowpipe. We also discuss basic data transformations and exporting of data from Snowflake.

Data Loading in Snowflake

Snowflake allows the loading of data through two primary methods. First, bulk data or large files can be loaded using the COPY command. The COPY command requires a virtual warehouse to load the data into a table. Data is loaded into a table and stored in the storage layer in the form of micro-partitions. When data is loaded into a table, one or more new micro-partitions are written to the storage, and the metadata for that table is updated, as shown in Figure 4.1.

FIGURE 4.1 Data loading

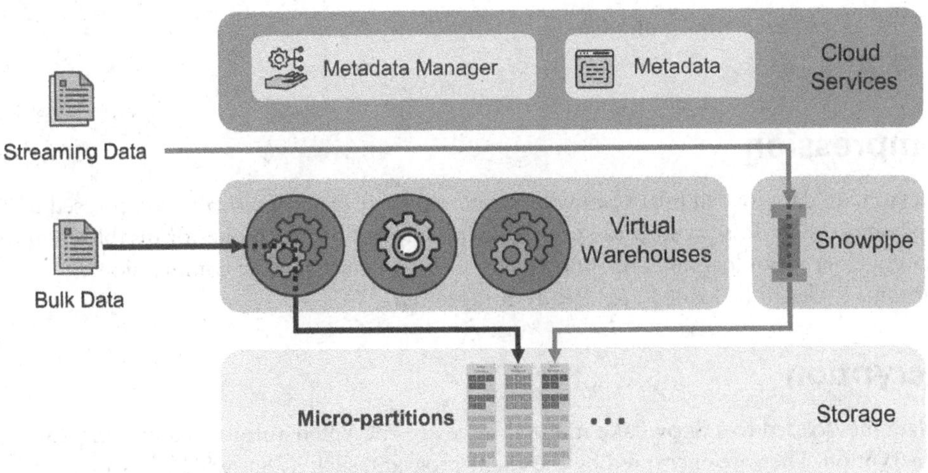

The metadata stores information about the micro-partitions, each column's range of values, and other optimization information. At the same time, additional metadata is created about the file that has been loaded into the table. Snowflake maintains metadata related to data loading and micro-partitions in its cloud services layer. The load metadata contains a variety of information, including the name of each file loaded into that table and the time stamp for the last load of a file. Using this load metadata, Snowflake ensures that it doesn't reprocess an already loaded file.

The load metadata expires after 64 days, after which, in specific scenarios, Snowflake skips loading old files for which the load status is unknown. You can load such files by setting the `LOAD_UNCERTAIN_FILES` option to `true` or by using the `FORCE` option, which loads all files regardless of their status.

The second method Snowflake allows for loading of data is continuous data loading using Snowpipe, a serverless service. Snowpipe permits micro-batch loading and is used when a constant stream of data, such as transactions or events, must be loaded quickly.

Supported File Formats for Loading Data

The following file formats are supported for loading data into Snowflake:

- Delimited text files—comma-separated values (CSV), tab-separated values (TSV), or files separated by any other single-byte delimiter
- JSON (JavaScript Object Notation)
- Parquet
- Avro
- ORC (Optimized Row Columnar)
- XML

Compression

By default, all data loaded into a Snowflake internal stage is automatically compressed using `gzip` compression. It is possible to specify other compression techniques or disable compression altogether when loading data. Snowflake can also detect specific compression algorithms if files to be loaded are already compressed.

Encryption

All data files loaded to a Snowflake internal stage are encrypted automatically using 256-bit encryption. They are encrypted by the client program, such as SnowSQL, before being uploaded to a Snowflake stage.

Files that are already encrypted can also be loaded into Snowflake, but an encryption key must be provided during the loading process.

What Is a Stage?

To understand the concept of a stage in Snowflake, you must know the role of staging in a data warehouse. A staging area is an intermediate storage location between the source systems and the data warehouse. Data extracted from a source system is transferred to a staging area through different means such as FTP. The staging area is also accessible to the data warehouse; therefore, the data in the staging area can easily be loaded into the data warehouse.

The staging area can be outside a data warehouse, so the data is first extracted from a source system and transferred to an intermediate area. Data is then loaded from the intermediate area into the data warehouse. This approach is shown in Figure 4.2.

FIGURE 4.2 Staging area outside a data warehouse

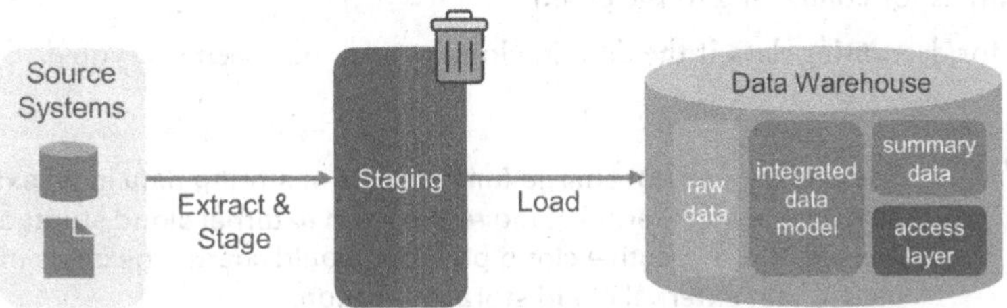

Alternatively, the staging area can be a location inside a data warehouse. Data from source systems is loaded into this staging area. Once the data is in the staging area, the data warehouse can easily process the data further into tables. This approach is shown in Figure 4.3.

FIGURE 4.3 Staging area inside a data warehouse

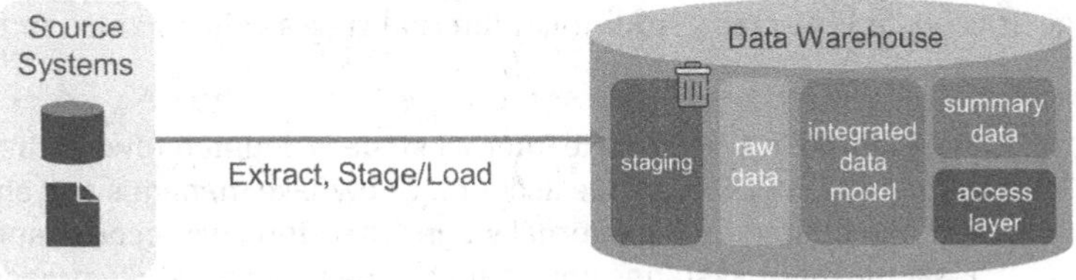

In Snowflake, the stage object plays the same role as the staging concept in data warehousing. Stages are used to assist in loading and unloading data in Snowflake. Data to be loaded into a Snowflake table must be made available in a Snowflake stage before it can be processed into a table. Once the data is in a stage, you can execute the `COPY` to load that data into a table. Similarly, when data is unloaded from a table, it is unloaded into a stage.

The stages in Snowflake can be divided into two types. *External stages* are stage objects mapped to external cloud storage. *Internal stages* store data internal to Snowflake and are managed by Snowflake. The internal stage type is further divided into three subtypes: table, user, and named internal stages. Let's take a look at each type.

External Stage

An external stage points to a storage location outside of Snowflake. Typically, an external stage refers to a storage location in a cloud platform such as an AWS S3 bucket. The external storage cloud location is managed not by Snowflake but rather by the organization owning that location. External stage definitions also contain additional information on connecting to the cloud storage location. This information includes the following:

- Path to the cloud storage
- Credentials for connecting to the cloud
- A key for decrypting data if the data in cloud storage has been encrypted

Snowflake does not charge for the costs of storing data in an external stage since an external stage refers to an external cloud storage location. Instead, the respective cloud provider would charge the costs of storing data in that external cloud storage location.

Internal Stages

As the name suggests, internal stages are internal to Snowflake, and Snowflake manages the storage for these stages. Files uploaded to an internal stage are stored and managed by Snowflake. Internal stages are mainly used for loading data from on-premises systems into Snowflake. Snowflake provides three types of internal stages: table stages, user stages, and named internal stages. By default, each table and each user in Snowflake are allocated an internal stage. It is possible to create additional internal stages called named internal stages.

Data stored in a Snowflake internal stage is counted toward the overall storage of your Snowflake account. Snowflake manages and charges for storage utilized by the internal stage. Therefore, we recommend that you clear the internal stages once data has been successfully processed.

Table Stage

Every table in Snowflake is automatically assigned a table stage. The table stage exists for the lifetime of a table and is dropped when the table is dropped. A table stage is a suitable option if you are aiming to load data into a single table. Files loaded into a table stage can only be loaded into the table associated with that stage. Multiple users can access a table stage, but a table stage can load data into only one table. Table stages have the following characteristics:

- A table stage cannot be altered or dropped; instead, they are created and allocated by default and available for the table's lifetime.
- They have the same name as the table and can be referenced using the `@%tablename` syntax.
- Table stages do not allow you to set the file format options. Instead, you must provide these options as part of the `COPY` command.
- Table stages do not support data transformation while loading the data.

User Stage

Every user in Snowflake is also assigned a stage by default. User stages are unique to a user, which means users cannot access each other's stages. However, user stages can be used to load multiple tables if required, unlike a table stage, which is tied to a table. User stages have the following characteristics:

- A user stage cannot be altered or dropped and is created and allocated for every Snowflake user.
- They can be accessed by using the `@~` syntax.
- User stages do not allow you to set the file format options; instead, you must provide these options as part of the `COPY` command.

Named Internal Stage

Named internal stages are internal stages that can be created, dropped, or altered as required. Compared to user and table stages, they provide more flexibility. Named internal stages can be used when regularly scheduled loads need to be performed. They have several other advantages over user and table stages:

- Named internal stages can be created, altered, and dropped.
- Because named internal stages are database objects, security and user access permissions can be applied to them.
- Named internal stages allow you to set the file format options, which means you can configure a stage once and use it for loading multiple files.

Figure 4.4 shows the stages we have discussed and how they are used to load data into Snowflake. The external stage points to a cloud storage object, and through an external stage, Snowflake can read and load data from cloud object storage. Notice how the external stage is linked to the cloud storage with a dotted line, signifying that it doesn't store any data but refers to cloud storage that stores the data.

FIGURE 4.4 Types of stages in Snowflake and their use

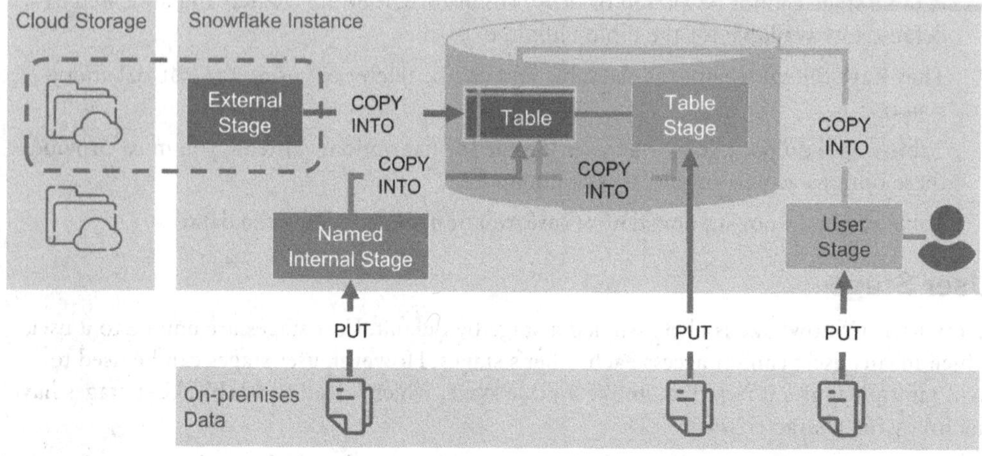

Named internal stages, table stages, and user stages are all examples of internal stages. Data must be uploaded to these stages through the PUT command using SnowSQL. Internal stages are typically used to load data from an on-premises system.

Data Loading via Internal Stages

In this series of exercises, we load data from on-premises CSV files. The exercises demonstrate the concept of loading data using the table stage, user stage, and the more flexible method of using an internal stage to load data.

Loading On-premises Data via the Table Stage

Exercise 4.1 walks you through the steps to load data from an on-premises system to a Snowflake table using a table stage. We treat our laptop as an on-premises system and use SnowSQL to upload the file into a table stage through the PUT command. Once the file is successfully uploaded into the table stage, we run the COPY command to load the file into the target table. Figure 4.5 illustrates the loading of on-premises data using SnowSQL and a table stage.

FIGURE 4.5 Loading on-premises data using SnowSQL and a table stage

EXERCISE 4.1

Loading On-premises Data from the Table Stage

1. You can access the example file (`customers.csv`) we are using in this exercise at the following URL. Download this file to your computer and store it in a folder accessible to the user you are logged in as.

   `https://snowpro-core-study-guide-downloads.s3.amazonaws.com/customers.csv`

2. Be sure to connect to your Snowflake account through SnowSQL. Use SnowSQL to PUT the `customers.csv` file into a table stage. Notice that SnowSQL is needed to upload the on-premises file but that other steps in this exercise can be run through the Snowflake web interface.

3. First, create a new database that will hold the Customer table in which you will load `customers.csv`:

```
CREATE DATABASE demo_data_loading;
```

4. Create the Customer table. The columns in this table relate to the data file that will be loaded into this table.

```
USE DATABASE demo_data_loading;
CREATE table customer
(
name STRING,
phone STRING,
email STRING,
address STRING,
```

EXERCISE 4.1 *(continued)*

```
postalCode STRING,
region STRING,
country STRING
);
```

5. Now that the table is created, Snowflake automatically creates a table stage and associates it with the table. You can validate that the stage has been created by executing a `LIST` command. Typically, the `LIST` command returns a list of files in that stage; however, you will get no results since you have not loaded any files.

```
LIST @%customer;
```

6. Next, you will upload files into the customer's table stage. To do so, you must log into your Snowflake instance via SnowSQL. SnowSQL must be run from the same machine where the files to be loaded are present. Using SnowSQL, run the following SQL to upload the `customers.csv` file into the Customer's table stage. The result of a successful PUT command is shown in the following screenshot.

```
PUT 'file:///<PATH>/customers.csv' @%customer;
```

```
SFADMIN#COMPUTE_WH@DEMO_DATA_LOADING.PUBLIC>PUT 'file:///C:/Users/john/customers.csv' @%customer;
+---------------+------------------+-------------+-------------+--------------------+--------------------+----------+---------+
| source        | target           | source_size | target_size | source_compression | target_compression | status   | message |
|---------------+------------------+-------------+-------------+--------------------+--------------------+----------+---------|
| customers.csv | customers.csv.gz |       10941 |        6192 | NONE               | GZIP               | UPLOADED |         |
+---------------+------------------+-------------+-------------+--------------------+--------------------+----------+---------+
1 Row(s) produced. Time Elapsed: 0.608s
```

7. Notice that the <PATH> placeholder in the preceding code needs to be replaced by the path where you have stored the `customers.csv` file. Also, note that the path should contain forward slashes rather than backslashes. So, if you are using Windows and the path to the file is `c:\Users\john\customers.csv`, then the path specified in the PUT statement should be `'file:///C:/Users/john/customers.csv'`.

8. Now you'll check which files are present in the table stage. To do so, run the `LIST` command using the following SQL. The following screenshot shows the command results, showing a single compressed file.

```
LIST @%customer;
```

```
SFADMIN#COMPUTE_WH@DEMO_DATA_LOADING.PUBLIC>LIST @%customer;
+------------------+------+----------------------------------+-------------------------------+
| name             | size | md5                              | last_modified                 |
|------------------+------+----------------------------------+-------------------------------|
| customers.csv.gz | 6192 | 5c3c2f222bf868e08ad41f30e38300ac | Sat, 9 Oct 2021 23:10:32 GMT |
+------------------+------+----------------------------------+-------------------------------+
1 Row(s) produced. Time Elapsed: 0.134s
```

9. Next you'll load the data from the table stage into the table using the COPY command. Provide the file format to the COPY command because it is essential for the loading

processing to make sense of the files in the stage. The file format in the following SQL instructs Snowflake to treat files in the stage as CSV files delimited by the pipe character and the first line as the column header, which must be skipped:

```
COPY INTO customer
FROM @%customer
file_format = (type = csv field_delimiter = '|' skip_header = 1);
```

The result of the command is shown in the following screenshot, demonstrating that 100 rows contained in the `customers.csv` file were successfully loaded into the Customer table.

```
SFADMIN#COMPUTE_WH@DEMO_DATA_LOADING.PUBLIC>COPY INTO customer
                                            FROM @%customer
                                            file_format = (type = csv field_delimiter = '|' skip_header = 1);
```

file	status	rows_parsed	rows_loaded	error_limit	errors_seen	first_error	first_error_line
customers.csv.gz	LOADED	100	100	1	0	NULL	NULL

10. We can now validate that rows were successfully loaded into the Customer table by executing the following SQL; the result will show 100 rows:

```
SELECT * FROM customer;
```

11. Now that the data is successfully loaded, you must clean up the stage; otherwise, the data in that stage will continue to contribute to storage costs. To do so, run the following SQL to delete the files in the stage:

```
REMOVE @%customer;
```

Data is automatically encrypted and transferred from the on-premises computer to the internal stage. The data is encrypted at the client's computer before the transfer, so the data in transit already has encryption applied to it. Data stored in an internal stage is stored in an encrypted format, which is aligned with the fact that all data in Snowflake, whether in tables, internal stages, or elsewhere, is always encrypted.

Loading On-premises Data via the User Stage

Next, Exercise 4.2 demonstrates how an on-premises file can be loaded into a table using a user stage. This exercise also introduces the concept of the file format object and how it can be reused for loading data into different tables.

We treat our laptop as an on-premises system and use SnowSQL to upload the file into a user stage through the `PUT` command. Once the file is successfully uploaded into the user stage, we run the COPY command to load the file into the target table. Although we use the user stage to load data into a single table in this example, using the same method you can upload multiple files into a user stage and load them to different tables. Figure 4.6 illustrates the loading of on-premises data using SnowSQL and a user stage.

FIGURE 4.6 Loading on-premises data via SnowSQL and a user stage

EXERCISE 4.2

Loading On-premises Data via the User Stage

1. The example file (vehicles.csv) we are using in this exercise can be downloaded from the following URL. Download this file to your computer and store it in a folder accessible to the user you are logged in as.

   https://snowpro-core-study-guide-downloads.s3.amazonaws.com/vehicles.csv

2. Be sure to connect to your Snowflake account through SnowSQL. You will use SnowSQL to PUT the vehicles.csv file into a user stage. Notice that SnowSQL is needed to upload the on-premises file but that other steps in this exercise can be run through the Snowflake web interface.

3. If it does not exist already, create a database that will hold the Vehicle table to load the vehicles.csv data:

   ```
   CREATE DATABASE IF NOT EXISTS demo_data_loading;
   ```

4. Create the Vehicle table. The columns in this table relate to the data file that will be loaded into the table.

   ```
   USE DATABASE demo_data_loading;
   CREATE table vehicle
   (
   Make STRING,
   ```

```
Model STRING,
Year NUMBER,
Category STRING
);
```

5. Next, you will upload files into the user stage. To do so, you must log into your Snowflake instance by using SnowSQL. SnowSQL must be run from the same machine where the files to be loaded are present. Using SnowSQL, run the following SQL to upload the `vehicles.csv` file into the user stage. A user stage is referenceable by using @~ in your query.

   ```
   PUT 'file:///<PATH>/vehicles.csv' @~;
   ```

6. Note that the `<PATH>` placeholder in the preceding code needs to be replaced by the path where you have placed the `vehicles.csv` file. Also, note that the path should contain forward slashes rather than backslashes. So, if you are using Windows and the path to the file is `c:\Users\john\vehicles.csv`, then the path specified in the `PUT` statement should be `'file:///C:/Users/john/vehicles.csv'`.

7. Now check which files are present in the user stage. To do so, run the `LIST` command using the following SQL. The result of the command is shown in the following screenshot, showing not just the `vehicles.csv` file in a compressed format but also other files with `worksheet_data` in their name. The files with `worksheet_data` in their name correspond to the worksheets in the classic web UI that you may have opened to create and execute SQL queries.

   ```
   LIST @~;
   ```

SFADMIN#COMPUTE_WH@DEMO_DATA_LOADING.PUBLIC>LIST @~;

name	size	md5	last_modified
vehicles.csv.gz	4992	3b4a81cb2aff072bf506d31e0e6b95ed	Sun, 10 Oct 2021 01:50:35 GMT
worksheet_data/95dc6a8e-bbd6-4458-9a2d-772043342ba9	1216	e656145bb621b321626566e1a838fd0f	Sat, 2 Oct 2021 06:37:17 GMT
worksheet_data/c1c83403-38c3-46a3-afdb-7a2b9bc8d692	432	c8a9cfd93ecf3f0f266721ea4158a820	Sun, 3 Oct 2021 11:15:52 GMT
worksheet_data/c90084cd-1935-4570-bda1-916a4258d1b8	448	952e2028ed0c626b681f942f2305e7ab	Sun, 10 Oct 2021 01:45:13 GMT
worksheet_data/cccc6b5e-8bb4-465e-aa24-61f1bfe54bbc	704	a02019ee59fc858be270f3f98866332f	Sun, 10 Oct 2021 00:05:01 GMT
worksheet_data/fb9771bb-e940-41c1-b6d7-41744e975d83	704	b254c3ce2dab916edbdea93876781a96	Sun, 3 Oct 2021 08:09:42 GMT
worksheet_data/metadata	1440	99b3d639587ef0fc5f31a4759297127e	Sun, 10 Oct 2021 01:45:14 GMT

8. Before running the `COPY` command to load this file into the Vehicle table, you must create a file format object. Snowflake allows you to create a file format definition that you can reuse with multiple file loads. You will create a file format definition that uses commas as the field delimiter, skips blank lines in the data, and indicates zero header rows in the file. The file format also indicates that fields are enclosed in double quotes.

   ```
   CREATE OR REPLACE FILE FORMAT CSV_No_Header_Blank_Lines
     type = 'CSV'
     field_delimiter = ','
     field_optionally_enclosed_by = '"'
   ```

EXERCISE 4.2 *(continued)*

```
skip_header = 0
skip_blank_lines = true;
```

9. Now you'll load the data from the user stage into the table using the COPY command. You must also provide the file format to the COPY command:

```
COPY INTO vehicle
FROM @~/vehicles.csv.gz
file_format = CSV_No_Header_Blank_Lines;
```

10. The following screenshot shows the result, demonstrating that 500 rows were successfully loaded into the Vehicle table. Also worth noting is that the number of rows processed is 512, but only 500 were loaded because the `vehicles.csv` file contains blank rows. In the file format definition, you instructed Snowflake to skip blank rows. If you had not done so, the load would fail with errors.

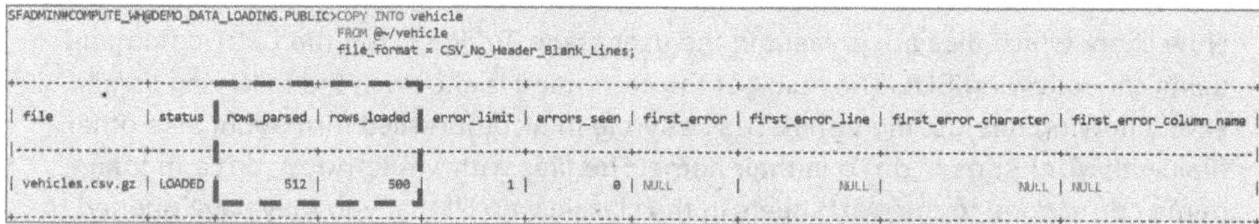

```
SFADMIN#COMPUTE_WH@DEMO_DATA_LOADING.PUBLIC>COPY INTO vehicle
                                            FROM @~/vehicle
                                            file_format = CSV_No_Header_Blank_Lines;
```

file	status	rows_parsed	rows_loaded	error_limit	errors_seen	first_error	first_error_line	first_error_character	first_error_column_name
vehicles.csv.gz	LOADED	512	500	1	0	NULL	NULL	NULL	NULL

11. You can now validate that rows were successfully loaded into the Vehicle table by executing the following SQL; the result will show 500 rows.

```
SELECT * FROM vehicle;
```

12. Now that the data is successfully loaded, you should clean up the stage; otherwise, the data in that stage will continue to contribute to storage costs. A user stage also stores worksheet data related to the classic web UI, so you cannot simply remove everything from the stage. To selectively delete files, run the following SQL:

```
REMOVE @~/vehicles.csv.gz;
```

File formats, external stages, and named internal stages are schema-level objects. They are created in the public schema of the selected database by default unless a different database and schema are specified at the time of their creation.

Loading On-premises Data via the Named Internal Stage

Exercise 4.3 demonstrates how an on-premises file can be loaded into a table using a named internal stage. This exercise also demonstrates how the file format configuration can be encapsulated in a named stage definition (something that cannot be done for user or table stages).

Like the previous two exercises, we treat our laptop as an on-premises system and use SnowSQL to upload the file into a named internal stage through the PUT command. Once the file is successfully uploaded into the named internal stage, we run the COPY command to load the file into the target table. Named internal stages are the most flexible and are used if there is a requirement to load multiple files regularly. Figure 4.7 illustrates the loading of on-premises data using SnowSQL and a named internal stage.

FIGURE 4.7 Loading on-premises data via SnowSQL and a named internal stage

EXERCISE 4.3

Loading On-premises Data via the Named Internal Stage

1. The example file (`locations.csv`) we are using in this exercise can be downloaded from the following URL. Download this file to your computer and store it in a folder accessible to the user you are logged in as.

   `https://snowpro-core-study-guide-downloads.s3.amazonaws.com/locations.csv`

2. Be sure to connect to your Snowflake account through SnowSQL. You will use SnowSQL to PUT the `locations.csv` file into a named internal stage. Notice that SnowSQL is needed to upload the on-premises file but that other steps in this exercise can be run through the Snowflake web interface.

3. If it does not exist already, create a database that will hold the Locations table to load the `locations.csv` data:

   ```
   CREATE DATABASE IF NOT EXISTS demo_data_loading;
   ```

4. Create the Locations table. The columns in this table relate to the data file that will be loaded into this table.

   ```
   USE DATABASE demo_data_loading;
   CREATE TABLE locations
   ```

EXERCISE 4.3 *(continued)*

```
(
    latitude NUMBER,
    longitude NUMBER,
    place STRING,
    CountryCode STRING,
    TimeZone STRING
);
```

5. Next, you'll create a file format object, which you will associate with the named internal stage later in this exercise. You will create a file format definition that uses the tab character as the field delimiter and indicates zero header rows in the file. If you need to list existing file formats, you can use `SHOW FILE FORMATS` to list file format objects available to you. You can use `DESCRIBE FILE FORMAT` to view details for a specific file format. If desired, you can create a new file format by cloning an existing file format.

```
CREATE OR REPLACE FILE FORMAT TSV_No_Headers
  type = 'CSV'
  field_delimiter = '\t'
  skip_header = 0;
```

6. Now create a named internal stage and associate the stage with the file format you just created. Attaching the file format with a stage removes the need to provide the file format in the `COPY` command.

```
CREATE OR REPLACE STAGE ETL_Stage
  file_format = TSV_No_Headers;
```

7. Next, you'll upload files into the named internal stage. To do so, you must log in to your Snowflake instance via SnowSQL. SnowSQL must be run from the same machine where the files to be loaded are present. Using SnowSQL, run the following SQL to upload the `locations.csv` file into the named internal stage:

```
PUT 'file:///<PATH>/locations.csv' @ETL_Stage;
```

8. Now check which files are present in the named internal stage. To do so, run the `LIST` command using the following SQL:

```
LIST @ETL_Stage;
```

9. Next, you'll load the data from the named internal stage into the table using the `COPY` command. You do not provide a file format in the `COPY` command because the named internal stage already has an associated file format.

```
COPY INTO locations
FROM @ETL_Stage;
```

10. You can now validate that rows were successfully loaded into the Locations table by executing the following SQL; the result will show 150 rows.

```
SELECT * FROM locations;
```

11. Now that the data is successfully loaded, you should clean up the stage by running the following SQL:

```
REMOVE @ETL_Stage;
```

The REMOVE command can be used to delete files from Snowflake's internal stages and external stages. To remove files from an external stage, necessary permissions must be configured in the cloud platform that allow Snowflake to perform the delete operation.

Data Ingestion Using the Named External Stage

Snowflake allows the loading of data from the following cloud storage services:

- Amazon S3
- Google Cloud Storage
- Microsoft Azure Blob Storage

As illustrated in Figure 4.8, Snowflake can access data in cloud storage locations through a named external stage. An external stage definition contains the URL to the location of the data, authentication settings, and other options that describe file formats.

FIGURE 4.8 Loading data from cloud storage via the external stage

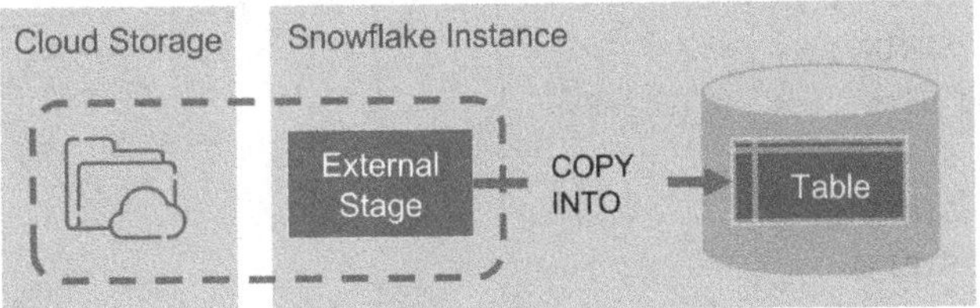

Snowflake supports loading data from any of the three supported cloud platforms regardless of which cloud platform hosts your Snowflake account.

Loading Data from Cloud Storage via the External Stage

Exercise 4.4 walks you through the steps to load data from an Amazon S3 bucket to a Snowflake table using an external stage. In an actual production scenario, the S3 bucket would be secured, and security configuration is required to enable a successful Snowflake connection to the S3 bucket. For convenience, we have used a public S3 bucket to demonstrate how the data loading from an external stage works.

EXERCISE 4.4

Loading Cloud Data via a Named External Stage

1. The example file (`prospects.csv`) we are using in this exercise is available at the following URL:

   `https://snowpro-core-study-guide.s3.amazonaws.com/dataloading/prospects/prospects.csv`

2. If it does not exist already, create a database that will hold the Prospects table to load the `prospects.csv` data.

```
CREATE DATABASE IF NOT EXISTS demo_data_loading;
```

3. Create the Prospects table. The columns in this table relate to the data file that will be loaded into this table.

```
USE DATABASE demo_data_loading;
CREATE TABLE prospects
(
    first_name STRING,
    last_name STRING,
    email   STRING,
    phone   STRING,
    acquired_date_time  DATETIME,
    city    STRING,
    ssn     STRING,
    job     STRING
);
```

4. Next, create a named external stage pointing to the S3 location containing the `prospects.csv` file. Note that you are pointing the stage to the folder that contains the `prospects.csv` file and not the file itself.

```
CREATE OR REPLACE STAGE prospects_stage
  url='s3://snowpro-core-study-guide/dataloading/prospects/'
  file_format = (type = 'CSV' field_delimiter = ','
  field_optionally_enclosed_by = '"' skip_header = 0);
```

5. Notice that because you used a public S3 location, you did not define any authentication configuration. In a real-world scenario, you need to define secure access to

connect to your S3 bucket properly. The details of these configurations are out of the scope for this book, but you can access the information for configuring access here:

https://docs.snowflake.com/en/user-guide/data-load-s3-config.html

https://docs.snowflake.com/en/user-guide/data-load-gcs-config.html

https://docs.snowflake.com/en/user-guide/data-load-azure-config.html

In such a case, the statement for creating the stage should look similar to the following:

```
CREATE OR REPLACE STAGE prospects_stage
  url='s3://snowpro-core-study-guide/dataloading/prospects/'
  storage_integration = <storage_integration_name>
  file_format = (type = 'CSV' field_delimiter = ','
  field_optionally_enclosed_by = '"' skip_header = 0);
```

6. Now load the data from the named external stage into the table using the COPY command:

```
COPY INTO prospects
FROM @prospects_stage;
```

7. You can now validate that rows were successfully loaded into the Prospects table by executing the following SQL, the result of which should show 1,000 rows.

```
SELECT * FROM prospects;
```

In this case, you have one file in the external stage, but if you had multiple files in the external stage, all files would have been loaded (assuming all have the correct structure).

This exercise used a public S3 bucket to simplify the process to keep the demonstration of the concept uncomplicated. In a real-world scenario, ensure that you use a secure bucket and perform the required security configurations on Snowflake.

If there are errors during load, the COPY command shows only the first error. You can use the VALIDATE command to view all errors encountered during a file load rather than just the first error.

Loading Data via the Snowflake Web UI

The classic Snowflake web user interface also provides capabilities for loading data into Snowflake. The loading process through the web UI follows a wizard-like interface to guide a user through the process. The wizard is intended to load only a limited number of small-sized files (up to 50 MB). The process is shown at a high level in the screenshots that follow.

You can access the data loading screen by clicking the database button on the top navigation screen, selecting a database, highlighting a table, and clicking the Load Data button, as shown in Figure 4.9. Alternatively, you can select the table, and the table view has a Load Data button that takes you to the same screen.

FIGURE 4.9 Accessing the Load Data wizard

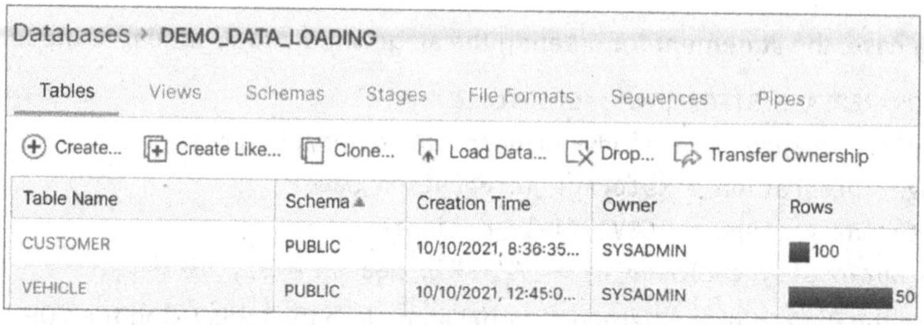
Databases › DEMO_DATA_LOADING
Tables
Views
Schemas
Stages
File Formats
Sequences
Pipes
Create...
Create Like...
Clone...
Load Data...
Drop...
Transfer Ownership
Table Name
Schema
Creation Time
Owner
Rows
CUSTOMER
PUBLIC
10/10/2021, 8:36:35...
SYSADMIN
100
VEHICLE
PUBLIC
10/10/2021, 12:45:0...
SYSADMIN
50

The Load Data wizard starts by asking you to select the compute warehouse to be used to execute the data loading process, as shown in Figure 4.10.

FIGURE 4.10 Selecting a compute warehouse

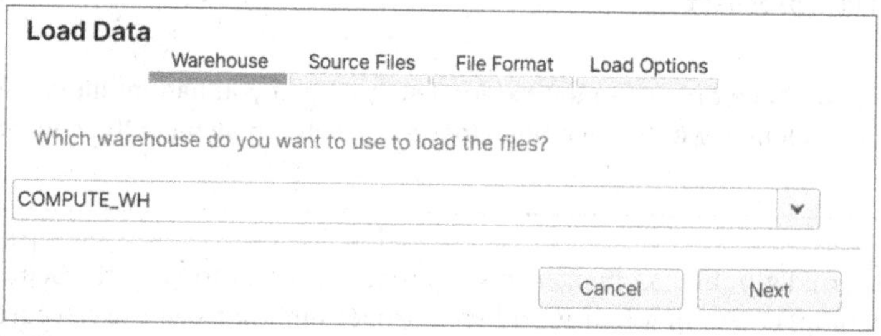
Load Data
Warehouse
Source Files
File Format
Load Options
Which warehouse do you want to use to load the files?
COMPUTE_WH
Cancel
Next

Once you've selected the virtual warehouse, click Next. The next screen asks you to select the files you want to load. These files can be on your computer so that you can select the file using your browser. Note that if you load files from your computer, the process uses `PUT` to upload the file into the table stage before loading the files into the target table.

The file selection screen also allows you to select an existing external stage or create a new external stage for data loading, as shown in Figure 4.11.

The next step is to select an existing file format or create a new format that matches the to-be-loaded file. The screen for choosing a file format is shown in Figure 4.12.

It is worth noting that data loading through the web user interface still uses the concept of stages and running the `COPY` command behind the scenes.

FIGURE 4.11 Selecting source files or stage for loading

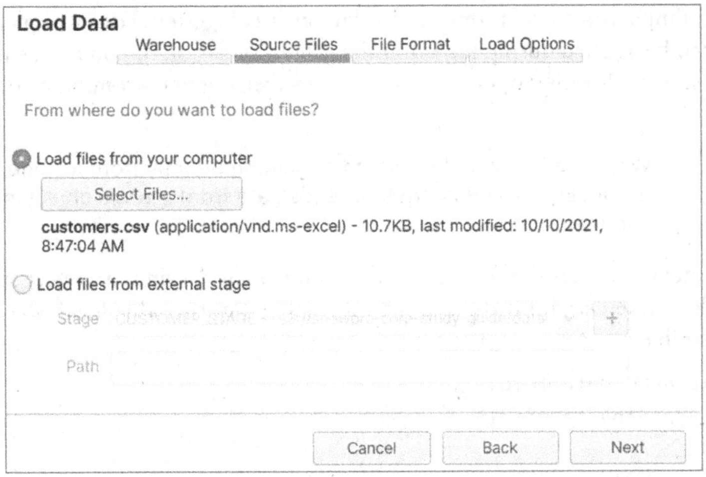

Load Data

Warehouse Source Files File Format Load Options

From where do you want to load files?

Load files from your computer

Select Files...

customers.csv (application/vnd.ms-excel) - 10.7KB, last modified: 10/10/2021, 8:47:04 AM

Load files from external stage

Stage

Path

Cancel Back Next

FIGURE 4.12 File Format screen

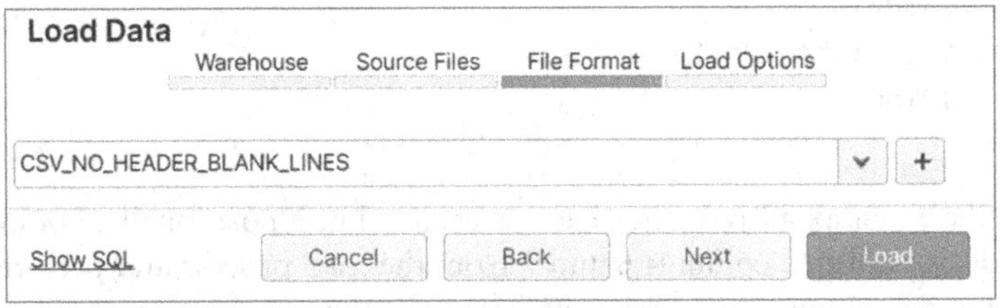

Load Data

Warehouse Source Files File Format Load Options

CSV_NO_HEADER_BLANK_LINES

Show SQL Cancel Back Next Load

Basic Data Transformations While Ingesting

Snowflake allows you to apply basic transformations to data while loading it into a table. The COPY command supports changing the order of columns, omitting one or more columns altogether, and casting data into specific data types during the ingestion process. The COPY command also supports truncating data that exceeds the target column width. The COPY command doesn't support joins, filtering, or aggregations.

In Exercise 4.4, you used the COPY command to load all the columns from a file in an external stage.

```
COPY INTO prospects
FROM @prospects_stage;
```

Using COPY in this manner is similar to performing a SELECT * query. In this case, the load process loads all columns in the file without any transformations. However, you can also do some simple transformations on the data as it is ingested. For example, basic transformations can be applied during ingestion that allow omission of columns, casting columns to a data type, or performing operations such as a substring operation on a column.

When loading a table, instead of loading directly from a stage, you can use a SELECT statement that reads data from a stage object in the COPY command.

As shown next, we treat the stage as a table and use the $ syntax to select specific columns. The file in Exercise 4.4 is used to load this table, but the table has fewer columns than the Prospects table in Exercise 4.4.

```
USE DATABASE demo_data_loading;
CREATE TABLE prospects_simple
(
    first_name STRING,
    last_name STRING,
    email   STRING,
    phone   STRING,
    acquired_date_time  DATE,
    job     STRING
);
```

Note that the $ syntax allows you to access each column positionally. For example, in the following code, we omitted columns 6 and 7 from the load process and performed a substring operation on column 5 to extract the data value from a date-time field:

```
COPY INTO prospects_simple
FROM (
        SELECT $1, $2, $3, $4,SUBSTR($5,1,10), $8
        FROM
        @prospects_stage
    );
```

You can test the SELECT statement separately before enclosing it within a COPY command. The ability to run the SELECT statement separately allows you to debug and get the data in the correct shape before loading it into the table.

Joins, filters, and aggregations are considered complex transformations and are not supported while ingesting the data. Therefore, joining, filtering, and aggregating data are supported after the data has been loaded into a table.

External Tables

In Snowflake, tables are typically entirely managed by the Snowflake engine. The data for these tables is usually loaded from on-premises systems or cloud storage. Table definitions and the metadata are stored in the cloud services layer, and the data for the table is stored in the storage layer using the Snowflake proprietary storage format.

However, Snowflake offers an alternate mechanism, using an external table, that provides the capability to create tables whose data is in external cloud storage. An external table's definition and metadata store information about file locations, filenames, and other properties. This enables you to query an external table in the same way a standard table is queried. External tables can be joined to other tables, and views can be created on an external table. External tables are read-only since they point to an external storage location; therefore, data manipulation language (DML) operations cannot be performed on an external table. Data in external tables do not contribute to Snowflake storage costs since the data for external tables resides outside of Snowflake.

External tables are handy for organizations with existing data lakes and large amounts of data in cloud object storage. External tables can be used to expose data from data lakes in scenarios where data is infrequently accessed or only a subset of data is to be queried. If all of the data is accessed or the frequency of access is high, it may be more cost-effective to store the data in a standard Snowflake table.

An external table can only be created against an external stage pointing to a cloud object storage location. An external table cannot be created against an internal stage.

In Exercise 4.5, you'll define an external table that reads data directly from cloud storage. External tables must use external stages to access the data in cloud storage. The data in external stages may be read as a variant data type, but by extracting individual columns out of the data, the table can be made to behave much like a standard Snowflake table.

EXERCISE 4.5

Create an External Table on Cloud Storage

1. The example file (`customers.csv`) we are using in this exercise can be accessed at the following URL:

   `https://snowpro-core-study-guide.s3.amazonaws.com/dataloading/external/customers.csv`

2. If it does not exist already, create a database:

```
CREATE DATABASE IF NOT EXISTS demo_data_loading;
```

EXERCISE 4.5 *(continued)*

3. Create an external stage pointing to the S3 path where the sample `customers.csv` file is stored:

```
CREATE OR REPLACE STAGE customer_stage
  url = 's3://snowpro-core-study-guide/dataloading/external/';
```

This S3 location was made public so that everyone can easily access the files for demonstration purposes. In a real-world scenario, your S3 locations would likely be secured, and you need to set up secure access to your S3 bucket.

4. Create the `customer_external` table on the external stage. Note that you have not provided any column names at the moment.

```
CREATE OR REPLACE EXTERNAL TABLE customer_external
  WITH location = @customer_stage
    file_format = (type = CSV field_delimiter = '|' skip_header = 1);
```

5. Next, select data from this external table to validate that everything is working correctly. To do so, run the following SQL. The expected results are shown in the following screenshot.

```
SELECT * FROM customer_external;
```

Row	VALUE
1	{"c1": "Benedict T. Weaver", "c2": "507-2889", "c3": "tellus.Suspendisse@litoratorquent.edu", "c4": "466-6280 Cursus Rd.", "c5":
2	{"c1": "Gemma X. Nelson", "c2": "190-5490", "c3": "sagittis.semper.Nam@idmollisnec.net", "c4": "953-2805 Vivamus St.", "c5": "Q
3	{"c1": "Amelia E. Mays", "c2": "1-148-965-3402", "c3": "interdum@consectetuereuismodest.net", "c4": "P.O. Box 802, 7698 Morbi
4	{"c1": "Adele D. Delacruz", "c2": "102-8437", "c3": "ipsum.Donec@gravidasitamet.co.uk", "c4": "Ap #511-6254 Aliquet St.", "c5": "E
5	{"c1": "Warren S. Gaines", "c2": "1-652-873-1969", "c3": "euismod@massaMauris.ca", "c4": "P.O. Box 552, 6384 Cursus St.", "c5":

6. Snowflake loads the data in a variant data type. You'll learn more about the variant data type in the "Semi-Structured Data" section next. You can access individual columns in this data type using the following syntax:

```
SELECT $1:c1 AS Name, $1:c2 as SSN, $1:c3 AS emailAddress,
$1:c4 AS Address, $1:c5 as Zip,$1:c6 AS Location, $1:c7 as Country
FROM customer_external;
```

7. It is not required to query the data as shown in the preceding SQL; instead, to improve the querying experience, the table definition can be updated so that data in the external file is mapped to (virtual) columns. Such tables can be queried like a standard table and do not require the syntax used in the previous statement. To redefine the `customer_external` table with the virtual columns, you can use the following SQL statement:

```
CREATE OR REPLACE EXTERNAL TABLE customer_external
(
   Name STRING as (value:c1::STRING),
   Phone STRING as(value:c2::STRING),
```

```
    Email STRING as(value:c3::STRING),
    Address STRING as(value:c4::STRING),
    PostalCode STRING as(value:c5::STRING),
    City STRING as(value:c6::STRING),
    Country STRING as(value:c7::STRING)
)
WITH location = @customer_stage
  file_format = (type = CSV field_delimiter = '|' skip_header = 1);
```

Query performance for an external table can be improved by creating a materialized view on the external table and refreshing it periodically.

Semi-Structured Data

Historically, we have dealt mainly with structured data composed of rows and columns and stored in a relational format, whether in a database, spreadsheet, or CSV files. With the explosion of data in the last decade, there has been a continuous increase in unstructured and semi-structured data. As a result, there has been an increased need for databases to handle these new types of data.

Semi-structured data may be defined as a somewhat structured form of data but without a rigid tabular or relational structure enforcement. Data typically contains tags or markers to separate data elements and enforce some form of structure. The elements of semi-structured data can grow or shrink over time, and there is no rigid enforcement of what elements must occur. IoT devices, applications, mobile devices, and sensors are an example of sources that generate semi-structured data.

Snowflake provides built-in support for handling a variety of semi-structured data formats. The following are the semi-structured data file types supported by Snowflake:

- JSON
- Avro
- ORC
- Parquet
- XML

The *VARIANT* Data Type and Semi-Structured Data

Snowflake provides the `VARIANT` data type, which can store any data, making it suitable for ingestion and querying semi-structured data. After JSON data has been loaded into a variant column, it can be accessed and traversed using SQL. As an example, consider the following JSON file loaded into a variant column called `val`:

```
{
   "first_name": "John",
```

```
    "last_name": "Smith",
    "address":{
                "address_line":"489 Kyle Stream",
                "city":"Port Gabriellafort",
                "state":"CT",
                "zip":"46873"
              },
    "employment_history": [{
            "name": "Wagner LLC",
            "from_date": "2018-01-15",
            "to_date": "2020-06-30"
        },
        {
            "name": "Rich Inc",
            "from_date": "2020-07-01"
        }
    ]
}
```

To access any first-level elements, use the column name followed by a colon (`:`) and then the JSON element name. For example, use `val:first_name` to access the value stored in the `first_name` JSON element.

To access second-level elements, use a dot after the first JSON element. For example, use `val:address.city` to access the internal elements contained in the address element.

The `VARIANT` data type can store any data type and can store up to 16 MB of uncompressed data for each row.

Loading NDJSON Data

NDJSON (newline delimited JSON) data is a JSON format in which each line in the file is a valid JSON in itself. It is a convenient format for storing semi-structured data so that it can be processed one row at a time. The NDJSON format is a suitable format for processing streaming semi-structured data. Please see `http://ndjson.org` for more details on the NDJSON format.

Exercise 4.6 demonstrates loading NDJSON data in a Snowflake table and accessing various JSON elements from the loaded data. The following snippet shows the first two rows of the NDJSON data used in the exercise, where each line in itself is a valid JSON.

```
{"ssn": "411-80-4180", "dob":"1981-01-20", "email": "thomaswilliam@example.org",
"first_name": "Isabella", "last_name": "Johns", "phone": "944-135-2471",
"city": "Timothyhaven", "job": "Land"}
```

```
{"ssn": "160-47-6605", "dob":"1972-05-16", "email": "melissa31@example.net",
"first_name": "Stephanie", "last_name": "Wade", "phone": "(344)886-2932x20449",
"city": "New Anthonyland", "job": "Teaching laboratory technician"}
```


EXERCISE 4.6

Loading NDJSON Data via an External Stage

1. The example file (`employees.json`) that we are using in this exercise can be downloaded from the following URL:

   `https://snowpro-core-study-guide.s3.amazonaws.com/dataloading/ndjson/employees.json`

2. The S3 URI to access this file via an external Snowflake stage is `s3://snowpro-core-study-guide/dataloading/ndjson/`.

3. If it does not exist already, create a database:

   ```
   CREATE DATABASE IF NOT EXISTS demo_data_loading;
   ```

4. Create a temporary table called `employee_temp` for loading the JSON data. Note that the table contains only one column of the `VARIANT` data type. You will load the JSON data into this column and then query various elements of the JSON.

   ```
   USE DATABASE demo_data_loading;
   CREATE TABLE employee_temp
   (
       rj VARIANT
   );
   ```

5. Next, you'll create an external stage pointing to the S3 path where the sample `employee.json` file is stored. Notice that you'll specify the file format as JSON so that Snowflake treats the data as JSON when loading it into the table.

   ```
   CREATE OR REPLACE STAGE employee_json_stage
     url = 's3://snowpro-core-study-guide/dataloading/ndjson/'
     file_format = (type = json);
   ```

   This S3 location was made public so that everyone could easily access the files for demonstration purposes. In a real-world scenario, your S3 locations would likely be secured, and you'd need to set up secure access to your S3 bucket.

6. Next, list this stage to ensure you can see the `employee.json` file. As a result of the following command, you should see a single row listing the `employee.json` file:

   ```
   LIST @employee_json_stage;
   ```

7. You'll load the JSON data into the `employee_temp` table. To do so, run the following SQL. This command should complete with 10 rows loaded into the table.

   ```
   COPY INTO employee_temp
   FROM @employee_json_stage;
   ```

EXERCISE 4.6 *(continued)*

8. Now, validate that the JSON data has been correctly loaded by running a simple SELECT on the table, which returns 10 rows; each row displays a single line of JSON data.

```
SELECT rj FROM employee_temp;
```

9. Next, you'll attempt to access individual elements in the JSON and convert the data into a relational form so that it can be used in querying and joined with other tables. To do so, use the (:) notation to access different fields, as shown in the following SQL:

```
SELECT rj:ssn, rj:dob, rj:email, rj:first_name, rj:last_name, rj:city, rj:phone, rj:job
FROM employee_temp;
```

The preceding statement shows results similar to what is shown in the following screenshot:

Row	RJ:SSN	RJ:DOB	RJ:EMAIL	RJ:FIRST_NAME	RJ:LAST_NAME	RJ:CITY	RJ:PHONE	RJ:JOB
1	"411-80-4180"	"1981-01-20"	"thomaswilliam@exa...	"Isabella"	"Johns"	"Timothyhaven"	"944-135-2471"	"Land"
2	"160-47-6605"	"1972-05-16"	"melissa31@exampl...	"Stephanie"	"Wade"	"New Anthonyland"	"(344)886-2932×20...	"Teaching laboratory...
3	"672-83-3743"	"1981-12-21"	"leeyvette@example...	"Jodi"	"Lane"	"Toddville"	"155-195-5268×374"	"Financial trader"
4	"859-65-5058"	"1987-11-30"	"michaeljensen@exa...	"Michael"	"Guerrero"	"Whitetown"	"+1-768-183-7046×...	"Control and instrum...

10. You may have noted that each value is enclosed in double quotes because it is still in a variant format. You can now apply the proper data type to each value and make the result a relational table. To do so, run the following SQL, which applies a data type to each column:

```
SELECT  $1:ssn::string,
        $1:dob::date,
        $1:email::string,
        $1:first_name::string,
        $1:last_name::string,
        $1:city::string,
        $1:phone::string,
        $1:job::string

FROM employee_temp;
```

11. Now that the data is in a relational format and correctly typed, it can be inserted and materialized into another table, or the preceding query can be converted into a view so that others may access the JSON data.

INSERT command can be used following the COPY command to further process data that has already been loaded into a temporary table. You can load data into an intermediate table and then perform further transformations on the data, finally inserting it into the final table using the INSERT command. `INSERT OVERWRITE` can be used to delete all the data from the table before inserting the new rows. You must have `DELETE` privileges on the target table to execute `INSERT OVERWRITE`.

If required, you can use sequences to generate unique values for a primary key column when inserting data. Sequences are Snowflake objects used to generate unique numbers across sessions and statements—that is, the value generated by a sequence is globally unique for that sequence.

Loading JSON Data

Exercise 4.7 demonstrates loading JSON data into Snowflake and using the `FLATTEN` function to explode the JSON into multiple rows. The following snippet shows a sample of the JSON data used in the exercise. We haven't shown the complete JSON structure due to space constraints. You will notice that the JSON file is nested and complex in structure. The `flights` array contains multiple flights, which further has the origin and destination information. We extract data from the `flights` array and present it in a tabular format in the exercise.

```
"provided_by": "ixata",
"provided_date": "2021-01-18",
"data_set": "flights_2021",
"world_wide": "true",
"flights": [{
        "airline": "Hawaiian Airlines",
        "origin": {
            "airport": "Cariri Regional airport",
            ....
        },
        "destination": {
            "airport": "Rosario airport",
            "iata": "ROS",
            ....
        },
        "stops": 3,
        "price": 830
    },
    {
        "airline": "Air France",
```

```
        "origin": {
            "airport": "Marignane airport",
            "iata": "MRS",
            ....
        },
        "destination": {
            "airport": "Las Palmas airport",
            ....
        },
        "stops": 3,
        "price": 374
    }
]
```

EXERCISE 4.7

Loading JSON Data via an Eternal Stage

1. The example file (`flights.json`) that we are using in this exercise can be downloaded from the following URL:

   `https://snowpro-core-study-guide.s3.amazonaws.com/dataloading/json/flights.json`

2. The S3 URI to access this file via an external Snowflake stage is `s3://snowpro-core-study-guide/dataloading/json`.

3. If it does not exist already, create a database:

   ```
   CREATE DATABASE demo_data_loading;
   ```

4. Create a temporary table called `flights_temp` for loading the JSON data. Note that the table contains only one column of the `VARIANT` data type. You will load the JSON data into this column and then query various elements of the JSON.

   ```
   USE DATABASE demo_data_loading;
   CREATE TABLE flights_temp
   (
       rj VARIANT
   );
   ```

5. Next, create an external stage pointing to the S3 path where the sample `employee.json` file is stored. Notice that you are specifying the file format as JSON so that Snowflake treats the data as JSON when loading it into the table.

   ```
   CREATE OR REPLACE STAGE flights_json_stage
     url = 's3://snowpro-core-study-guide/dataloading/json/'
     file_format = (type = json);
   ```

   This S3 location was made public so that everyone could easily access the files for demonstration purposes. In a real-world scenario, your S3 locations would likely be secured, and you need to set up secure access to your S3 bucket.

6. Now load the JSON data into the `flights_temp` table. To do so, run the following SQL. This command should complete with one row loaded into the table.

```
COPY INTO flights_temp
FROM @flights_json_stage;
```

7. Next, validate that the JSON data has been correctly loaded by running a simple SELECT on the table, which returns one row, which is the complete JSON file that we just loaded.

```
SELECT * FROM flights_temp;
```

8. Now, you'll attempt to access individual elements in the JSON and convert the data into a relational form. To do so, use the (:) notation to access different fields, as shown in the following SQL. It is straightforward to access the root elements since they are not nested.

```
SELECT rj:data_set::String as data_set_name, rj:provided_by::String as
provided_by from flights_temp;
```

9. However, the flights data is contained in an array. We use the FLATTEN function to explode the array values into their respective rows using the following SQL. The result set shows that each entry in the `flights` array has been expanded into an individual row, as shown in the following screenshot.

```
SELECT
    rj:data_set::String as data_set_name, rj:provided_by::String as provided_by,
    value
FROM
    flights_temp
    , lateral flatten( input => rj:flights );
```

Row	DATA_SET_NAME	PROVIDED_BY	VALUE
1	flights_2021	ixata	{ "airline": "Hawaiian Airlines", "destination": { "airport": "Rosario air
2	flights_2021	ixata	{ "airline": "Air France", "destination": { "airport": "Las Palmas airpor
3	flights_2021	ixata	{ "airline": "West Air (China)", "destination": { "airport": "General Abe
4	flights_2021	ixata	{ "airline": "Shenzhen Airlines", "destination": { "airport": "Eldorado I
5	flights_2021	ixata	{ "airline": "Jeju Air", "destination": { "airport": "Sepinggan airport", "
6	flights_2021	ixata	{ "airline": "Air Canada", "destination": { "airport": "Hopkins Internati
7	flights_2021	ixata	{ "airline": "United Airlines", "destination": { "airport": "Mineral'nyye
8	flights_2021	ixata	{ "airline": "Frontier Airlines", "destination": { "airport": "Kahului airp
9	flights_2021	ixata	{ "airline": "Shenzhen Airlines", "destination": { "airport": "Pinto Mart
10	flights_2021	ixata	{ "airline": "China Eastern Airlines", "destination": { "airport": "Hopki

10. Now that the JSON data has been expanded, you can access individual elements in each row and create a relational view running the following SQL. The results are shown in the following screenshot.

```
SELECT
    rj:data_set::String as data_set_name, rj:provided_by::String as provided_by,
```

EXERCISE 4.7 *(continued)*

```
        value:airline::String AS airline,
        value:origin.airport::String as orig_airport,
        value:origin.city::String as orig_city,
        value:destination.airport::String as dest_airport,
        value:destination.city::String as dest_city
    FROM
        flights_temp
        , lateral flatten( input => rj:flights );
```

Row	DATA_SET_NAME	PROVIDED_BY	AIRLINE	ORIG_AIRPORT	ORIG_CITY	DEST_AIRPORT	DEST
1	flights_2021	ixata	Hawaiian Airlines	Cariri Regional air...	Juazeiro do Norte	Rosario airport	Rosa
2	flights_2021	ixata	Air France	Marignane airport	Marignane	Las Palmas airport	Telde
3	flights_2021	ixata	West Air (China)	Tromso Langnes ...	Tromso	General Abelardo...	Tijua
4	flights_2021	ixata	Shenzhen Airlines	Chongqing Jiang...	Chongqing	Eldorado Internati...	Fonti
5	flights_2021	ixata	Jeju Air	John F Kennedy I...	Jamaica	Sepinggan airport	Balikp

The FLATTEN function can be used to convert semi-structured data into a relational representation.

Unstructured Data

Unstructured data doesn't have the organization or a predefined schema that would make storage and analysis easy. Therefore, it requires some special preprocessing before it can be analyzed further. Some examples of unstructured data are voice recordings from call center operations, video data from traffic cameras, or data from a social media feed.

Snowflake provides support for storing, managing, and processing unstructured data through URLs, directory tables, and UDFs for processing unstructured data. Figure 4.13 shows the high-level process for processing unstructured data.

The directory table acts as a catalog of the stage object and provides a list of files in the stage. A directory table can provide a Snowflake-hosted file URL to each file in the stage. A user-defined function (UDF) then iterates over the list of files, extracting meaningful information from each file. The extracted information is then loaded into a target table, where it can be queried like any other relational table. If desired, you can use a stream object to monitor the directory table for changes and schedule a task that triggers the UDF to process only the new files listed by the directory table.

Directory Tables

The directory table is a catalog for the stage object and provides a list of stage files. Directory tables are not independent database objects; instead, they are implicit objects on top of a stage. They store metadata about files in a stage and can be queried to provide Snowflake-hosted file URLs for the files in a stage. Snowflake charges separately for directory tables, including costs for event notification and refresh of the table metadata.

FIGURE 4.13 Loading unstructured data

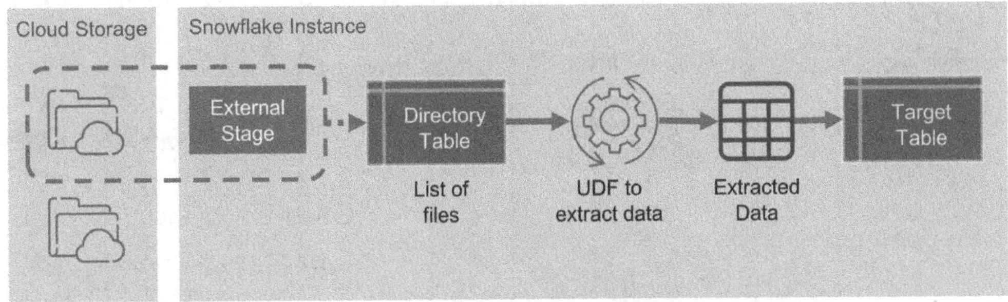

Types of URLs Used to Access Unstructured Files

Once the unstructured data is in external cloud storage or the internal Snowflake stage, Snowflake allows access to the files through different types of URLs:

Scoped URL Scoped URLs provide temporary access to a staged file. The URL expires after 24 hours. Only the user who generated the scoped URL can use the URL to access the file. The `BUILD_SCOPED_FILE_URL` function is used to generate a scoped URL

File URL A file URL provides permanent access to a staged file—that is, the URL never expires. It can be accessed by a custom application through REST API calls but requires that the role specified in the REST API call has privileges on the stage. The `BUILD_STAGE_FILE_URL` function is used to generate a file URL.

Pre-signed URL Pre-signed URLs can be used to allow external users to access or download files without authenticating to Snowflake or providing an authorization token. Pre-signed URLs expire after the length of time specified in the `expiration_time` argument. A pre-signed URL can be obtained by calling the `GET_PRESIGNED_URL` function.

Unloading Data from Snowflake

So far, we have investigated various methods of loading data into Snowflake. Snowflake also provides a mechanism for exporting data out of Snowflake, also called unloading the data. The mechanism underpinning unloading of data is the exact mechanism used for data loading, except it is reversed. Data from tables and views can be extracted to Snowflake's internal and external stages through the `COPY` command. Once the data is in an internal stage, you can download it to your computer using the `GET` command (see Figure 4.14). Data extracted to external stages is generally available using cloud storage access mechanisms, such as accessing the S3 bucket directly that was referenced by the external stage.

FIGURE 4.14 Data unload mechanisms in Snowflake

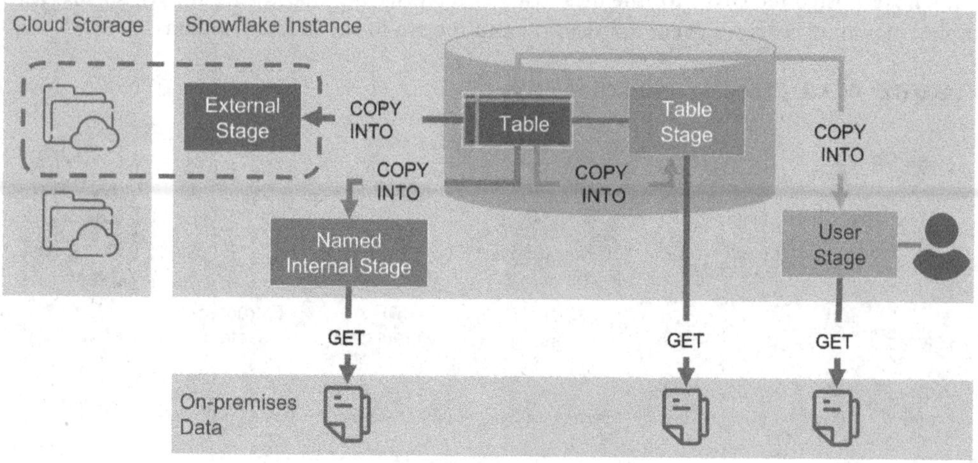

File Formats Supported for Unloading

Snowflake supports a more extensive set of file types for data loading, but not all of these file types are available when unloading the data. The following file formats are supported for unloading data:

- Delimited text files—comma-separated (CSV), tab-separated (TSV), or files separated by any other single-byte delimiter
- JSON—only the newline delimited JSON (NDJSON) format is supported for unloading
- Parquet

Data cannot be unloaded to the following file formats, although they are supported for loading data:

- Avro
- ORC
- XML

Compression

By default, all data unloaded from Snowflake is automatically compressed using `gzip` compression. It is possible to specify other compression techniques or altogether disable compression when unloading data.

Encryption

All data files unloaded to a Snowflake internal stage are encrypted automatically using 256-bit encryption. When the files from the internal stage are downloaded to a local disk, they are decrypted.

Data unloaded to an external stage is not encrypted automatically, but it can be encrypted if an encryption key is provided to encrypt the files.

Data Unloading Considerations

Snowflake unloads data to multiple files, where the maximum size of each file is 16 MB by default. The maximum size can be changed by using the `MAX_FILE_SIZE` parameter, allowing up to 5 GB per file. The default behavior of unloading data to multiple files can be changed by setting the `SINGLE` parameter to `true`, resulting in data exported to a single file.

When exporting to CSV files, you can set the `EMPTY_FIELD_AS_NULL` parameter to `false` and the `FIELD_OPTIONALLY_ENCLOSED_BY` parameter to double quotes ("") to ensure that NULL values are distinguishable from an empty string in the exported file.

Snowflake truncates the values of floating-point number columns to (15,9) when they are unloaded to CSV or JSON files. Floating-point numbers are not truncated when unloaded to a Parquet file.

Unload Data to an On-premises System via an Internal Stage

Exercise 4.8 demonstrates how data already loaded into Snowflake can be unloaded (or extracted) out of a table. Although *unload* is a misleading term because it could be perceived as data being downloaded and removed from Snowflake, Snowflake uses *unload* to describe the export of data. Unload of data in Snowflake is accomplished with the `COPY` command, with the source and the target of the `COPY` command interchanged.

In this exercise you'll export data from the Customer table, previously loaded in Exercise 4.1. You create a new named internal stage, unload data from the Customer table into the stage, and then use SnowSQL to download that data onto your laptop.

EXERCISE 4.8

Unloading Data via a Named Internal Stage

1. Start by choosing the database where your table is and creating the file format and new internal stage:

```
USE DATABASE demo_data_loading;
```

2. Create a file format object that defines the exported file's format. You will create a file format definition that uses the tab character as the field delimiter.

```
CREATE OR REPLACE FILE FORMAT Export_TSV_With_Headers
  type = 'CSV'
  field_delimiter = '\t'
  file_extension = ".csv";
```

3. Next, create a named internal stage and associate the stage with the file format you just created. Attaching the file format with a stage removes the need to provide the file format in the COPY command.

```
CREATE OR REPLACE STAGE Export_Stage
  file_format = Export_TSV_With_Headers;
```

EXERCISE 4.8 (continued)

4. Unload the data from the named internal stage from the table using the COPY command:

```
COPY INTO @Export_Stage
FROM customer;
```

5. Validate that the data export was successful by listing the files in the internal stage. To do so, run the following SQL. You should see the results shown in the following screenshot.

```
LIST @Export_Stage;
```

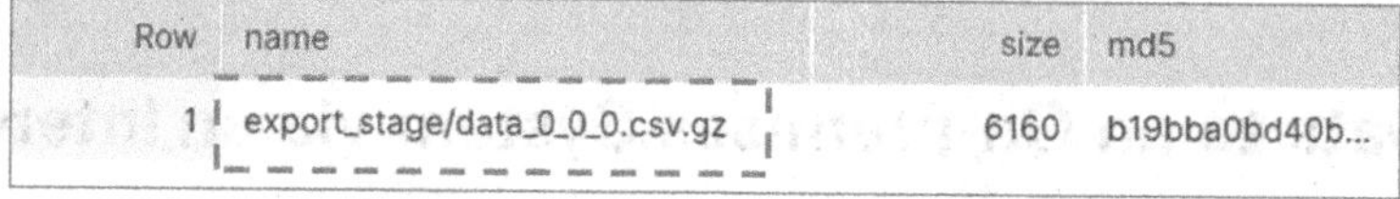

Row	name	size	md5
1	export_stage/data_0_0_0.csv.gz	6160	b19bba0bd40b...

Note that the data was automatically compressed as it was exported out. This is because Snowflake automatically compresses unloads.

6. Next, download these exported files from the internal stage to your computer. To do so, using SnowSQL run the following:

```
GET  @Export_Stage 'file://<PATH>/';
```

Please note that you must replace the <PATH> placeholder in the code with the folder where you would like the files to be downloaded. Also, note that the path should contain forward slashes rather than backslashes.

7. Once you run the GET command, Snowflake downloads the csv.gz files in the stage to your local computer, from where they can be extracted using an appropriate file compression program.

Snowflake automatically compresses the data when unloading or exporting data to a stage. The data in a Snowflake stage is stored encrypted and is encrypted in transit. SnowSQL decrypts the data before storing it on the local filesystem when the GET command is executed.

Load Near-Real-Time Streaming Data

Snowflake supports the loading of continuous data through a serverless service called Snowpipe. Snowpipe allows you to load data in micro-batches. This technique is typically used when a steady stream of data, such as transactions or events, needs to be loaded and the data must be made quickly available to businesses. Snowpipe can load data within minutes of new data arriving in a stage.

Snowpipe is serverless and has its own compute capacity, which means that Snowpipe doesn't depend on virtual warehouses for processing. The compute capacity and scaling up and down of a Snowpipe is managed automatically by Snowflake. The cost for a Snowpipe is also billed separately from virtual warehouse costs.

Snowpipe is serverless and is managed, scaled up, and scaled down automatically without requiring any intervention from the user. Costs for Snowpipe are charged separately from virtual warehouse costs.

How Snowpipe Works

Snowpipe's definition contains a COPY command that Snowflake utilizes to load the data. The COPY command provides information on the location of the data and the target table in which the data is to be loaded. Although a COPY command is in a Snowpipe's definition, a Snowpipe cannot be run like a SQL command. A Snowpipe must be triggered by a notification from cloud services or manually triggered via a REST API call, as shown in Figure 4.15.

FIGURE 4.15 Loading data through Snowpipe

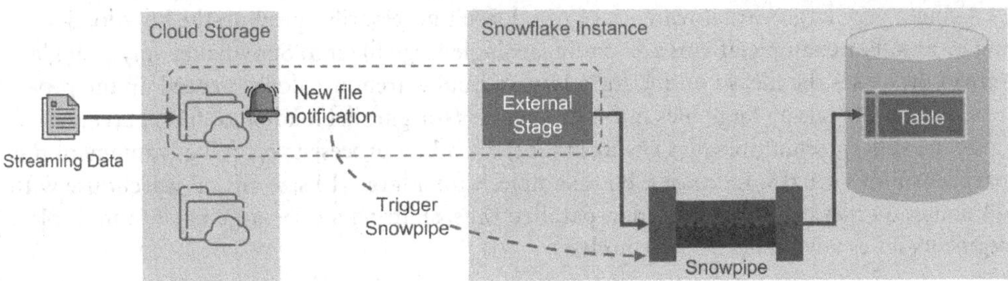

Once triggered, the Snowpipe executes the COPY command contained in its definition and loads the newly arrived data into the target table.

A typical definition of a Snowpipe may look similar to the following. Note that the main body of the Snowpipe definition consists of the COPY command. Also, note that the following statement is just an example and may not necessarily work in your Snowflake setup without additional configuration.

```
CREATE OR REPLACE PIPE load_prospects_pipe
auto_ingest = true
AS COPY INTO prospects
FROM @prospects_stage
file_format = (type = 'CSV' field_delimiter = ',' field_optionally_enclosed_by
= '"' skip_header = 0);
```

Snowpipe can load data from external or internal stages. You must trigger a Snowpipe through the REST API when using internal stages with Snowpipe.

Optimizing Data Loading and Unloading

Consider organizing your data in a folder structure instead of keeping all files in a single bucket. A properly organized folder structure with an appropriate subfolder scheme can improve the performance of loads. This is because listing files in a folder during the COPY operation requires time, and if all files are kept in a single folder, the listing operation takes longer to complete, thus impacting the loads. Organizing your files into folders and subfolders and passing a granular path in the COPY command allow Snowflake to look into just the segment of the folders that need to be processed instead of scanning the whole bucket.

For optimal loading performance through the COPY command, it is recommended to have the file size approximately 100–250 MB after compression. This applies both to regular loads and for data loaded through Snowpipe.

Bulk Load Optimization

Loading of bulk files in Snowflake using the COPY command is straightforward, but specific optimizations must be considered to ensure the best performance for loading files.

Using a very large virtual warehouse size doesn't necessarily speed up the bulk loading of files. For example, if you are loading a single large file into Snowflake, only a single thread processes the file, so opting for a large virtual warehouse doesn't speed up the process. Instead, break up large files into multiple files for parallel loading of files. Having a large file split into multiple files ensures that the loading process takes full advantage of the parallelism of virtual warehouses. For example, with a large (L) size virtual warehouse with 64 nodes, 64 files can be processed in parallel; thus, splitting a very large file into multiple segments takes advantage of these nodes.

Optimizing Snowpipe Loads

Ensure that large files are split into 100 to 250 MB size chunks (after compression). Ensure a granular folder structure and specify paths to ensure that the loading activity is not spending time scanning the cloud storage folder.

Optimizing Data Unloading

It is advisable to unload data to multiple files to ensure that the unloading process can take advantage of Snowflake parallelism. To do so, set the SINGLE parameter to true in your COPY command. Also, consider NULL values when exporting the data, as your target system may require NULL values represented in a specific way.

To obtain higher efficiency for your queries during development, you can use estimating functions such as HyperLogLog to find the approximate number of distinct values in a data set. Similarly, when exploring a table's data, you can use the SAMPLE or TABLESAMPLE keyword to return a subset of table rows.

Summary

This chapter focused on how to load data into Snowflake. Snowflake provides methods to load data bulk using the COPY command and in a continuous manner using the Snowpipe functionality. We covered the concept of stages and how Snowflake provides external stages to load data from cloud storage and internal stages for loading data from on-premises systems. We also looked at how to load and process semi-structured data such as JSON data.

Exam Essentials

Understand the concept of stages. Stages help load and unload data in Snowflake. Data must first be available in a Snowflake stage before processing into a Snowflake table. Once the data is staged, it may be copied into a table using the COPY command. Snowflake's stages fall into two categories: external stage and internal stages. Internal stages are further subdivided into named internal stages, user stages, and table stages. Snowflake assigns a stage to every table and every user by default. Named internal stages can be created or dropped as required. They are more flexible than user and table stages.

Be able to describe the purpose of external tables. External tables provide the capability to create tables for which the data is in external cloud storage. They can be queried like a regular table. They can be connected to other tables and have views developed on them. Because external tables point to external storage, DML operations cannot be done on external tables.

Understand how Snowflake supports semi-structured data. Snowflake has built-in support for semi-structured data. It supports ingestion and processing of JSON, Avro, ORC, Parquet, and XML formats. Snowflake's VARIANT data type may hold any data, making it well suited for semi-structured data loading and processing.

Understand methods for managing unstructured data. Snowflake supports URLs, directory tables, and UDFs for processing unstructured data. The directory table is a catalog of a stage's files. A directory table can provide a Snowflake-hosted UR for each staged file. A user-defined function (UDF) iterates across the list of files, extracting data. Scoped URLs provide temporary access to a staged file. A file URL provides permanent access to a staged file—that is, the URL never expires. Pre-signed URLs allow external users to access files without authenticating.

Know how to unload data. Snowflake also allows you to export data from it. The technique for unloading data is the same as for ingesting data but in reverse. The COPY command is used to extract data from tables and views to Snowflake's internal and external stages.

Be able to describe the purpose of Snowpipe. Snowflake allows continuous data loading using Snowpipe, a serverless service. Snowpipe permits micro-batch loading. It is used when a steady stream of data must be loaded quickly, such as transactions or events. Snowpipe can load data minutes after it enters a stage.

Review Questions

1. Which of the following features in Snowflake allows creating tables through which you can query data in an external stage without loading it first?
   - **A.** Materialized views
   - **B.** External tables
   - **C.** Snowpipe
   - **D.** COPY
2. True or False: Snowpipe is designed to load small volumes of data that is arriving continuously.
   - **A.** True
   - **B.** False
3. Which of the following statements are true for external tables? (Choose three.)
   - **A.** External tables can be joined with other tables.
   - **B.** Views can be created on external tables.
   - **C.** Update queries can be run on external tables.
   - **D.** External tables are read-only.
4. Which of the following statements are true for Snowpipe? (Choose two.)
   - **A.** Snowpipe uses an active virtual warehouse to load data.
   - **B.** Snowpipe makes use of Snowflake's serverless computing resources.
   - **C.** Snowflake automatically scales up and down the Snowpipe resource.
   - **D.** Snowpipe's compute resources are managed through a virtual warehouse that you must expand yourself.
5. Which of the following is true about Snowpipe? (Choose two.)
   - **A.** The cost of Snowpipe is calculated and billed separately from the cost of virtual warehouse use.
   - **B.** Snowpipe utilizes shared virtual warehouse computational resources for processing.
   - **C.** Snowpipe is serverless and so does not require virtual warehouse resources.
   - **D.** Snowpipe consumption costs are included in the virtual warehouse compute.
6. Which one of the following data loading methods uses virtual warehouse resources? (Choose all that apply.)
   - **A.** Loading data using COPY command through an external stage
   - **B.** Loading data using COPY command through an internal stage
   - **C.** Data loading through Snowpipe
   - **D.** Unloading data to an external stage using the COPY command

7. Which of the following can be used to load data using the COPY command? (Choose two.)
   - **A.** External stage
   - **B.** Internal stage
   - **C.** Web pages
   - **D.** REST APIs

8. Snowflake supports which semi-structured file formats? (Choose all that apply.)
   - **A.** Parquet
   - **B.** JSON
   - **C.** HTML
   - **D.** Avro
   - **E.** XML

9. When exporting or unloading data from Snowflake, which of the following file formats are supported for unloading? (Choose all that apply.)
   - **A.** Avro
   - **B.** ORC
   - **C.** XML
   - **D.** CSV
   - **E.** Parquet

10. What is the amount of uncompressed data that a column of VARIANT data type can store for a single row?
    - **A.** 8 MB
    - **B.** 16 MB
    - **C.** Unlimited
    - **D.** 32 MB

11. The load metadata for a table expires after how many days?
    - **A.** 64 days
    - **B.** 32 days
    - **C.** Never
    - **D.** 256 days

12. Which of the following can be a target location when using the COPY INTO <*location*> command? (Choose two.)
    - **A.** A named internal stage
    - **B.** A named external stage
    - **C.** A local folder
    - **D.** Cloud storage location, such as an S3 bucket

13. Which of the following statements are true regarding data loading? (Choose all that apply.)
    A. `GET` is used to download files from a Snowflake internal stage to a local folder.
    B. `PUT` is used to upload files into a Snowflake internal stage from a local folder.
    C. `REMOVE` can be used to remove files from internal stages and external stages.
    D. `GET` and `PUT` cannot be executed from the Worksheets view.
    E. `LOAD` is used to load files into a table from an internal stage.

14. Which of the following transformations are *not* supported by the `COPY` command? (Choose three.)
    A. `JOIN`
    B. `GROUP BY`
    C. `FLATTEN`
    D. `CONCAT`
    E. `CAST`

15. Snowpipe supports loading data continuously. Snowpipe can load data from which of the following objects? (Choose two.)
    A. External stages
    B. Internal stages
    C. Temporary tables
    D. Transient tables

16. True or False: When you use the `PUT` command, the data is encrypted on the client machine before uploading it.
    A. False
    B. True

17. What is the recommended file size to optimize the load process?
    A. 100–250 MB
    B. 25–50 MB
    C. 5–10 MB
    D. 500 MB

18. Which of the following is true regarding data unloading in Snowflake? (Choose all that apply.)
    A. By default, Snowflake unloads data to multiple files.
    B. By default, Snowflake unloads data to a single file.
    C. The size of each file is 16 MB by default but can be configured to a maximum of 5 GB per file.
    D. The size of each file is fixed at a maximum of 16 MB.

Data Pipelines

THE SNOWPRO CORE EXAM TOPICS COVERED IN THIS CHAPTER INCLUDE THE FOLLOWING:

✓ **Domain 1.0: Snowflake Data Platform Features and Architecture**

- 1.3 Outline Snowflake's catalog and objects.
  - Streams
  - Tasks

✓ **Domain 4.0: Data Loading and Unloading**

- 4.2 Outline different commands used to load data and when they should be used.
  - STREAM
  - TASK

Snowflake provides the capability to schedule SQL statements and stored procedures through the concept of tasks. This chapter introduces you to tasks and walks you through creating a simple task and a complex task tree consisting of more than one task. The chapter also touches on streams, which is Snowflake's method of providing change data capture capability.

Introducing Tasks

Snowflake tasks are used to execute a SQL statement or to call a stored procedure on a schedule. Tasks are suitable for scenarios where there is a need to run SQL statements or stored procedures regularly. For example, you can use tasks to refresh data in a table used in a report, keep aggregate tables up-to-date, load data into Snowflake, export data out of Snowflake, or even perform maintenance actions on a schedule.

Snowflake tasks can be executed based on a schedule or triggered manually using the EXECUTE TASK command.

Multiple tasks can be connected to perform multiple actions if needed. Also, tasks can be used with streams to perform continuous data processing.

Scheduling a Task

Tasks can be created using the CREATE TASK command. The basic syntax for creating a task is as follows. Note that a simplified syntax is shown here. For the complete syntax, please refer to Snowflake's documentation.

```
CREATE TASK <task_name>
  { WAREHOUSE = <string> } | { USER_TASK_MANAGED_INITIAL_WAREHOUSE_SIZE =
<string> }
  SCHEDULE = '{ <num> MINUTE | USING CRON <expr> <time_zone> }'
  AFTER <predecessor_task>
AS
  <sql>;
```

To create a task, you must specify the SQL statement you would like to execute when the task is run. Another essential aspect is specifying whether a warehouse or Snowflake-managed compute resources will be used; more about that later in this chapter. The `CREATE`

TASK statement can also specify the schedule for executing the task. You can specify the schedule in minutes or by using a CRON expression.

Exercise 5.1 demonstrates the creation of a simple task with a recurring schedule. In this exercise, you'll create a task that aggregates data from a table and inserts the aggregated data into another table. The intent is to simulate a real-world scenario where a table used for reporting will be populated on a schedule.

Snowflake tasks can be scheduled based on time or by using CRON expressions. A Snowflake task can also be triggered manually by using the EXECUTE TASK command.

EXERCISE 5.1

Simple Task to Load Data into a Table

1. Begin by creating a database and a table. Name the table **customer_report** and the database **test_tasks.** We will use sample data from the **snowflake_sample_data** database. The purpose of **customer_report table is** to store the money spent by each customer in the sample database.

```
USE ROLE SYSADMIN;
CREATE OR REPLACE DATABASE test_tasks;

CREATE TABLE test_tasks.public.customer_report
(
  customer_name STRING,
  total_price   NUMBER
);
```

2. Use the following SQL to prepare the data that you will load into this table. The SQL joins the Customer and the Order table to produce a customer-level spending report. You can run this SQL to get familiarized with the results and the number of rows produced by this query.

```
SELECT c.c_name as customer_name,SUM(o.o_totalprice) AS total_price
FROM snowflake_sample_data.tpch_sf1.orders o
INNER JOIN snowflake_sample_data.tpch_sf1.customer c
ON o.o_custkey = c.c_custkey
GROUP BY c.c_name;
```

3. Next, you'll create a Snowflake task called generate_customer_report, which you'll use to execute a scheduled INSERT statement. You specify COMPUTE_WH as the virtual warehouse, which is used to execute the SQL contained in this task. (If you have created another virtual warehouse and prefer to use that, you can provide its name in the statement.) You'll specify a recurring schedule of 5 minutes, which indicates that the INSERT statement will be executed every 5 minutes.

EXERCISE 5.1 *(continued)*

```
CREATE TASK generate_customer_report
WAREHOUSE=COMPUTE_WH
SCHEDULE = '5 MINUTE'
AS
INSERT INTO test_tasks.public.customer_report
SELECT c.c_name as customer_name,SUM(o.o_totalprice) AS total_price
FROM snowflake_sample_data.tpch_sf1.orders o
INNER JOIN snowflake_sample_data.tpch_sf1.customer c
ON o.o_custkey = c.c_custkey
GROUP BY c.c_name;
```

4. Note that we specified 5 minutes for demonstration purposes only; using a 5-minute recurring schedule means that the job runs every 5 minutes and uses virtual warehouse resources. Suspend this task after you have understood the concepts and performed your testing; otherwise, this recurring job can result in a significant bill as it will keep the associated virtual warehouse in a resumed state.

5. It is worth noting *that new Snowflake tasks are created in a suspended state*. So, it does not start executing automatically until you explicitly set the status to resumed. You can validate that a new task is created in a suspended state by viewing the task's properties using the following statement. The state column in the result set shows *suspended*, as you can see in the following screenshot.

   ```
   SHOW TASKS LIKE 'generate_customer_report';
   ```

warehouse	schedule	predecessors	state	definition
COMPUTE_WH	5 MINUTE		suspended	INSERT INTO test_tasks.public.customer_report SELECT c.c_nam

6. Since new Snowflake tasks are created in a suspended state, you must set the task status to RESUME to ensure that the task starts running on the defined schedule. To do so, run this command:

   ```
   ALTER TASK generate_customer_report RESUME;
   ```

   You may encounter an error stating `Cannot execute task, EXECUTE TASK privilege must be granted to owner role`. This error indicates that the user role you are using doesn't have the required privileges.

7. To provide the required privileges, switch the role to ACCOUNTADMIN and run the following command. Modify the role name if needed. The code assumes you have given the privileges to the SYSADMIN role.

   ```
   USE ROLE ACCOUNTADMIN;
   GRANT EXECUTE TASK ON ACCOUNT TO ROLE SYSADMIN;
   ```

8. Now switch the role back to SYSADMIN and resume the task:

```
USE ROLE SYSADMIN;
ALTER TASK generate_customer_report RESUME;
```

9. You can watch the task execution by querying the task_history() table function, as shown in the following code. Note that the task will run based on the provided schedule, so the following query may not return any results until the first execution of the task. Be sure to provide the task name in uppercase—the SQL code will not return any results if you provide the task name in lowercase.

```
USE ROLE ACCOUNTADMIN;
SELECT name, state,
    completed_time, scheduled_time,
    error_code, error_message


FROM TABLE(information_schema.task_history())
WHERE name = 'GENERATE_CUSTOMER_REPORT';
```

You can see a history of a task's execution by using the task_history() table function. This function returns the last 7 days of the history of the executed tasks and the scheduled executions within the next 8 days.

10. Once the task has been successfully executed on the defined schedule, you'll see a result similar to this:

	NAME	STATE	COMPLETED_TIME	...	SCHEDULED_TIME	ERROR_CODE	ERROR_MESSAGE
1	GENERATE_CUSTOMER_REPORT	SCHEDULED	null		2021-12-09 23:47:31.581 -0800	null	null
2	GENERATE_CUSTOMER_REPORT	SUCCEEDED	2021-12-09 23:42:46.021 -0800		2021-12-09 23:42:31.581 -0800	null	null

11. You can also validate that the task was executed successfully by counting the number of rows in the customer_report table, which is the table where the task should have inserted new rows. The following count query should show 99,996 rows:

```
SELECT COUNT(*) FROM test_tasks.public.customer_report;
```

12. Since this task was intended for testing purposes and the schedule was set for a very short interval, you must suspend the task; otherwise, it will keep on executing every 5 minutes, consuming valuable compute resources, and will result in an increased bill. To suspend the task, run the following SQL:

```
ALTER TASK generate_customer_report SUSPEND;
```

New tasks are created in a suspended state and must be set to resume in order for them to start executing according to the defined schedule. Only roles with the EXECUTE TASK privilege can resume a task.

Real World Scenario

Scheduling Automatic Refresh of Reporting Aggregates

In the business of online sales, a retail organization collects all customer transactions at a detail level in a transaction table in their data warehouse. The transactions are inserted into the table every hour. The reporting team has created an aggregate table on top of the Transactions table, which they refresh manually. The reporting team now requires that the aggregate table be automatically refreshed hourly. The administrators created a new task that refreshes the aggregated data on an hourly schedule to meet their requirements.

Connecting Multiple Tasks in a Task Tree

Multiple Snowflake tasks can be connected in a tree-like structure that starts with a single root node and can have multiple child nodes. The concept is shown in Figure 5.1. The task tree starts with a root node and can have one or many child tasks. The tasks relate to each other via task dependency—that is, the child task is dependent on the parent task. So, the parent task must complete before a child task runs.

FIGURE 5.1 Multiple tasks tree

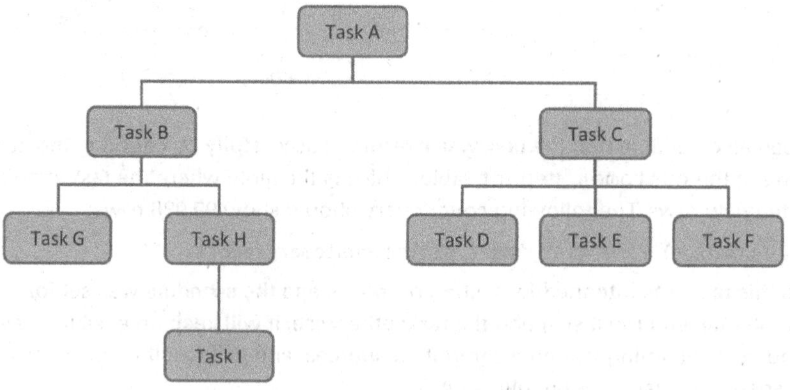

A task can only have a single parent task; however, one parent task can have multiple child tasks.

A task can have a maximum of 100 child tasks, and a complete tree of tasks is limited to a maximum of 1,000 tasks, including the root task.

Creating and Connecting Multiple Tasks

Tasks can be connected to a predecessor task using the AFTER clause in the task Data Definition Language (DDL). A simplified syntax is shown here, with emphasis on the AFTER clause. The AFTER clause can be used while creating or altering a task.

```
CREATE TASK <task_name>
  { WAREHOUSE = <string> } | { USER_TASK_MANAGED_INITIAL_WAREHOUSE_SIZE =
<string> }
  SCHEDULE = '{ <num> MINUTE | USING CRON <expr> <time_zone> }'
  AFTER <predecessor_task>
AS
  <sql>;
```

Exercise 5.2 demonstrates the creation of a simple task tree in which two tasks are connected. The second task runs when the first task has completed successfully. For simplicity, you'll use the task you created in Exercise 5.1. In that exercise, you created a task, `generate_customer_report`, that aggregates data from a table and inserts the aggregated data into another table. But if you run the `generate_customer_report` task several times, it will keep appending data to the table. So, you'll add a predecessor step in Exercise 5.2 that deletes all rows from the target table before loading it with new data.

EXERCISE 5.2

Creating a Simple Task Tree

1. Begin by switching to the `test_tasks` database:

```
USE DATABASE test_tasks;
```

2. Next, you'll create a new Snowflake task called `delete_customer_report`, which you will use to delete all data from the `customer_report` table. You'll specify `COMPUTE_WH` as the virtual warehouse, which is used to execute the SQL contained in this task. (If you have created another virtual warehouse and prefer to use that, you can provide its name in the statement.) You'll specify a recurring schedule of 5 minutes, which indicates that the DELETE statement will be executed every 5 minutes. Make sure that you are creating this task using the same role that you used to create the `generate_customer_report` task in Exercise 5.1.

```
CREATE TASK delete_customer_report
WAREHOUSE=COMPUTE_WH
SCHEDULE = '5 MINUTE'
AS
DELETE FROM test_tasks.public.customer_report;
```

3. We used 5 minutes for demonstration purposes only; using a 5-minute recurring schedule means that the job runs every 5 minutes and uses virtual warehouse resources. Suspend this task after you have understood the concepts and performed your testing; otherwise, this recurring job can result in a significant bill as it will keep the associated virtual warehouse in a resumed state.

EXERCISE 5.2 *(continued)*

4. Next, you'll alter the `generate_customer_report` task that you created in Exercise 5.1. Then, you'll remove the schedule from the `generate_customer_report` task because it will become a child task in the following steps. To do so, run the following SQL:

```
ALTER TASK generate_customer_report UNSET SCHEDULE;
```

5. Next, add the `delete_customer_report` task as the parent of the `generate_customer_report` task. To do so, run the ALTER command, as shown here:

```
ALTER TASK generate_customer_report ADD AFTER delete_customer_report;
```

6. Since new Snowflake tasks are created in a suspended state, you must set the task status to `RESUME` to ensure that the task starts running on the defined schedule. Also, because you suspended the `generate_customer_report` task at the end of the previous exercise, you must now set it to `RESUME`. Note that any child tasks must be set to `RESUME` first because once a root task is set to `RESUME`, you cannot change the status of any tasks in that task tree.

```
ALTER TASK generate_customer_report RESUME;
ALTER TASK delete_customer_report RESUME;
```

7. You can watch the task execution by querying the `task_history()` table function, as shown in the following code. Note that the task will run based on the provided schedule, so the following query may not return any results until the first execution of the task. Provide the task name in uppercase, since the SQL does not return any results if you provide the task name in lowercase.

```
SELECT name, state,
    completed_time, scheduled_time,
    error_code, error_message

FROM TABLE(information_schema.task_history())
WHERE name IN ('DELETE_CUSTOMER_REPORT','GENERATE_CUSTOMER_REPORT');
```

8. Once the task has been successfully executed on the defined schedule, the code should return a result similar to the following screenshot. The highlighted row shows the execution of the two tasks you linked together. The `delete_customer_report` task ran first, followed by the `generate_customer_report` task. The first row in the result shows that the root task—that is, `delete_customer_report`—is scheduled for the subsequent execution. The last row shows the execution from Exercise 5.1.

	NAME	STATE	COMPLETED_TIME	...	SCHEDULED_TIME	ERROR_CODE	ERROR_MESSAGE
1	DELETE_CUSTOMER_REPORT	SCHEDULED	null		2021-12-10 01:28:19.620 -0800	null	null
2	GENERATE_CUSTOMER_REPORT	SUCCEEDED	2021-12-10 01:23:37.660 -0800		2021-12-10 01:23:31.639 -0800	null	null
3	DELETE_CUSTOMER_REPORT	SUCCEEDED	2021-12-10 01:23:31.639 -0800		2021-12-10 01:23:19.600 -0800	null	null
4	GENERATE_CUSTOMER_REPORT	SUCCEEDED	2021-12-09 23:42:46.021 -0800		2021-12-09 23:42:31.581 -0800	null	null

9. Since you created these tasks for testing purposes and have set the schedule for a very short interval, you should suspend the tasks; otherwise, you may incur costs. To do so, run the following SQL. Note that you must suspend the root task before making changes to any child tasks.

```
ALTER TASK delete_customer_report SUSPEND;
ALTER TASK generate_customer_report SUSPEND;
```

All tasks in a tree of tasks must have the same task owner—that is, the same role should have the OWNER privilege on all the tasks in a tree.

User-Managed and Serverless Tasks

You have specified a virtual warehouse in the previous exercises when creating a task and have used the following syntax for creating your tasks thus far:

```
CREATE TASK <task_name>
  WAREHOUSE = <string>
  SCHEDULE = '<num> MINUTE'
  AFTER <predecessor_task>
AS
  <sql>;
```

When you specify a virtual warehouse for a task, you are indicating that you want the task to use that specific virtual warehouse during execution. The virtual warehouse should already be created and available for use. Additionally, the virtual warehouse should either be running or set to automatically resume so that when the task executes, it can use the virtual warehouse compute resources.

When using this approach, you are responsible for creating, managing, and specifying a right-sized virtual warehouse for your tasks. You are also responsible for making sure the virtual warehouse is running or set to automatically resume.

Snowflake-Managed Compute or Serverless Tasks

The serverless compute model allows you to use computer resources managed by Snowflake. The compute resources may be scaled up or down by Snowflake as required, based on each task's workload demands. With serverless tasks, you are not required to manage the compute resources or ensure that a virtual warehouse is running or set to automatically resume in order for your tasks to work. However, creating a serverless task varies slightly from the standard CREATE TASK syntax. A simplified syntax follows:

```
CREATE TASK <task_name>
  USER_TASK_MANAGED_INITIAL_WAREHOUSE_SIZE = <string>
  SCHEDULE = '<num> MINUTE'
```

```
  AFTER <predecessor_task>
AS
  <sql>;
```

Instead of specifying a virtual warehouse name, you are now specifying an initial warehouse size through the USER_TASK_MANAGED_INITIAL_WAREHOUSE_SIZE parameter. The size can be any standard virtual warehouse size available, ranging from X-Small to 6X-Large.

Note that serverless tasks was a preview feature when we were writing this book, but we expect that the feature will become generally available.

Exercise 5.3 demonstrates the creation of a simple serverless task with a recurring schedule. You'll create a serverless task that takes a snapshot of orders every 5 minutes. The intent is to simulate a real-world scenario with business requirements to track the order trend near real time.

EXERCISE 5.3

Creating a Simple Serverless Task

1. Begin by creating a database and a table. Name the table **order_count**. The table's purpose is to store orders.

```
CREATE OR REPLACE DATABASE test_tasks;

CREATE TABLE test_tasks.public.order_count
(
  Snapshot_time TIMESTAMP,
  total_orders   NUMBER
);
```

2. Use the following SQL to prepare the data that you will load into this table. The SQL sums the total price in the Order table.

```
SELECT CURRENT_TIMESTAMP as snapshot_time,COUNT(*) AS total_orders
FROM snowflake_sample_data.tpch_sf1.orders o
GROUP BY 1;
```

3. Next, you'll create a serverless Snowflake task called generate_order_count, which you use to execute an INSERT statement on schedule. You do not specify a virtual warehouse but instead provide an initial warehouse size, which indicates to Snowflake that you intend to create a Snowflake-managed serverless task. In addition, you'll specify a recurring schedule of 5 minutes.

```
CREATE TASK generate_order_count
USER_TASK_MANAGED_INITIAL_WAREHOUSE_SIZE = 'XSMALL'
```

```
SCHEDULE = '5 MINUTE'
AS
INSERT INTO test_tasks.public.order_count
SELECT CURRENT_TIMESTAMP as snapshot_time, COUNT(*) AS total_orders
FROM snowflake_sample_data.tpch_sf1.orders o
GROUP BY 1;
```

4. You may encounter an error stating `Missing option(s): [WAREHOUSE]`. This can mean that your role doesn't have the required privileges. To provide the privileges to create serverless tasks, run the following as an ACCOUNTADMIN and rerun the previous step again:

   ```
   USE ROLE ACCOUNTADMIN;
   GRANT EXECUTE MANAGED TASK ON ACCOUNT TO SYSADMIN;
   ```

5. Once you have created the tasks, you must set the task status to RESUME since new Snowflake tasks are created in a suspended state. To do so, run the following command:

   ```
   ALTER TASK generate_order_count RESUME;
   ```

6. You can watch the task execution by querying the `task_history()` table function, as shown in the following code. Note that the task will run based on the provided schedule, so the following query may not return any results until the first execution of the task. Be sure to provide the task name in uppercase.

   ```
   SELECT name, state,
       completed_time, scheduled_time,
       error_code, error_message

   FROM TABLE(information_schema.task_history())
   WHERE name IN ('GENERATE_ORDER_COUNT');
   ```

7. Once the serverless task has successfully executed on the defined schedule, the previous code should return a result similar to the following screenshot.

	NAME	STATE	COMPLETED_TIME	SCHEDULED_TIME	ERROR_CODE	···	ERROR_MESSAGE
1	GENERATE_ORDER_COUNT	SCHEDULED	null	2022-03-01 04:41:24.278 -0800	null		null
2	GENERATE_ORDER_COUNT	SUCCEEDED	2022-03-01 04:36:28.838 -0800	2022-03-01 04:36:24.258 -0800	null		null

8. You can also validate that the task was executed successfully by selecting all rows from the `order_count` table:

   ```
   SELECT * FROM test_tasks.public.order_count;
   ```

9. Since you created this task for testing, you should suspend it; otherwise, its execution will incur a cost. To do so, run the following SQL. You can also drop the task altogether if you prefer.

   ```
   ALTER TASK generate_order_count SUSPEND;
   ```

You created a simple serverless task that executes on a 5-minute schedule and inserts the order count into another table. A serverless task differs from a user-managed task in a few aspects, including creating the task, billing, and viewing the task execution history.

Billing for Serverless Tasks

With user-managed tasks that use a defined virtual warehouse, billing is straightforward and is based on the time duration for which a virtual warehouse was in a running state. For example, the virtual warehouse may be idle during that time or fully utilized; regardless, the bill will be based on the duration while the virtual warehouse is in a running state. This billing approach is similar to the typical virtual warehouse usage billing.

But for serverless tasks, the billing is calculated differently. Snowflake calculates the bill for serverless tasks based on the actual compute usage. The bill is based on the actual usage of compute resources and the cloud services usage charges. For the compute resources, Snowflake credits are charged per the compute hour used by the task execution. Snowflake applies a multiplier of 1.5 to the Snowflake credit calculation to cover the management cost of serverless tasks.

Serverless task history can be found in both the `task history()`table function and the `serverless_task history()`table function.

Introducing Streams

Streams are a Snowflake feature that allows you to track data updates made to a table. A stream can track any data changes made to a table's data, including inserts, updates, and deletes. This process, commonly known as change data capture (CDC), enables users and processes to determine what changed in a table since the last time.

Streams can be queried like tables, allowing users to read and process the data available through a stream similar to how they can read and process data from a table. Streams can even be combined with tasks to process change data on a schedule.

Streams don't contain any data; think of them as bookmarks that encapsulate the changes. After you have queried or consumed the latest changes, the bookmark moves and points to future changes as they occur. Figure 5.2 illustrates this concept by displaying the table's journey over time as different Data Manipulation Language (DML) changes (inserts/updates/deletes) are performed. A single stream has been defined on the table. The stream is queried at various points in time, and every time it is queried, the stream returns a different set of changes that have occurred since the last querying of the stream.

Capture Changes Using Streams

Exercise 5.4 demonstrates creating a simple stream to track inserts, updates, and deletes made to the customer table. Once a new customer is inserted, you can use a SQL statement to process the new customer into another table. In the latter part of the exercise, you combine your stream with a task to process changes automatically using a schedule.

FIGURE 5.2 Streams and change data capture

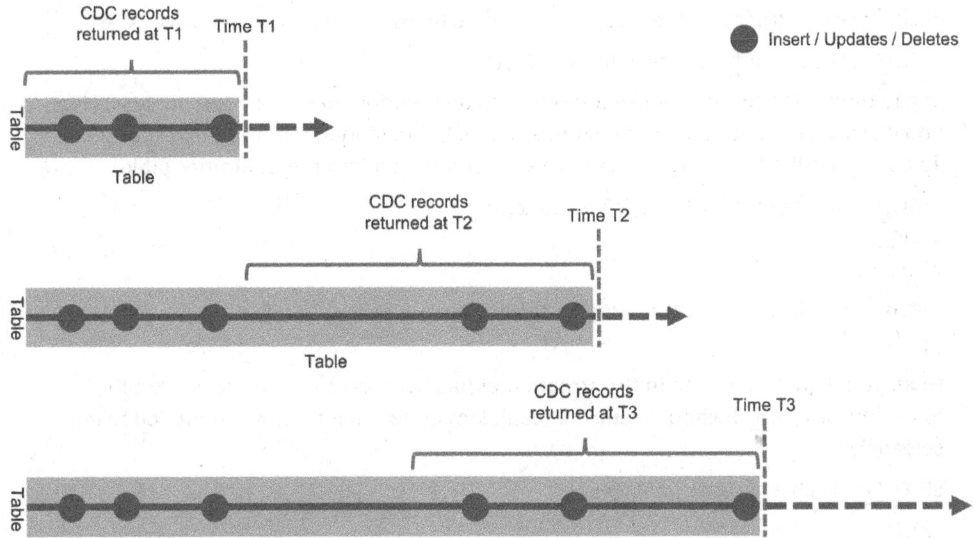

EXERCISE 5.4

Creating a Stream to Track and Process Changes

1. Begin by creating a database and a table. Name the database **test_streams** and the table **Customer**. The table is intended to contain all customers who have signed up.

```
CREATE OR REPLACE DATABASE test_streams;

CREATE TABLE test_streams.public.customer
(
  Customer_Name  STRING,
  Customer_Email STRING,
  Discount_Promo BOOLEAN
);
```

2. Next, create another table called `discount_list` that will be used to contain only those customers' emails who have signed up through a promotion and who are eligible for a discount voucher:

```
CREATE TABLE test_streams.public.discount_voucher_list
(
  Customer_Email STRING
);
```

EXERCISE 5.4 *(continued)*

3. Next, create a stream on the Customer table using the simple syntax shown here:

```
CREATE STREAM customer_changes ON TABLE customer;
```

4. In a real-world scenario, the Customer table can be populated by a load process. Here, you'll use `INSERT` statements to simulate data being loaded into the Customer table. To do so, run the following SQL, which inserts one row into the Customer table.

```
INSERT INTO test_streams.public.customer
VALUES
(
  'John Smith', 'john.smith@personal.unknown','Y'
);
```

5. Next, you'll query the data in the stream that has been captured. To do so, run the following SQL, which should return a result similar to what's shown in the following screenshot.

```
SELECT * FROM customer_changes;
```

	CUSTOMER_NAME	CUSTOMER_EMAIL	DISCOUNT_PROMO	METADATA$ACTION	METADATA$ISUPDATE	METADATA$ROW_ID
1	John Smith	john.smith@personal.unknown	TRUE	INSERT	FALSE	5a2d8601efb6d239d7e7f85528a68401982d3811

6. To consume the data from a stream, you must query and process the data into another table. Since you need to insert emails of all discount-eligible customers into the `discount_voucher_list` table, you'll use the following SQL. You select only those customers for whom the `Discount_Promo` flag is set to `True`. You are also processing only the `INSERT` events and ignoring any `UPDATE` events in the stream.

```
INSERT INTO test_streams.public.discount_voucher_list
SELECT Customer_Email FROM customer_changes WHERE Discount_Promo = 'Y'
AND METADATA$ACTION = 'INSERT' AND METADATA$ISUPDATE = FALSE;
```

7. Once you have run the SQL, you'll see that any qualifying records are inserted into the target table, and the stream will no longer show any rows.

8. You can further test how the stream behaves by adding more rows and updating an existing row:

```
UPDATE test_streams.public.customer SET Customer_Email = 'john.smith@official
.known' WHERE Customer_Name = 'John Smith';

INSERT INTO test_streams.public.customer
VALUES
(
  'Akram Khan', 'akram.khan@new.organisation','Y'
```

```
);

INSERT INTO test_streams.public.customer
VALUES
(
  'Jane Doe', 'jane.doe@jane.industries','N'
);
```

9. Now, review what the stream contains after the preceding update and inserts were executed. To do so, run the following SQL; the results appear in the following screenshot. Note that the UPDATE command is represented with two entries in the stream, one a `DELETE` entry and the second entry an `INSERT`.

```
SELECT * FROM customer_changes;
```

	CUSTOMER_NAME	CUSTOMER_EMAIL	DISCOUNT_PROMO	METADATA$ACTION	METADATA$ISUPDATE	METADATA$ROW_ID
1	John Smith	john.smith@official.known	TRUE	INSERT	TRUE	f7b087ef0cb6e4dacfa081682dee5760
2	John Smith	john.smith@personal.unknown	TRUE	DELETE	TRUE	f7b087ef0cb6e4dacfa081682dee5760
3	Akram Khan	akram.khan@new.organisation	TRUE	INSERT	FALSE	0b3dca2087ec14bb2218ec0ab304aaa
4	Jane Doe	jane.doe@jane.industries	FALSE	INSERT	FALSE	a60cffc9bdb607b5ffd944638fd167aec

10. You'll now combine the concept of streams and tasks together. Rather than rerunning the SQL in step 6, you can create the SQL in step 6 as a task and schedule it on a regular interval so that when change data is captured, the task automatically inserts the data into the `discount_voucher_list` table. To do so, create a new task using the following SQL. You'll use the SYSTEM$STREAM_HAS_DATA system function to ensure that the task skips execution if there is no data in the stream.

```
CREATE TASK process_new_customers
USER_TASK_MANAGED_INITIAL_WAREHOUSE_SIZE = 'XSMALL'
SCHEDULE = '5 MINUTE'

WHEN SYSTEM$STREAM_HAS_DATA('customer_changes')
AS
INSERT INTO test_streams.public.discount_voucher_list
SELECT Customer_Email FROM customer_changes WHERE Discount_Promo = 'Y'
AND METADATA$ACTION = 'INSERT' AND METADATA$ISUPDATE = FALSE;

ALTER TASK process_new_customers RESUME;
```

11. Once the task has been executed, you will see new rows inserted into the `discount_voucher_list` table.

Summary

We have covered the constructs of tasks and streams in this chapter. Tasks are used for scheduling SQL statements or stored procedures in Snowflake, while streams are used for change data capture. Streams may be combined with tasks to perform automatic processing of change data. We went through several exercises that reinforce the concept of tasks and streams and demonstrated how the two can be combined. We also looked at how the schedule history for tasks can be retrieved and how tasks may be connected to create a task tree.

Exam Essentials

Understand the concept of tasks. Snowflake tasks are used to schedule SQL statements or stored procedures. Snowflake tasks can be executed on a schedule as well as triggered manually. Tasks are generated in a suspended state and must be set to resume to begin executing according to the given schedule.

If needed, multiple tasks can be linked to create a task tree. The `AFTER` clause in the task DDL connects tasks to their predecessors. All tasks in a tree of tasks must have the same task owner—the same role should have the `OWNER` privilege on all the tasks in a tree. A task can have up to 100 child tasks, and a task tree can have up to 1,000 tasks, including the root task.

Tasks can use a user-managed virtual warehouse or Snowflake-managed compute resources. However, tasks' basic syntax and capabilities remain the same regardless of the computing model. The billing for a task with a user-managed virtual warehouse is encapsulated in the billing for that virtual warehouse. However, for serverless tasks that use Snowflake-managed compute resources, the billing is done separately and is based on the amount of compute used for processing that task. It is worth noting that Snowflake applies a multiplier of 1.5 when calculating credit usage for serverless tasks.

Serverless task history can be found in both the `task history()` table function and the `serverless_task history()` table function.

Understand how streams are used for change data capture. Streams are a Snowflake feature that allows you to track data updates made to a table. A stream can track table data changes such as inserts, updates, and deletes. This capability, also known as change data capture (CDC), allows users and processes to see what has changed in a table since the last consumption of data.

Streams can be queried like tables, allowing users to read and process data in the same way as tables. They can even be combined with tasks to process change data on a schedule.

Review Questions

1. Which of the following is a way to view task execution history for tasks that use a user-managed virtual warehouse?
   - **A.** `SELECT task_execution_history` from the session.
   - **B.** Query the `task_execution_history` table in the system schema.
   - **C.** Query the `information_schema.task_history()` table function.
   - **D.** It is not possible to view the task execution history.
2. Which of the following privileges is required to set a task to resumed state?
   - **A.** `EDIT TASK` privilege
   - **B.** `EXECUTE TASK` privilege
   - **C.** `RESUME TASK` privilege
   - **D.** `ADMIN TASK` privilege
3. Which of the following are valid scheduling approaches for tasks? (Choose all that apply.)
   - **A.** `ON EVENT`
   - **B.** Using `CRON`
   - **C.** `<num> MINUTE`
   - **D.** `ON DATE`
4. You have just created a new task. What would be the initial state of this task?
   - **A.** Suspended
   - **B.** Active
   - **C.** Resumed
   - **D.** Running
5. Which of the following is true regarding task trees? (Choose all that apply.)
   - **A.** Multiple tasks connected in a parent-child relationship form a task tree.
   - **B.** Only the root node can have a schedule in a task tree.
   - **C.** Tasks can have multiple parents.
   - **D.** All tasks in a tree of tasks must have the same task owner.
6. Which of the following is true regarding serverless tasks? (Choose all that apply.)
   - **A.** Serverless tasks use Snowflake-managed compute resources.
   - **B.** Serverless tasks are billed differently and have a 1.5 multiplier when calculating credit usage.
   - **C.** Snowflake scales the compute up and down for serverless tasks as per workload requirements.
   - **D.** Serverless tasks cannot have any child tasks.

7. Streams are a Snowflake mechanism that provides which of the following functionalities?
   A. Message queue capabilities
   B. Change data capture
   C. Data archival
   D. Scheduled execution of SQL

8. Streams can capture which of the following changes in a table? (Choose all that apply.)
   A. `INSERT`s
   B. `UDPDATE`s
   C. `DELETE`s
   D. Table structure changes
   E. Table name changes

9. Which of the following is true regarding streams? (Choose all that apply.)
   A. Streams can be queried like a table.
   B. Once a stream is created, it cannot be dropped unless the whole table is dropped.
   C. Multiple streams can be created on the same table.
   D. Streams don't contain any data but are bookmarks to the data changes.

Continuous Data Protection

THE SNOWPRO CORE EXAM TOPICS COVERED IN THIS CHAPTER INCLUDE THE FOLLOWING:

✓ **Domain 1.0: Snowflake Data Platform Features and Architecture**

- 1.3 Outline Snowflake's catalog and objects.
  - Tables Types

✓ **Domain 6.0: Data Protection and Data Sharing**

- 6.1 Outline continuous data protection with Snowflake.
  - Time Travel
  - Fail-Safe
  - Data encryption
  - Replication

Snowflake provides a comprehensive set of features that protect data from malicious actions and human error in a Snowflake environment. These features include data encryption at rest and in transit, authentication and authorization controls, multifactor authentication, and network-level policies to control access. Snowflake also provides some novel features that help protect and recover data in the event of human error. For example, Time Travel and the undrop feature allow data recovery after it has been inadvertently modified. This chapter introduces the components of continuous data protection and covers Time Travel, Fail-safe, the undrop functionality, and the concept of transient and temporary tables in detail. Authentication, authorization, multifactor authentication, and other security topics are covered in more depth in Chapter 9, "Security."

Components of Continuous Data Protection

Snowflake provides several data protection features, including encryption, role-based access, authentication and authorization, Time Travel, and Fail-safe. Data encryption, access control, and network policies are introduced in this chapter; access control and multifactor authentication are covered in more detail in Chapter 9, "Security."

Data Encryption

Snowflake automatically encrypts all customer data by default using AES-256 bit encryption. Snowflake encrypts data *at rest*, meaning that the data has been stored on disk. Data in transit is also automatically encrypted to provide maximum security. Data loaded via an internal stage or unloaded to an internal stage is automatically encrypted by Snowflake.

Access Control

Snowflake provides authentication and fine-grained authorization capabilities. By default, access to a Snowflake instance is controlled via standard authentication, protected through a username and password specific to Snowflake. However, additional configuration can be performed to enable single sign-on (SSO) in which authentication is provided by an external identity provider such as Okta or Microsoft Active Directory Federation Services (ADFS). Snowflake also provides authorization capabilities through a role-based access control model.

Snowflake also supports multifactor authentication (MFA) for enhanced security during the authentication process. With MFA, users are required to provide information in addition to the username and password to complete the authentication process. The additional information can be an SMS or a token sent to a mobile app or a notification sent to a mobile app to approve the login process.

Network Policies

Network policies enable you to limit access to your Snowflake instance by allowing only a defined list of IP addresses to connect. You can also allow limit access by blocking specific IP addresses.

Time Travel

Snowflake provides a novel data protection capability that allows you to query, retrieve, and recover historical data in tables. Sometimes, data may be accidentally altered or deleted due to human error, and you want to recover such data with minimum hassle. Before Snowflake's Time Travel feature, the standard approach for recovering from accidental data loss was to recover the data from a backup. With Snowflake's Time Travel capabilities, any user can read data as it existed at a point in time with minimum fuss. Time Travel duration can be between one and 90 days and depends on the Snowflake edition and the configuration for a specific table.

Fail-safe

Fail-safe storage is an extension of Time Travel that keeps data for an additional seven days beyond the Time Travel duration. Fail-safe provides additional protection from data loss; however, only Snowflake support can recover data from Fail-safe storage.

Replication and Failover/Failback

The primary purpose of replication is to support failover/failback in Snowflake, although replication is also used to enable cross-region data sharing. Replication and failover/failback allows an organization to recover from failures and unexpected outages, execute planned failover, and support migration activities across regions. If there is a significant problem with cloud services in a particular region, Snowflake won't work until the problem is fixed and services are back up and running. Therefore, replicating your critical account objects to another Snowflake account in a different region ensures data durability and availability.

Snowflake supports database replication, account object replication, and client redirects, which together provide business continuity capabilities in Snowflake. Account replication in Snowflake enables customers to create replication groups that specify what objects to replicate, where to replicate, and on what schedule. Account replication also enables the creation of failover groups that allow customers to specify which objects to fail over in case of a failure. Database replication allows replicating and storing read-only copies of a single database.

Snowflake charges for data replication, including the data transfer, and computes costs for replication. The data transfer costs are dependent on the cloud platform, the region of the source account, and the target account platform and region. In addition to these costs, the storage costs of the replicated data are charged separately.

Time Travel and Fail-safe

Micro-partitions are the key to understanding how Time Travel works in Snowflake. Snowflake stores data for a table in one or more micro-partitions. Micro-partitions corresponding to a table are tracked in metadata maintained in the cloud services layer. As new data is added to a table, new micro-partitions are added. The concept of micro-partitions is illustrated in Figure 6.1.

FIGURE 6.1 Snowflake stores data in micro-partitions.

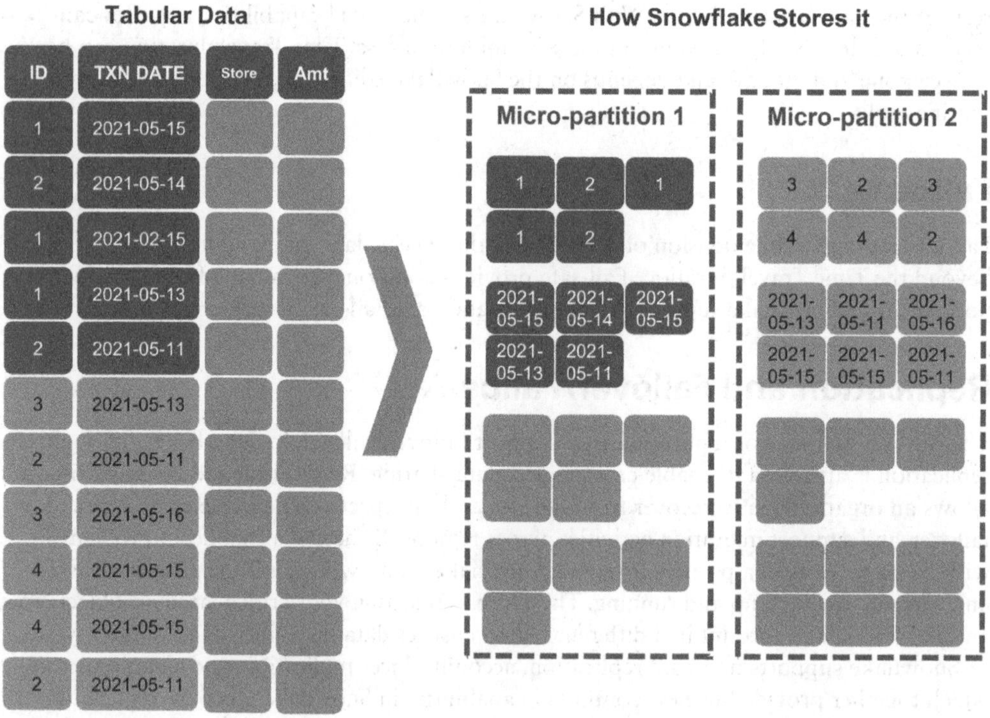

The micro-partitions are immutable, which means they cannot be changed once written. The immutability has implications when data in a table is updated or deleted. Because the micro-partitions are immutable, the data within them cannot be altered. When data in a table is updated, new micro-partitions are created that contain the updated data. The new micro-partitions logically replace existing micro-partitions containing the data as it existed before the update. The metadata for the table is updated to reflect the new micro-partitions, and the replaced micro-partitions are marked as deleted, as illustrated in Figure 6.2.

FIGURE 6.2 Snowflake stores data in micro-partitions.

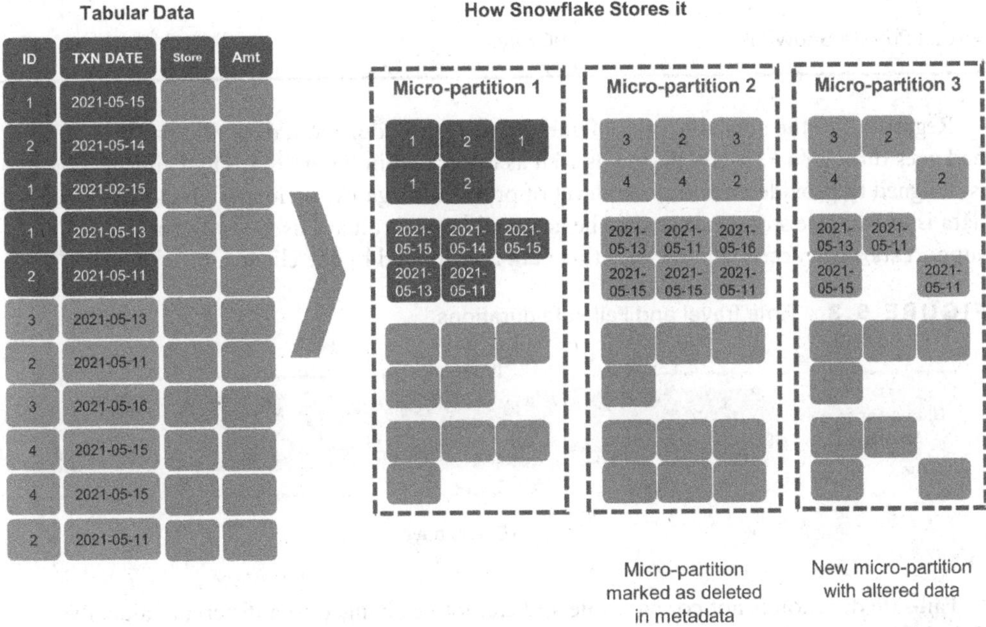

It is important to note that the micro-partitions that have been replaced and marked as deleted still exist physically on the disk and can be read if needed. This forms the foundations of the Time Travel capability in Snowflake. With Time Travel, users can read data from a table as it existed at a point in time, and all Snowflake is doing behind the scenes is reading data from historical micro-partitions, which were marked as deleted.

Snowflake keeps these historical micro-partitions for a defined period after they are purged. For a defined period, data in these historical micro-partitions can be accessed by an ordinary user. This period is referred to as the Time Travel period. Depending on the Snowflake edition, the Time Travel period can be from one day to 90 days. The Time Travel period can also be configured between zero days to the maximum allowable days constrained by the respective Snowflake edition. Table 6.1 illustrates the maximum allowed Time Travel duration for each Snowflake edition.

TABLE 6.1 Time Travel durations for various Snowflake editions

Snowflake edition	Maximum allowed Time Travel duration
Standard	1 day
Enterprise	90 days

TABLE 6.1 Time Travel durations for various Snowflake editions *(continued)*

Snowflake edition	Maximum allowed Time Travel duration
Business Critical	90 days
Virtual Private Snowflake	90 days

Regardless of the available or configured Time Travel duration, data that has been modified goes through a Fail-safe period as well as illustrated in Figure 6.3. The Fail-safe storage is designed to provide an additional level of protection against accidental data loss. When data is in Fail-safe storage, it cannot be accessed by an ordinary user—only Snowflake support staff can access and recover this data if requested by the client.

FIGURE 6.3 Time Travel and Fail-safe durations

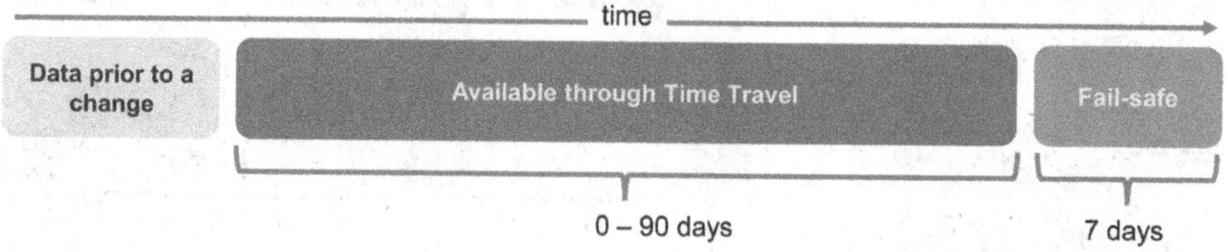

Fail-safe duration is not configurable and cannot be changed to a different value. By default, data goes through seven days of Fail-safe storage. However, Snowflake provides special table types, called transient and temporary tables, that don't have the Fail-safe capability.

Data that is in Fail-safe can be recovered only by Snowflake support. The Fail-safe storage can be used to recover data by Snowflake support in extreme scenarios where data has been lost or damaged due to unforeseen errors.

Time Travel can be set to zero days at a table, schema, or database level. However, it is not possible to change the Fail-safe duration, and it stays fixed at seven days. Temporary and transient tables don't have any Fail-safe.

Time Travel in Action

To support Time Travel, Snowflake provides additional syntax in SQL. To access table data as it existed at a specific point in time, you can use the following syntax, which provides an exact time stamp to see data at the desired point in time:

```
SELECT ...
FROM ...
```

```
AT ( TIMESTAMP => <timestamp>);
```

Sometimes specifying an exact time stamp is not feasible. For example, when you know someone updated the data within the last 3 hours, but you do not know the exact time stamp, the following syntax can be used, using the offset from the current time. The offset value specific is the time difference in seconds from the current time.

```
SELECT ...
FROM ...

AT ( OFFSET => <time_difference>);
```

Snowflake can also perform Time Travel to a point in time when a query was run by specifying a query ID in a Time Travel query. Using the BEFORE syntax, a Time Travel query returns data as it existed before the query was executed. The AT syntax shows the data as it existed once the query was executed.

```
SELECT ...
FROM ...

AT|BEFORE ( STATEMENT => <id>);
```

In the following exercises, we walk you through each of these Time Travel syntaxes.

Time Travel to a Point in Time

Exercise 6.1 focuses on retrieving data as it existed at a point in time. In this exercise, you'll populate a table with sample data, note the current time, and wait for some time before updating all the rows. You'll then use Time Travel to see the data as it existed at the point in time before the update was run.

EXERCISE 6.1

Traveling to a Point in Time

1. Begin by creating a database and a table. To understand the concept of Time Travel, you need a table with data. Since Snowflake provides a database with sample data, you'll use the Customer table in the sample database as a source for a new Customer table. Use the CREATE TABLE AS SQL syntax to create the Customer table with data:

```
CREATE DATABASE test_timetravel;

CREATE TABLE test_timetravel.public.CUSTOMER
AS SELECT * FROM SNOWFLAKE_SAMPLE_DATA.TPCH_SF1.CUSTOMER;
```

2. Next, validate that the new table indeed has data populated. To do so, run the following SQL. You should see 150,000 returned as the row count, which indicates that the table was created successfully with data.

```
SELECT COUNT(*) FROM CUSTOMER;
```

EXERCISE 6.1 ***(continued)***

3. The following steps will simulate an accidental update of the data in this table. The goal is to accidentally corrupt the data and then demonstrate how data can be accessed before the update. Before running the update, locate the current time stamp by running the following SQL. Take note of the result of this SQL as we will use the time stamp value in a later step.

```
SELECT CURRENT_TIMESTAMP;
```

4. Now, run a query that simulates an accidental update. For example, the following query sets the `c_phone` column to `NULL` for all rows in the Customer table.

```
UPDATE CUSTOMER SET c_phone = NULL;
```

5. Validate that the column has been set to `NULL` by running a `SELECT` query.

```
SELECT * FROM CUSTOMER;
```

6. Next, you'll use the Time Travel capability to access the data as it existed before you ran the update. You will use the time stamp that you noted in step 3.

```
SELECT * FROM CUSTOMER
BEFORE(TIMESTAMP => '<timestamp>'::timestamp_ltz);
```

Replace the `<timestamp>` placeholder with the value from step 3. For example, the SQL may look like the following after replacing the `<timestamp>` placeholder:

```
SELECT * FROM CUSTOMER
BEFORE(TIMESTAMP => '2021-11-22 02:06:17.411 -0800'::timestamp_ltz);
```

7. The previous step returns the data in the Customer table as it existed before the given time stamp. Because you recorded the time stamp before running the "accidental" update, you can use the time stamp value to access the data before the update. In the result set returned by step 7, pay special attention to the `c_phone` column and validate that the column contains no `NULL` values.

In this exercise, you used Time Travel SQL extensions and the time stamp syntax to view the data as it existed at a particular time. The Time Travel feature is relatively straightforward to use and can be easily included in standard SQL statements.

Time Travel to an Offset from the Current Time

Exercise 6.2 focuses on retrieving data as an offset from the current point in time. In this exercise, you'll populate a table with sample data, and wait for 5 minutes before deleting all the rows. You'll then use Time Travel to see the data as it existed 5 minutes ago.

EXERCISE 6.2

Traveling to an Offset from the Current Time

1. Begin by creating a database and a table. To understand the concept of offset-based Time Travel, you need a table with data. Since Snowflake provides a database with sample data, use the Nation table in the sample database as a source for a new Nation table. Use the `CREATE TABLE AS` SQL syntax to create the Nation table with data.

```
CREATE OR REPLACE DATABASE test_timetravel;

CREATE TABLE test_timetravel.public.NATION
AS SELECT * FROM SNOWFLAKE_SAMPLE_DATA.TPCH_SF1.NATION;
```

2. Next, validate that the new table indeed has data populated; to do so, run the following SQL, which should return a non-zero row count:

```
SELECT COUNT(*) FROM NATION;
```

3. The following step simulates an accidental deletion of the data from this table to demonstrate how data can be accessed as it existed before the delete:

```
DELETE FROM NATION;
```

4. Validate that the data has been deleted from the Nation table by counting the rows; the result from the following query should be 0:

```
SELECT COUNT(*) FROM NATION;
```

5. Since you want to use the offset capabilities of Time Travel, you must wait before proceeding with the next step. The next step assumes a lapsed time of 5 minutes.

6. You'll now use the Time Travel capability to access the data as it existed 5 minutes ago. To do so, you'll supply –300 as the offset value to the current time. The offset is the duration in seconds, and –300 equals 5 minutes in the past.

```
SELECT * FROM NATION
BEFORE(OFFSET => -300);
```

The previous step returns the data in the Nation table as it was 5 minutes ago, which is also the time before the delete statement was run.

We used Time Travel SQL extensions and the offset syntax in this exercise to see the data as it existed as an offset to the current time.

Time Travel to see data as it existed before a DML query

Exercise 6.3 focuses on retrieving data as it existed before a Data Manipulation Language (DML) query was executed. A DML query modifies the data in a table. Using Time Travel, it is possible to see the data before modification. In this exercise, you'll populate a table with sample data, delete all data and note the Query ID of the delete statement. You'll then use Time Travel and Query ID to see the data as it existed before the `DELETE` statement execution.

EXERCISE 6.3

Retrieve Data as It Existed before a DML Query

1. Begin by creating a database and a table. To understand how to use Time Travel to retrieve data as it existed before a DML query was run, you need a table with data. Since Snowflake provides a database with sample data, use the Supplier table in the sample database as a source for a new Supplier table. Use the `CREATE TABLE AS` SQL syntax to create the Supplier table with data:

EXERCISE 6.3 *(continued)*

```
CREATE OR REPLACE DATABASE test_timetravel;

CREATE TABLE test_timetravel.public.SUPPLIER
AS SELECT * FROM SNOWFLAKE_SAMPLE_DATA.TPCH_SF1.SUPPLIER;
```

2. Next, validate that the new table indeed has data populated; to do so, run the following SQL, which should return a non-zero row count:

```
SELECT COUNT(*) FROM SUPPLIER;
```

3. The following step simulates an accidental deletion of the data in this table. The goal is to demonstrate how data can be accessed as it existed before this statement was executed. Ensure that you take note of the Query ID when running the following statement. The next steps show how to find the Query ID.

```
DELETE FROM SUPPLIER;
```

4. If you are using Snowsight or the new Snowflake web UI, the Query ID can be found by clicking the ellipsis in the right corner and selecting Copy Query ID, as shown in the following screenshot.

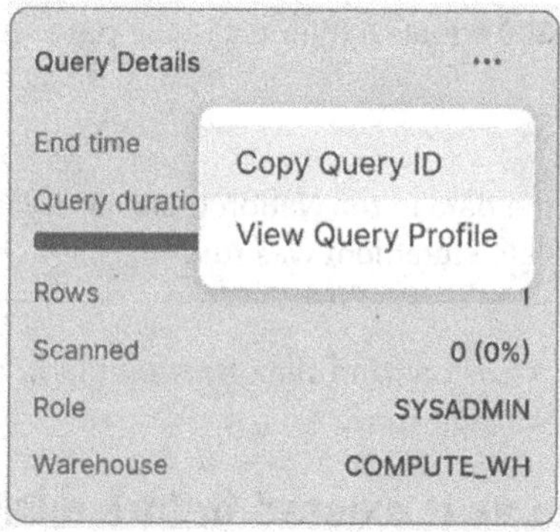

If you are using the classic Snowflake web UI, you can find the Query ID as shown in this screenshot:

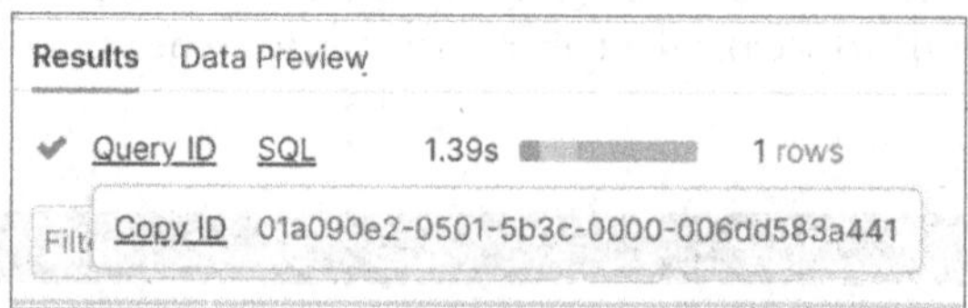

5. Next, you'll select the data as it existed before the DELETE statement was executed. Use the statement syntax in the Time Travel query as shown in the following code:

```
SELECT * FROM SUPPLIER
BEFORE(statement => '<query_id>');
```

6. Replace the <query_id> placeholder with the value from step 4; for example, the SQL may look like the following after replacing the <query_id> placeholder:

```
SELECT * FROM SUPPLIER
BEFORE(statement => '01a07a99-0501-5b3c-0000-006dd583a375');
```

The previous step returns the data in the Supplier table as it was before the DELETE statement was run.

Undrop Using Time Travel

Snowflake also provides the ability to recover dropped tables, schemas, and databases using Time Travel. When tables, schemas, or databases are dropped, they are not immediately removed from the system but instead are available to be restored for the duration of Time Travel. When a table is dropped, the physical data for the table is retained on the disk, and the table is marked as deleted in the metadata. An undrop operation simply sets the table's status to non-deleted to restore the table.

The undrop functionality applies to tables, schemas, and databases. That means you can restore complete databases or schemas, along with their child objects.

In the following exercise, we create a simple table, drop it, and restore it using the undrop syntax.

EXERCISE 6.4

Undrop a Dropped Table

1. Begin by creating a database and a table that you'll use to understand the undrop functionality. Since Snowflake provides a database with sample data, you can use the Part table in the sample database as a source for a new Part table. Use the CREATE TABLE AS SQL syntax to create the Part table with data:

```
CREATE OR REPLACE DATABASE test_timetravel;

CREATE TABLE test_timetravel.public.PART
AS SELECT * FROM SNOWFLAKE_SAMPLE_DATA.TPCH_SF1.PART;
```

2. Next, you'll drop the table. Once the table is dropped, you can run a SELECT to validate that the table is indeed dropped. The SELECT statement should fail.

```
DROP TABLE test_timetravel.public.PART;
```

3. Now you'll undrop the table, which is quite simple in syntax, as shown in the following SQL. By executing the undrop, you'll recover the table to its previous state.

```
UNDROP TABLE test_timetravel.public.PART;
```

4. Validate that the table is restored by counting the number of rows in the table.

```
SELECT COUNT(*) FROM test_timetravel.public.PART;
```

Time Travel and Fail-safe Storage Costs

Snowflake charges for data stored for Time Travel purposes and Fail-safe storage. The storage costs apply because historical micro-partitions are retained to provide Time Travel and Fail-safe functionality. The storage cost for Time Travel and Fail-safe is calculated every 24 hours from when the data was changed and depends on the number of days the data is maintained. The number of days data is maintained depends on the type of the table being used and the way Time Travel is configured.

Figure 6.4 illustrates how Time Travel for each update to a table is maintained separately. Each update to a table goes through its own Time Travel and Fail-safe period cycle.

FIGURE 6.4 Time Travel and Fail-safe storage for different updates

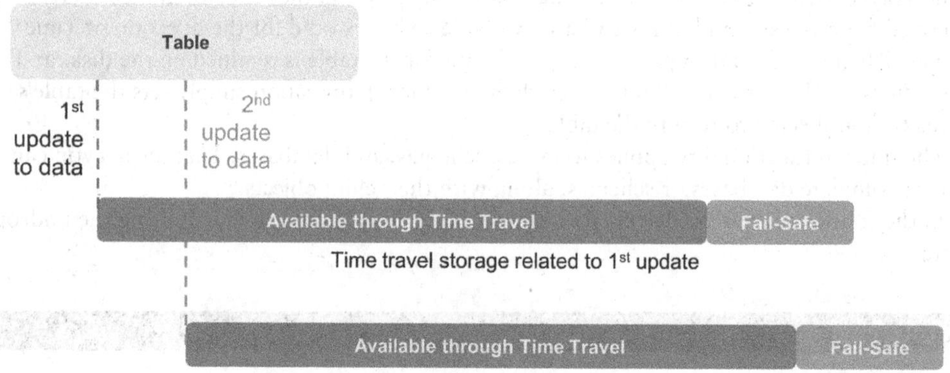

Snowflake provides two table types, temporary and transient tables, that don't have a Fail-safe capability to avoid costs associated with Time Travel and Fail-safe storage. Additionally, temporary tables and transient tables only have up to one day of Time Travel, which helps to minimize costs. Transient and temporary tables are a good choice for scenarios where data is required to be stored for a short period of time. Table 6.2 compares permanent, temporary, and transient tables.

TABLE 6.2 Time Travel comparison of permanent, temporary, and transient tables

Table type	Maximum Time Travel period	Fail-safe period
Permanent (Standard edition)	1 day	7 days
Permanent (Enterprise edition and above)	90 days	7 days
Temporary	1 day	0 days
Transient	1 day	0 days

Temporary Tables

Temporary tables can only have up to one day of Time Travel and no Fail-safe period. Temporary tables exist only in the session in which they were created, and as soon as the session is closed, temporary tables cease to exist. However, since they are limited to a session, they are not visible to other users or other sessions. Once the session is closed, data stored in a temporary table is completely removed from the system and is no longer recoverable. Note that the Time Travel for a temporary table is only available as long as the session is active.

The syntax for creating a temporary table is similar to creating a permanent table. The `TEMPORARY` keyword is used when creating temporary tables, as shown in the following code:

```
CREATE TEMPORARY TABLE <table_name> ...
```

Transient Tables

Transient tables are similar to temporary tables in that they have up to one day of Time Travel and have no Fail-safe. Transient tables are not limited to a session and are not automatically removed once a session is closed. Therefore, transient tables are available to other sessions and other users with the required privileges. Transient tables are ideal for situations where data is required to be stored temporarily and is required to be shared across sessions. Since transient tables are not tied to a session, they must be dropped explicitly. The syntax for creating a transient table is as follows, with the addition of the `TRANSIENT` keyword to the standard create table syntax:

```
CREATE TRANSIENT TABLE <table_name> ...
```

The Time Travel period can be changed for an object by running the `ALTER` command and specifying the Time Travel days through `data_retention_time_in_days`. For example:

```
ALTER TABLE <table_name> SET data_retention_time_in_
days=<number_of_days>;
```

Summary

This chapter introduced some of the components of continuous data protection in Snowflake. The chapter focused specifically on the Time Travel functionality provided by Snowflake, allowing easy access to data that may have been accidentally modified or deleted. Standard SQL queries can be modified using the Time Travel SQL extensions to access historical data in a table. In addition to Time Travel, Snowflake also has the concept of Fail-safe, which provides additional capabilities for data recovery. Since Time Travel and Fail-safe storage both have associated costs, Snowflake provides temporary and transient tables that don't have any Fail-safe storage and are more cost-effective for scenarios where data needs to be stored temporarily.

Exam Essentials

Know the components of continuous data protection in Snowflake. Snowflake's data protection features include encryption, role-based access, authentication, authorization, Time Travel, and Fail-safe. Snowflake defaults to encrypting all customer data at rest or in transit using AES-256 bit encryption. Snowflake provides authentication, fine-grained authorization capabilities, single sign-on (SSO), and multifactor authentication (MFA). Network policies allow you to restrict access to your Snowflake instance by IP address from a network security perspective. Additionally, Snowflake provides Time Travel and Fail-safe storage.

Time Travel Snowflake offers a novel data protection capability that allows you to query, retrieve, and recover historical data from tables. Users can read data as it existed at a specific point in time with minimal effort. Time Travel duration can range between one and 90 days, depending on the Snowflake edition and the configuration for a specific table. All Snowflake editions allow Time Travel; however, the Standard edition is limited to a maximum of one day of Time Travel. Starting from the Enterprise edition, up to 90 days of Time Travel is possible. Time Travel duration can be changed for tables, schema/database, or account level.

Fail-safe Fail-safe storage is a Time Travel extension that keeps data for seven days after the Time Travel period has ended. Fail-safe storage provides additional data loss protection; however, only Snowflake support can recover data from Fail-safe storage. Fail-safe duration is seven days for permanent tables and cannot be configured. Fail-safe cannot be turned off. However, certain table types such as transient tables and temporary tables don't have Fail-safe storage, making them suitable for temporary workloads.

Undrop When tables, schemas, or databases are dropped, they are not immediately deleted from the system but remain recoverable for the duration of Time Travel. The actual data is kept on the disk when a table is dropped, although the table is marked as dropped. To undrop a table, Snowflake simply sets its status to non-deleted. Undrop works on tables, schemas, and databases.

Review Questions

1. Which of the following Snowflake editions provide Time Travel capability? (Choose all that apply.)
   - A. Enterprise
   - B. Standard
   - C. Business Critical
   - D. Virtual Private Snowflake
2. Which of the following is the minimum Snowflake edition that provides 90 days of Time Travel?
   - A. Enterprise
   - B. Standard
   - C. Business Critical
   - D. Virtual Private Snowflake
3. True or False: Time Travel requires extra storage, which results in additional costs.
   - A. True
   - B. False
4. What is the maximum amount of Time Travel duration possible when using Snowflake Standard edition?
   - A. 7 days
   - B. 90 days
   - C. One day
   - D. Zero days
5. What is the maximum amount of Time Travel possible for a temporary table?
   - A. 7 days
   - B. 90 days
   - C. One day
   - D. Zero days
6. Which of the following table types don't provide any Fail-safe storage? (Choose all that apply.)
   - A. Permanent tables
   - B. Temporary tables
   - C. Transient tables
   - D. Aggregate tables

7. Data that has entered Fail-safe storage can be accessed by which of the following?
   A. Any user
   B. Snowflake support
   C. IT staff
   D. Administrators
8. What is the maximum amount of Time Travel possible for a transient table?
   A. 7 days
   B. 90 days
   C. 1 day
   D. 0 days
9. What is the maximum allowable duration for Time Travel for a permanent table in the Snowflake Enterprise edition?
   A. 7 days
   B. 90 days
   C. 0 days
   D. One day
10. True or False: It is possible to disable Fail-safe for certain databases, schemas, or tables.
    A. True
    B. False
11. True or False: Fail-safe storage is a way for Snowflake customers to access historical data that may have been accidentally deleted.
    A. False
    B. True
12. Which of the following objects can be undropped? (Choose all that apply.)
    A. Databases
    B. Tables
    C. Schemas
    D. External stages
    E. File formats

Chapter

7

Cloning and Data Sharing

THE SNOWPRO CORE EXAM TOPICS COVERED IN THIS CHAPTER INCLUDE THE FOLLOWING:

✓ **Domain 1.0: Snowflake Data Platform Features and Architecture**

- 1.1 Outline key features of the Snowflake Cloud Data platform.
  - Data Cloud/Data Exchange/Partner Network
- 1.3 Outline Snowflake's catalog and objects.
  - Shares

✓ **Domain 2.0: Account Access and Security**

- 2.3 Outline data governance capabilities in Snowflake.
  - Secure views

✓ **Domain 6.0: Data Protection and Data Sharing**

- 6.1 Outline continuous data protection with Snowflake.
  - Cloning
  - Replication
- 6.2 Outline Snowflake data sharing capabilities.
  - Account types
  - Data Marketplace and Data Exchange
  - Private data exchange
  - Access control options
  - Shares

Snowflake's unique architecture, reliance on micro-partitions, excellent cloud services layer, and metadata management underpin several novel features. These features include zero-copy cloning and data sharing without moving the data. This chapter describes zero-copy cloning and how it works before taking you through some hands-on exercises on cloning. The chapter then describes data sharing and how it works, and describes the three high-level approaches to data sharing in Snowflake.

Zero-Copy Cloning

Cloning, or zero-copy cloning, is a feature provided by Snowflake that allows users to create a clone of a table, schema, or database without physically copying the data. Cloning provides immediate benefits by reducing the need for extra storage and fast speed of the copy operation. Since cloning does not physically copy data, the process is much faster than a traditional copy operation. It does not require additional storage space because there is no physical copying of data.

A snapshot of the data present in the cloning source is taken and is made available in the cloned object. The source object and the cloned object are independent of each other, and you can perform data modification operations on either object without affecting the other.

Although the `CLONE` command can create a copy of various Snowflake objects, we will focus on cloning tables, schemas, and databases in this chapter. The following object types are supported for cloning.

Objects that contain data:

- Databases
- Schemas
- Tables
- Streams

Other objects supported for cloning:

- Stages
- File formats
- Sequences
- Tasks
- Streams

The objects that contain data are cloned using the zero-copy cloning technique, which we discuss in detail in this chapter.

When tables, schemas, or databases are cloned, the cloned object doesn't contribute to the overall storage until data manipulation language (DML) operations are performed on the source or target, adding new data or updating existing data.

How Zero-Copy Cloning Works

Let's discuss how zero-copy cloning works under the covers. In Chapter 2, "Snowflake Architecture," you learned that Snowflake stores its data in the form of micro-partitions. Micro-partitions are the reason zero-copy cloning is so fast and efficient. Snowflake does not copy any micro-partitions; instead, within its metadata, it points the cloned table to the existing micro-partitions. This concept is illustrated in Figure 7.1. The figure illustrates that the cloned table, T2, was cloned from the source table, T1, which has three micro-partitions. When initially cloned, T2 shares T1's micro-partitions. Because this is a metadata-only operation, there is no data movement or additional storage requirements. The operation is very fast and does not require a running virtual warehouse.

FIGURE 7.1 Zero-copy cloning and micro-partitions

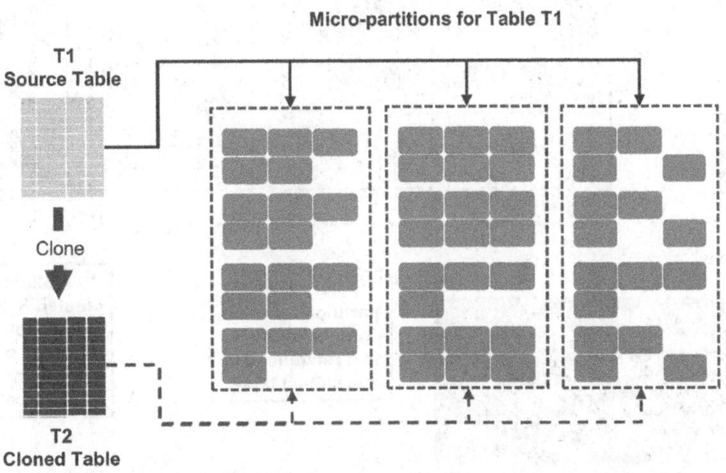

Although cloning is fast because it is a metadata operation, it is not always immediate. For huge tables with millions of micro-partitions, cloning may take some time while the metadata is updated.

Earlier, you also learned that the source object and the cloned object are independent of each other. You can perform data modification operations to either object without affecting the other. This is because Snowflake is tracking the micro-partitions in the metadata for each table independently. Snowflake updates the micro-partition information for only the updated table when either table is updated.

This concept is illustrated in Figure 7.2, which builds on the example shown in Figure 7.1. Here, data in the source table, T1, has been updated. Because of the update, one of the micro-partitions is no longer part of the table and is shown deemphasized in the figure. However, note that the micro-partition which is no longer part of table T1 is still part of the cloned table, T2. Finally, an additional micro-partition is added to T1, shown as the highlighted micro-partition in Figure 7.2.

FIGURE 7.2 Updates to the source table in a cloning scenario

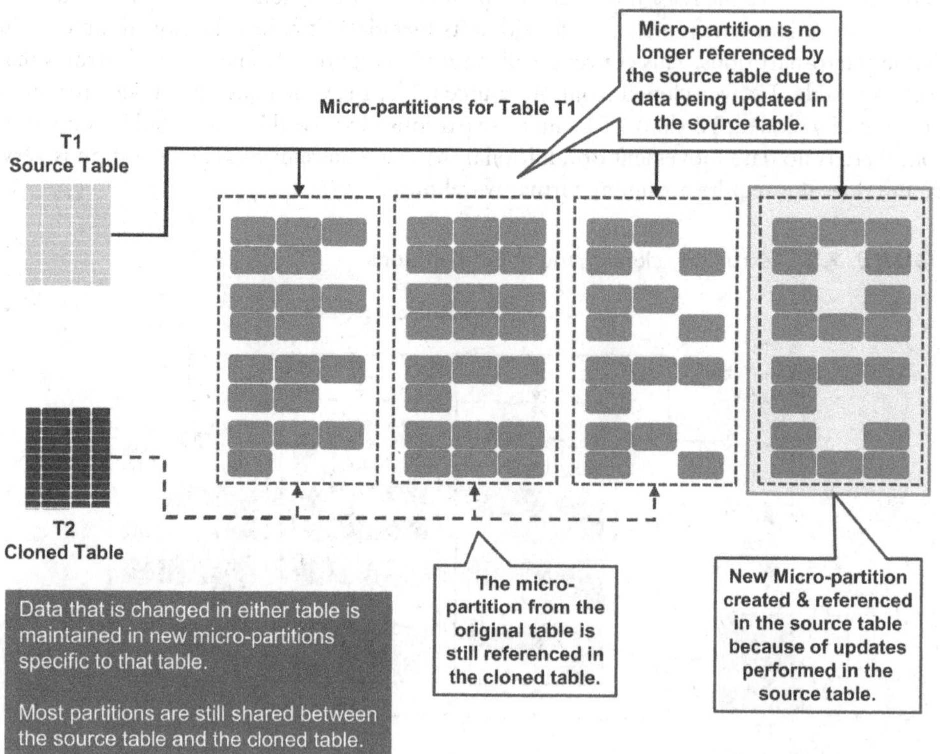

It is worth noting that there is no additional storage requirement for the cloned table when a table is cloned. However, as new data is inserted or updates are performed to either table, micro-partitions may be added or removed. If new micro-partitions are added, then additional storage costs are charged.

Figure 7.3 illustrates the scenario when data in a cloned table is changed. As shown in the figure, data in the cloned table, T2, was updated, resulting in a new micro-partition to be written out. Consequently, one of the micro-partitions in the source table, T1, is no longer pointed to by the cloned table.

FIGURE 7.3 Updates to the cloned table in a cloning scenario

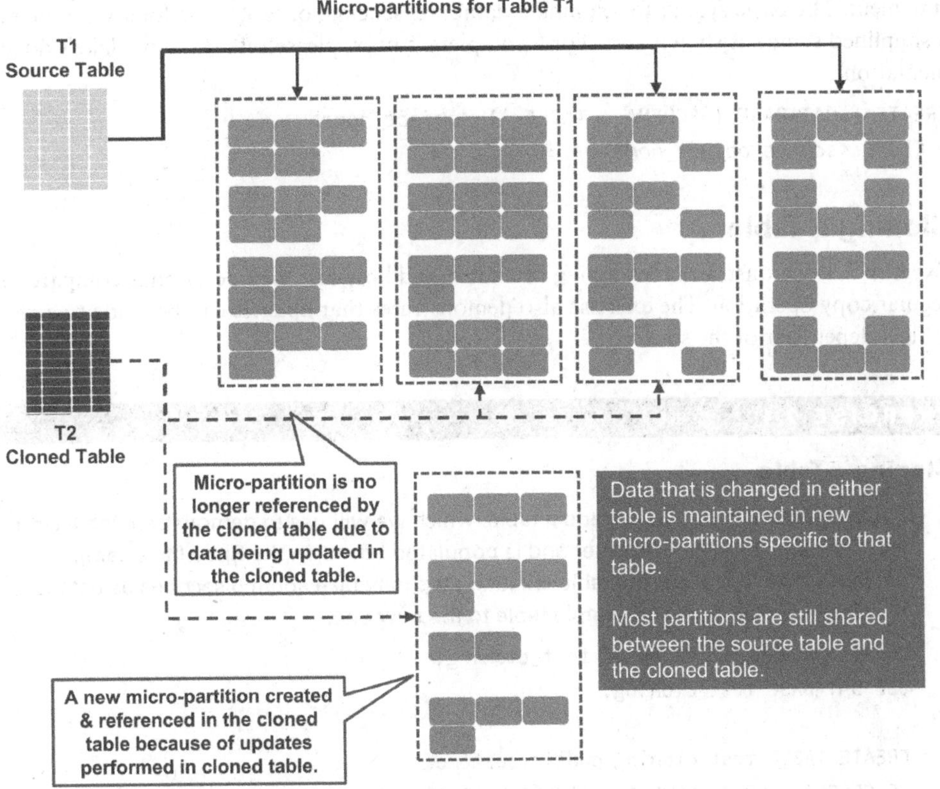

Cloning is a great feature for making copies of data for debugging purposes or for standing up replicas of whole production environments. It minimizes the need for additional storage requirements for cloned objects. Additional storage is only required when data is inserted or updated in either the source or the cloned table, resulting in additional micro-partitions to be written out and consequently additional storage and charges.

Internal named stages cannot be cloned. When a database or schema is cloned, any Snowpipes that reference an internal named stage are not cloned. Also, external tables cannot be cloned.

Database, Schema, and Table Cloning

Although cloning can be performed for various objects, this chapter focuses on database, schema, and table cloning. Zero-copy cloning is not limited to tables but can be performed even at a schema or database level. When a complete schema or database is cloned, all objects in that schema are made available in the cloned schema.

Databases, schemas, and tables can be cloned using the CLONE syntax in the CREATE statement. The basic syntax for cloning a database, schema, or table is as follows. Note that a simplified syntax is shown here. For a complete syntax, please refer to Snowflake's documentation.

```
CREATE { DATABASE | SCHEMA | TABLE  } <object_name>
  CLONE <source_object_name>;
```

Cloning a Table

Exercise 7.1 demonstrates the cloning of a table and how fast the operation is compared to a regular copy operation. The exercise also demonstrates that updates can be made to a cloned table independent of the source.

EXERCISE 7.1

Cloning a Table

1. Begin by creating a database and a table, which we will use to demonstrate table cloning. The table is called Customer and is populated based on the Snowflake sample database data. Note that the table creation step may take about 5 seconds as data is physically copied from the sample table to the new one.

```
CREATE OR REPLACE DATABASE test_cloning;
USE DATABASE test_cloning;

CREATE TABLE test_cloning.public.customer
AS SELECT * FROM SNOWFLAKE_SAMPLE_DATA.TPCH_SF10.CUSTOMER;
```

2. Validate the row count in the Customer table using the following SQL; the result should be 1.5 million rows.

```
SELECT COUNT(*) from customer;
```

3. At this stage, go ahead and suspend your virtual warehouses, as the next step demonstrates that cloning doesn't invoke any compute but instead is a metadata operation.

4. Clone the table using zero-copy cloning; the syntax is straightforward, as shown in the following SQL. The statement should execute almost immediately as it is a metadata operation.

```
CREATE TABLE customer_copy clone customer;
```

5. Check your virtual warehouse status. Suppose you have not run any other query except the clone query. In that case, the virtual warehouse remains suspended, indicating that the cloning has happened at a metadata and a cloud services level.

6. Validate the row count in the cloned customer table; the result should be 1.5 million rows.

```
SELECT COUNT(*) from customer_copy;
```

7. Next, we'll demonstrate that the source table and cloned table updates happen independently. Although cloned tables share the same data and hence the same micro-partitions, updates can be made to either table, which will not impact the other table. Run the following SQL to update a subset of rows in the customer_copy table. The UPDATE statement should impact 300,276 rows.

```
UPDATE customer_copy SET C_MKTSEGMENT = 'STRUCTURE' WHERE C_MKTSEGMENT =
'BUILDING';
```

8. Now view how the tables differ by running the following SQL, the result of which is shown in the following screenshot.

```
SELECT C_MKTSEGMENT, COUNT(*) from customer GROUP BY 1;
```

	C_MKTSEGMENT	COUNT(*)
1	MACHINERY	300,441
2	FURNITURE	299,496
3	HOUSEHOLD	299,751
4	AUTOMOBILE	300,036
5	BUILDING	300,276

9. Run the same SQL, but this time for the cloned table; the following screenshot shows the results.

```
SELECT C_MKTSEGMENT, COUNT(*) from customer_copy GROUP BY 1;
```

	C_MKTSEGMENT	...	COUNT(*)
1	MACHINERY		300,441
2	HOUSEHOLD		299,751
3	FURNITURE		299,496
4	AUTOMOBILE		300,036
5	STRUCTURE		300,276

Notice that the tables are retaining updates independently.

We cloned a table using the zero-copy cloning method, a metadata operation that is fast to complete. As opposed to physical copying of data, zero-copy cloning of a table doesn't move any data but instead points to the same micro-partitions as the source table. However, from the time the table was cloned, the two tables can exist independently—that is, updates, inserts, and deletes can be performed to either table, and they do not impact the other table.

Cloning a Database

Exercise 7.2 tackles the cloning of a complete database, demonstrating that database child objects like schemas and tables are recursively cloned when a database is cloned.

EXERCISE 7.2

Cloning a Database

1. We'll reuse the database you created in Exercise 7.1, but we'll add a new schema to that database and new tables. To add a new table to the public schema, run the following SQL:

```
USE DATABASE test_cloning;

CREATE TABLE test_cloning.public.nation
AS SELECT * FROM SNOWFLAKE_SAMPLE_DATA.TPCH_SF10.NATION;
```

2. Next, add an additional schema and add a table to the new schema using the following SQL:

```
USE DATABASE test_cloning;

CREATE SCHEMA sub_schema;

CREATE TABLE test_cloning.sub_schema.region
AS SELECT * FROM SNOWFLAKE_SAMPLE_DATA.TPCH_SF10.REGION;
```

3. Once the additional schema and tables have been created, review the structure using the database tree in the Snowflake web UI. The databases, schemas, and table should look similar to this screenshot:

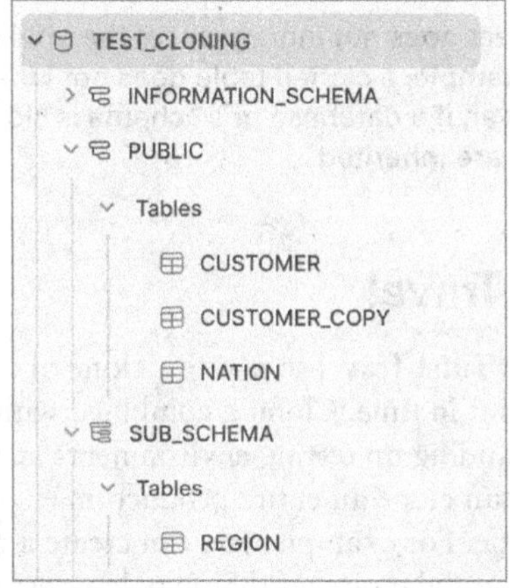

4. Now, use the following SQL to clone the whole database using zero-copy cloning. The statement should execute almost immediately since it is a metadata operation.

```
CREATE DATABASE cloned_database clone test_cloning;
```

5. Once the preceding statement has completed execution, you will see a new database named cloned_database. Expand the database tree in the Snowflake web user interface and notice that the schemas and tables from the source database have all been cloned as part of the database cloning. The result looks similar to the following screenshot.

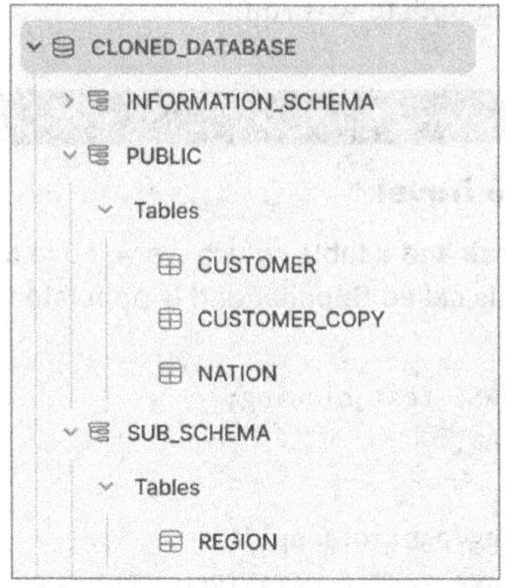

We cloned a complete database in this exercise. Cloning a database results in all child schemas of that database and objects contained inside those schemas being cloned recursively.

A cloned object does not inherit any of the privileges from the source object; for example, a cloned table does not inherit any granted privileges. However, if a database or a schema is cloned, privileges on the child objects are inherited.

Cloning with Time Travel

Cloning can be combined with Time Travel to create a clone of a table, a database, or a schema as they existed at a point in time. Cloning combined with Time Travel is a powerful feature that can be used for standing up testing environments at a point in time for debugging or testing purposes. You can clone an entire production environment through this feature while traveling back in time. For example, you can create a replica of production one month ago and use it to debug old data issues that may have escaped detection. The syntax for cloning with Time Travel is similar to the usual cloning syntax, except it includes the Time Travel extensions in the syntax, as shown here:

```
CREATE { DATABASE | SCHEMA | TABLE  } <object_name>
  CLONE <source_object_name>
[ { AT | BEFORE } ( { TIMESTAMP => <timestamp> | OFFSET => <time_difference> |
STATEMENT => <id> } ) ]
```

Exercise 7.3 demonstrates the concept of cloning a table while traveling back in time. In this exercise, you create a table, populate it with some data, update the data, and then clone the table as it existed before the update was run.

EXERCISE 7.3

Cloning a Table with Time Travel

1. Begin by creating a database and a table, which we will use to demonstrate cloning with Time Travel. The table is called Supplier and is populated based on the Snowflake sample database data.

```
CREATE OR REPLACE DATABASE test_cloning;
USE DATABASE test_cloning;

CREATE TABLE test_cloning.public.supplier
AS SELECT * FROM SNOWFLAKE_SAMPLE_DATA.TPCH_SF10.SUPPLIER;
```

2. Next, run an update query on the table data to demonstrate the cloning with Time Travel. Run the following SQL and make sure that you have noted the query ID, which we will use in the next steps. You can review Exercise 6.3 to understand how to obtain the query ID for a SQL statement.

```
UPDATE test_cloning.public.supplier SET S_NAME = NULL;
```

3. Validate that S_NAME is set to NULL for all rows by running the following SQL. The query should result in zero rows.

```
SELECT * FROM test_cloning.public.supplier WHERE S_NAME IS NOT NULL;
```

4. Next, clone the table using zero-copy cloning with Time Travel; the syntax is straightforward, as shown in the following SQL. Please replace *<query_id>* with the query ID you noted in step 2.

```
CREATE TABLE supplier_copy clone supplier
BEFORE (STATEMENT => '<query_id>');
```

5. The preceding statement creates a clone of the Customer table as it existed before the UPDATE statement was run. Therefore, the cloned table will have the S_NAME still populated and not set to NULL. To validate this, run the following SQL. You should see several records returned as a result, which indicates that the table has data before the update.

```
SELECT * FROM test_cloning.public.supplier_copy WHERE S_NAME IS NOT NULL;
```

In this exercise, we cloned a table while traveling back in time, demonstrating that we can make clones of tables as they existed at a point in time. Cloning with Time Travel is a novel feature that simplifies standing up testing environments and helps debug and fix data issues that may have occurred over time.

Secure Data Sharing in Snowflake

Like Time Travel and Cloning, Secure Data Sharing does not move data; instead, it is a metadata operation. Secure Data Sharing is performed through Snowflake's cloud services and the metadata layer. There is no movement or copying of data during a data sharing operation; instead, the shared table references the original table and its underlying micro-partitions. This ensures that a sharing operation is almost instantaneous and that any updates in the source table are automatically and immediately reflected in the shared table. Figure 7.4 illustrates the concept of Secure Data Sharing and how it is achieved. Data is shared by a data provider, any Snowflake account that creates a share and makes it available to other accounts to consume. A data consumer is any account that creates a database from the share and consumes data shared by the provider.

There is no data movement during data sharing since the source table's micro-partitions are referred to in the cloned table. Therefore, there are no additional storage requirements either, which means there are no storage costs for the consumer.

FIGURE 7.4 Data sharing and micro-partitions

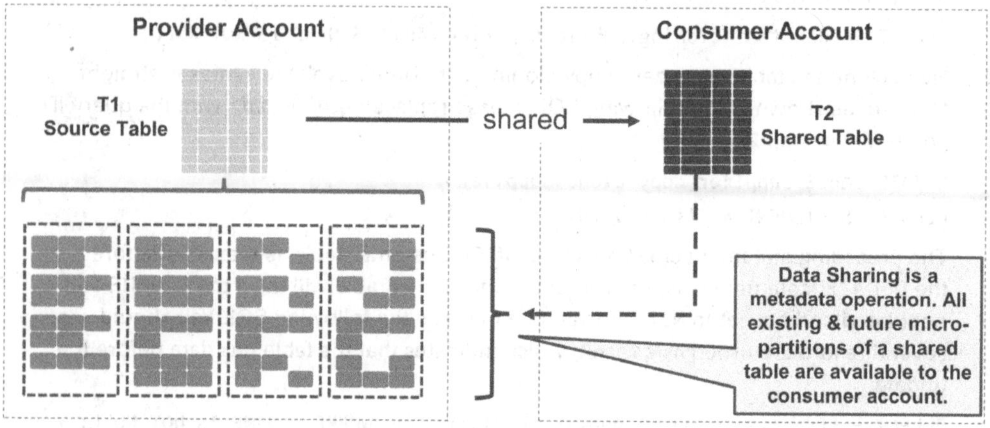

Typically, a Snowflake account can share data within the same cloud provider and region as the account itself. If you want to share data with other Snowflake accounts that are in another region or a different cloud provider, data must be replicated to the target region and the target cloud provider. To set up replication, designate one or more databases as primary databases on the source account. On the target account, create a database as a replica of the source database, followed by a share containing the replicated database.

Snowflake Offerings for Data Sharing

Snowflake provides three types of product offerings for Secure Data Sharing, all of which utilize the sharing mechanisms discussed in the preceding section. The Secure Data Sharing product offerings provided by Snowflake are as follows:

Direct Sharing Account-to-account data sharing.

Snowflake Data Marketplace Consume free and paid datasets provided by various data providers. It's possible to publish your own datasets as well.

Data Exchange A private data marketplace created and controlled by the customer to publish and consume data internally and with limited external parties.

Direct Sharing

Direct Sharing is the simplest form of data sharing used to share data from one account to another. Direct sharing uses the concept of data providers, data consumers, and the share object to share data with other Snowflake accounts. As explained previously, no actual data is copied or transferred between accounts during sharing. The sharing is achieved through metadata operations in the cloud services layer. Therefore, the data consumer incurs no additional storage costs because the provider account stores and pays for the data storage. However, the consumer account must pay for the compute resources used to run queries on the shared data.

Let's discuss a few key data sharing concepts through the high-level process for Direct Sharing, shown in Figure 7.5.

FIGURE 7.5 Direct Sharing

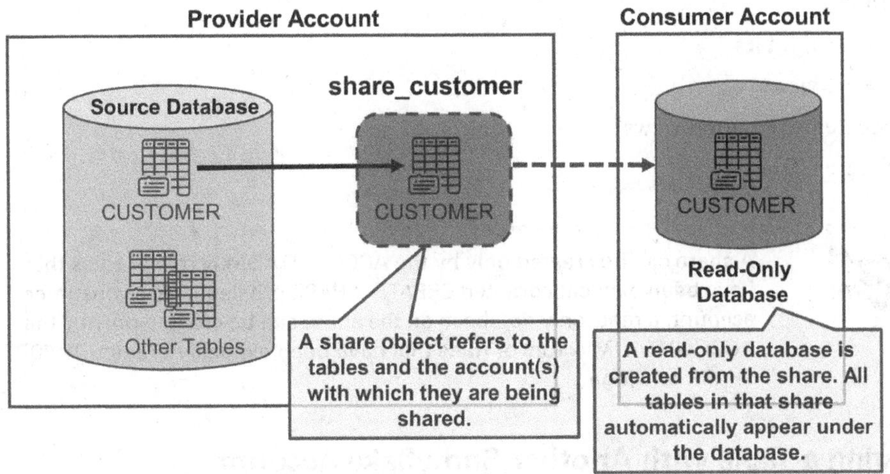

A Provider account is where the data sharing journey begins. Any Snowflake account can be a data provider that can share one or more objects with one or more Snowflake accounts.

A data provider starts by creating a Share object. A Share object can be thought of as a container of all the information required for sharing an object. Each Share object contains the following:

- Objects that are being shared, such as tables. Tables can be added to a share by granting the share `SELECT` access to the tables.
- Database and schema containing the shared object. The Share object must be provided `USAGE` access to the schema and the shared object database.
- One or more Snowflake accounts with which data is being shared, also known as *consumers*.

Once a consumer's account number is added to a share, the share starts appearing in the consumer account. The consumer then creates a read-only database on the Share object and can see all of the shared objects under that read-only database.

The high-level flow for Direct Sharing is shown in Figure 7.6.

FIGURE 7.6 Process flow for direct data sharing

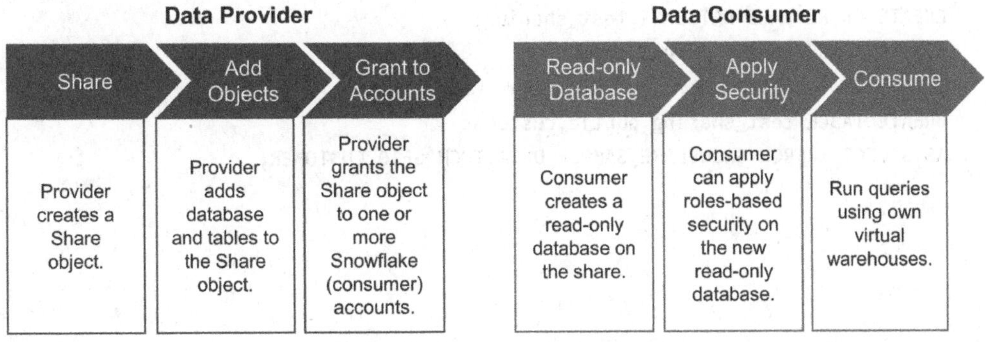

The following types of objects can be shared through direct data sharing:

- Tables
- External tables
- Secure views
- Secure materialized views
- Secure UDFs

A share can be created only by the ACCOUNTADMIN role or roles that have been explicitly granted `CREATE SHARE` privilege. As a consumer account, a read-only database on the share can be created only by the ACCOUNTADMIN role or roles that have been explicitly granted `IMPORT SHARE` privilege.

Sharing a Table with Another Snowflake Account

Exercise 7.4 demonstrates sharing of a table with another Snowflake account. We create a new Share object, add a new table to that Share object, add the necessary grants, and make the Share object available to a consumer. Then, as the consumer account we create a read-only database using the share and can then consume the shared data.

Notice that you need two Snowflake accounts for this exercise, one to act as a data provider and the other as a data consumer. For this exercise, we suggest that the two accounts you use be on the same cloud provider and in the same region. Although Snowflake supports data sharing across regions and cloud providers, it requires data replication to be set up, which is beyond the scope of this chapter.

Note that we use the ACCOUNTADMIN role for creating and managing the share. Alternatively, a role with the `CREATE SHARE` privilege can be used.

EXERCISE 7.4

Sharing a Table with Another Snowflake Account

Run the following steps while logged into the Provider account:

1. Begin by creating a database and a table, which we will use to demonstrate data sharing:

```
CREATE OR REPLACE DATABASE test_sharing;
USE DATABASE test_sharing;

CREATE TABLE test_sharing.public.customer
AS SELECT * FROM SNOWFLAKE_SAMPLE_DATA.TPCH_SF10.CUSTOMER;
```

2. Next, switch to the ACCOUNTADMIN role for the required privileges and create the Share object.

   ```
   USE ROLE ACCOUNTADMIN;
   CREATE SHARE shr_customer;
   ```

3. To add a table to a share, the required syntax is to grant the share SELECT access to the table. For example, the following SQL adds the Customer table to the shr_customer Share object. However, you will notice that this statement fails because we haven't granted the required privileges on the database and schema containing the Customer table.

   ```
   GRANT SELECT ON TABLE test_sharing.public.customer TO SHARE shr_customer;
   ```

4. You must provide USAGE privilege on the database and the schema to the Share object before doing step 3. To do so, run the following SQL:

   ```
   GRANT USAGE ON DATABASE test_sharing TO SHARE shr_customer;
   GRANT USAGE ON SCHEMA test_sharing.public TO SHARE shr_customer;
   ```

5. Let's grant the SELECT access on the table to the share again, using the following SQL:

   ```
   GRANT SELECT ON TABLE test_sharing.public.customer TO SHARE shr_customer;
   ```

6. The final step is to add one or more consumer accounts to the share. To find the account name for a Snowflake account, you can revisit Exercise 3.1, which describes a simple method to find the account name. Alternatively, in the new Snowflake web user interface, the bottom left of the screen also shows account information. Note that you need the consumer account name in the following statement:

   ```
   ALTER SHARE shr_customer ADD ACCOUNT = <consumer_account_name>;
   ```

Run the following steps while logged into the consumer account:

7. While logged into the consumer account, you must create a database on the share, as shown in the following SQL. You must replace the provider account name with the name of the account that created the share and shared the data. Note that you must use the ACCOUNTADMIN role or another role that has explicitly been granted the IMPORT SHARE privilege.

   ```
   USE ROLE ACCOUNTADMIN;
   CREATE DATABASE customer_data FROM SHARE <provider_account_name>.shr_customer;
   ```

8. Once the database has been created, you can query the Customer table in the read-only database just like any other table. For example:

   ```
   SELECT * FROM customer_data.public.customer;
   ```

In the preceding exercise, we shared a table from one Snowflake account to another by creating a Share object, adding a table to the share, and adding a consumer account.

It is possible to add multiple consumer accounts to a single share, simultaneously sharing the data with several consumers.

Sharing Tables That Exist in Different Databases

If you need to share data from multiple tables that exist in different databases, creating a secure view is an option. Since multiple databases cannot be added to a single share, Snowflake's suggested approach is to create secure views in a single database. The views can point to different tables in different databases. The secure views may also be used to join data from different tables and present the data as a single view for sharing. The concept is illustrated in Figure 7.7. The figure illustrates four tables shared from three different databases. A new database is created solely for sharing to share these tables optimally. Several secure views are created in this new database, pointing directly to a table or joining data from multiple tables. This shared database and the secure views are then shared with the consumer accounts.

FIGURE 7.7 Sharing secure views

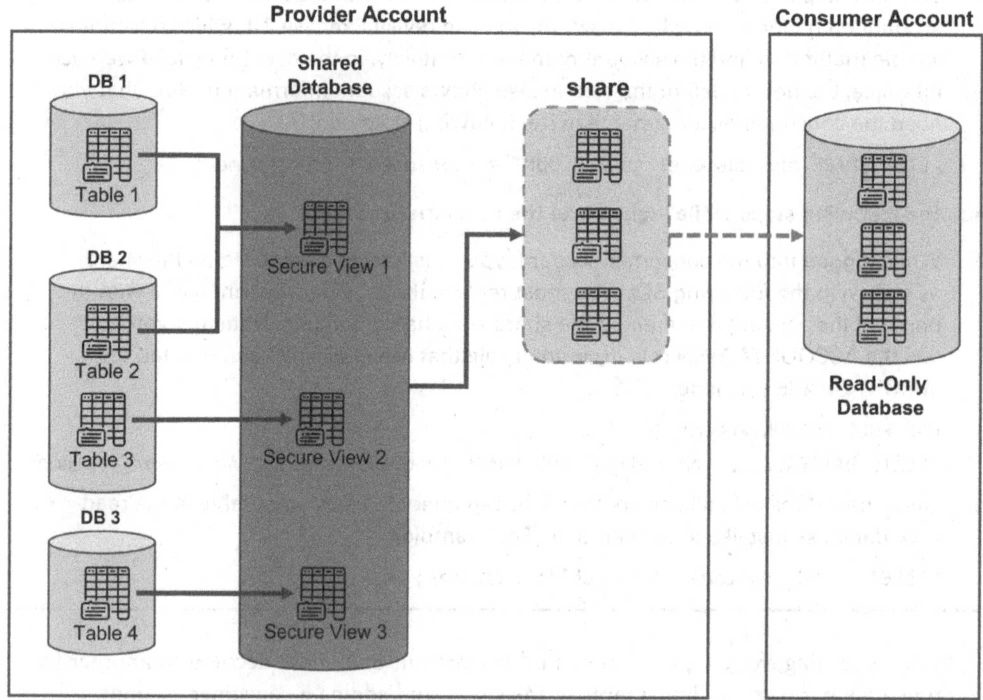

Sharing secure views is almost identical to sharing a table; however, an additional step is required to provide the Share object with the `REFERENCE USAGE` privilege on the databases underlying the secure views. For example, in the scenario shown in Figure 7.7, the Share object needs to have `REFERENCE USAGE` granted on the DB 1, DB 2, and DB 3 databases. The syntax for a reference usage grant follows:

```
GRANT REFERENCE USAGE ON DATABASE <database_name> TO SHARE <share_name>;
```

Sharing with a Non-Snowflake User

We have so far discussed sharing data with other Snowflake accounts. It is possible in Snowflake to share data with a non-Snowflake user by creating an account for the non-Snowflake user. This *reader account* is created by the data provider for sharing. The data provider then creates an initial administrator user and a virtual warehouse in the new reader account. The sharing process is the same as sharing with any other Snowflake account. The concept of data sharing through a reader account is illustrated in Figure 7.8.

FIGURE 7.8 Secure Data Sharing with non-Snowflake users

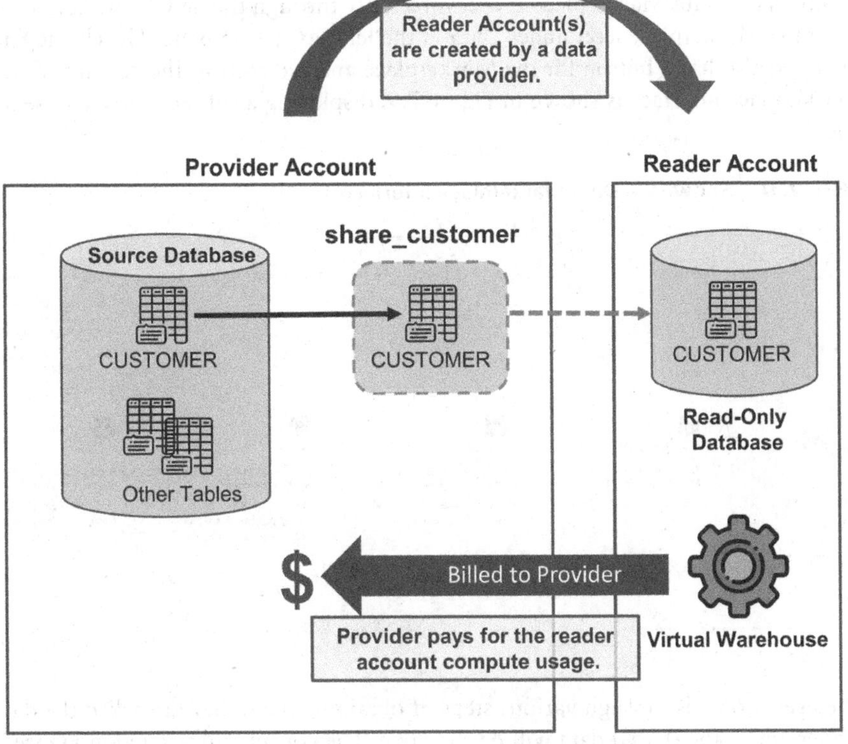

Because the data provider creates the reader account, all reader account's compute costs are billed to the provider account. Any virtual warehouse usage by the reader account is added to the compute costs of the provider account.

Snowflake Data Marketplace

Snowflake Data Marketplace is a marketplace for discovering and accessing third-party datasets that have been made available by various organizations. These third-party datasets are often offered for a cost but they can sometimes be available for free. Once you have obtained access to a dataset, the dataset is available in your Snowflake account just like any other table, and you can join the dataset with existing tables. Snowflake accounts can also publish datasets to Snowflake Data Marketplace and monetize them.

Snowflake Data Marketplace uses the same underlying principles that underpin data sharing and were explained earlier in this chapter.

Snowflake Data Marketplace is available to all Snowflake accounts except Virtual Private Snowflake (VPS) accounts. The Data Marketplace is also not available for Microsoft Azure Government; however, its support is planned.

The Snowflake Data Marketplace is accessible only through the new Snowflake web interface, using the Marketplace icon under Data in the left navigation pane. The classic Snowflake interface also has a button for the Marketplace and redirects to the new interface. The Data Marketplace interface is shown in Figure 7.9, displaying a subset of free datasets available.

FIGURE 7.9 Snowflake Data Marketplace interface

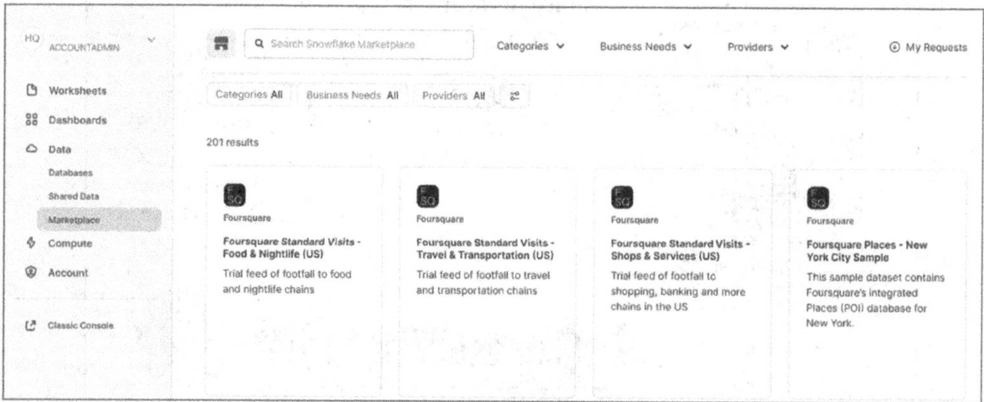

As the user proceeds through various steps of obtaining data, they are asked the database name under which the shared data will be available. The concept, illustrated in Figure 7.10, is similar to how a read-only database is required to be created during direct data sharing.

FIGURE 7.10 Get Data button in the Data Marketplace

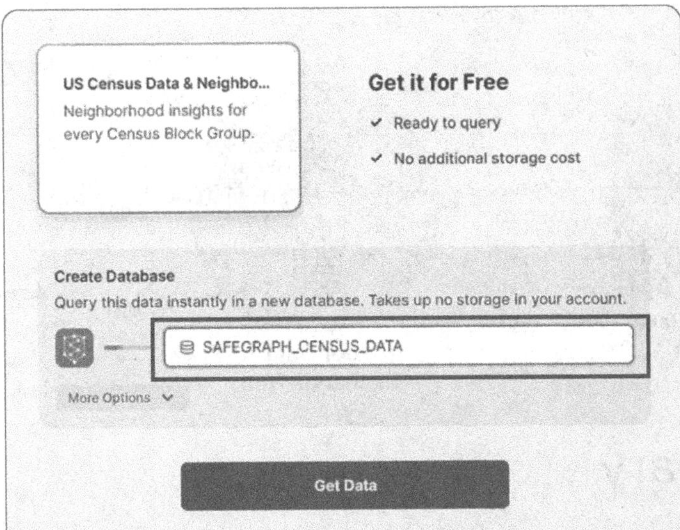

Only users with the `IMPORT SHARE` privilege can create databases from the Snowflake Data Marketplace.

Snowflake Data Marketplace has two types of data listings:

Standard Data Listings Provide immediate access to the published dataset. This type of listing is used for providing generic data that any organization can use.

Personalized Data Listings Provide customized datasets that can be requested and are provided on demand. Personalized data listings may produce data specific to each consumer.

Data Exchange

Data Exchange is your own private data sharing hub that can be used to share data among a selected group of invite-only members. The account owning the Data Exchange is responsible for inviting members and specifying whether they can share, consume, or do both. The concept of Data Exchange is illustrated in Figure 7.11, demonstrating that the owning account creates and controls a Data Exchange hub. Member accounts can be set to either consume, publish, or both. The result is a hub where members specified by the owning account can exchange and share data.

The purpose of Data Exchange is to allow enterprises to share data with trusted partners, suppliers, vendors, and customers. Data Exchange functionality is available to all Snowflake accounts except VPS Snowflake accounts. The functionality may not be enabled by default, and, if not enabled, requires a Snowflake support request to enable.

FIGURE 7.11 Data Exchange

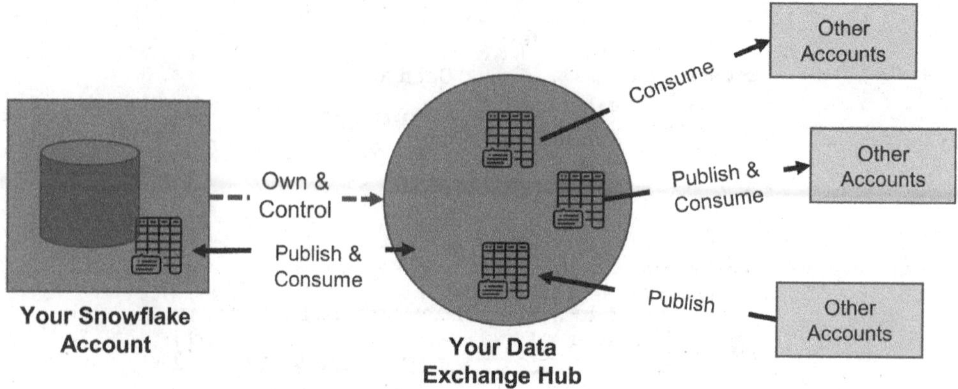

Summary

This chapter discussed cloning and data sharing, two novel features provided by Snowflake. You can create instant copies of tables, schemas, and databases by using zero-copy cloning without additional storage costs. You can also combine cloning with Time Travel. The chapter included two cloning exercises to demonstrate these concepts.

This chapter also described data sharing in Snowflake. Like cloning, data sharing is also almost instantaneous and doesn't move data. We practiced the steps for direct data sharing with another account and discussed Data Marketplace and Data Exchange, two other mechanisms for data sharing.

Exam Essentials

Be familiar with zero-copy cloning and how it works. Snowflake's zero-copy cloning functionality lets users make clones of tables, schemas, and databases without physically copying data. Cloning reduces the demand for extra storage and speeds up the copy process. Because cloning does not duplicate data physically, it is substantially faster than physical copying. The cloned object contains a snapshot of the data in the cloning source. The source and cloned objects are independent, so you may modify data on either without impacting the other. Micro-partitions are the reason behind rapid and efficient zero-copy cloning. No micro-partitions are copied, but metadata points the cloned table to the existing micro-partitions. Additional storage is not required for the cloned table when cloning a table. However, as new data is stored or updated in either table, micro-partitions may be created or deleted, and additional storage may be required.

Although cloning is a fast operation, as a metadata process, it may not be instantaneous. Large tables with millions of micro-partitions may take longer to clone while updating metadata. Cloning and Time Travel can be used together to generate a clone of a table, database, or schema at a specific point in time. Named internal stages and external tables are some objects that can't be cloned. Cloning a database copies all its child schemas and objects; however, Snowpipes that reference an internal named stage are not copied. A cloned object does not inherit any of the parent object's privileges. However, when you clone a database or schema child objects inherit the rights.

Understand data sharing in Snowflake. Data sharing, like Time Travel and cloning, is a metadata operation. Snowflakes cloud services and the metadata layer facilitate data sharing. During data sharing, no data is moved or copied; instead, the shared table refers to the original table and its micro-partitions. That way, any changes in the source table are automatically mirrored in the shared table.

Snowflake's data sharing products include Direct Sharing, Snowflake Data Marketplace, and Data Exchange. Direct Sharing is the simplest method of sharing data across accounts. The provider account stores and pays for the data; the consumer incurs no additional storage expenses. The consumer, however, pays for the compute resources required to conduct queries on shared data.

Any Snowflake account can be a data provider, sharing data with other Snowflake accounts. A data provider first creates a share, a container for all the data necessary to share an object. Share objects contain shared objects, the shared object's database, schema, and one or more Snowflake accounts (consumers) with whom data is shared. The consumer sees the shared objects by creating a read-only database on the share object. Only the ACCOUNTADMIN role or roles with the `CREATE SHARE` privilege can create a share. Similarly, only the ACCOUNTADMIN role or roles specifically allowed the `IMPORT SHARE` privilege can create a read-only database on the share as a consumer account.

It is possible in Snowflake to share data with a non-Snowflake user, which is done by creating a reader account. Because the data provider creates and owns the reader account, all the reader account's compute costs are billed to the provider account.

Snowflake Data Marketplace allows users to search for and access third-party datasets made public by various organizations. Datasets are typically supplied for a fee or for free. Once accessed, a dataset becomes a table in your Snowflake account, and you may join it with other tables. Snowflake accounts may also sell datasets on the Data Marketplace.

Data Exchange is a private data sharing hub where you may share data with a small number of accounts. The Data Exchange owner invites members and specifies whether they can share, consume, or do both.

Review Questions

1. Which of the following are true regarding cloned tables? (Select all that apply.)
   - **A.** Cloning physically copies data from one table to another.
   - **B.** A cloned table does not contribute to the overall storage.
   - **C.** Cloning is a metadata operation.
   - **D.** Cloning is almost instantaneous.
2. True or False: Cloning is a metadata operation.
   - **A.** True
   - **B.** False
3. Which of the following can be cloned? (Select all that apply.)
   - **A.** Databases
   - **B.** Schemas
   - **C.** Tables
4. True or False: After cloning, any updates to the cloned table automatically update the source table.
   - **A.** True
   - **B.** False
5. Which of the following are true regarding cloning? (Select all that apply.)
   - **A.** Cloning a database does not copy any of its child schemas or their objects.
   - **B.** Cloning a database copies all of its child schemas and their objects.
   - **C.** A database cannot be cloned.
   - **D.** If a database or schema is cloned, child object privileges are copied.
6. Which of the following is correct regarding cloning? (Select all that apply.)
   - **A.** Internal named stages cannot be cloned.
   - **B.** A Snowflake account can be cloned.
   - **C.** When a database or schema is cloned, any Snowpipes that reference an internal named stage are not cloned.
7. Which of the following are Snowflake's product offerings for Secure Data Sharing? (Select all that apply.)
   - **A.** Direct Sharing
   - **B.** Data Monetization
   - **C.** Snowflake Data Marketplace
   - **D.** Data Exchange

8. A data provider has shared a set of tables with a consumer through a share. The consumer has created a read-only database on the share and can successfully see and read the table data. If the data provider adds new tables to the share, which of the following statements apply?
   - A. The consumer is required to drop and re-create the database on the share to see the new tables.
   - B. The new tables automatically appear in the read-only database.
   - C. It is not possible to add tables to a share after it has been shared with a consumer.
9. A data provider has shared a set of tables with a data consumer who is a Snowflake customer. Who is billed for the compute usage when the consumer runs queries on the shared data?
   - A. The data provider
   - B. The data consumer
10. A data provider has shared a set of tables with a non-Snowflake user. The data provider created a reader account to enable the sharing. Who is billed for the compute usage when the consumer runs queries on the shared data?
    - A. The data provider
    - B. The data consumer
11. Is it possible to add multiple consuming accounts to a single share?
    - A. Yes
    - B. Only if you are an Enterprise customer
    - C. No
    - D. Only when using AWS as the cloud provider
12. Which of the following roles can create a Share in Snowflake? (Select all that apply.)
    - A. ACCOUNTADMIN
    - B. SECURITYADMIN
    - C. SYSADMIN
    - D. A role that has been granted the `CREATE SHARE` privilege
13. Which of the following roles can create a read-only database from a share in Snowflake? (Select all that apply.)
    - A. ACCOUNTADMIN
    - B. SECURITYADMIN
    - C. SYSADMIN
    - D. A role that has been granted the `IMPORT SHARE` privilege

14. Which of the following is true regarding Data Exchange in Snowflake? (Select all that apply.)

A. Data Exchange is your own private data sharing hub where you can share data with an invite-only group of people and organizations.

B. Participating members can share, consume, or do both, depending on their privileges.

C. The account owning the Data Exchange is responsible for inviting members.

D. Data Exchange allows businesses to share data among a limited set of trustworthy partners, suppliers, vendors, and customers.

15. Which of the following is true regarding Data Marketplace in Snowflake? (Select all that apply.)

A. Snowflake accounts can also publish and monetize datasets on the Marketplace.

B. Snowflake Data Marketplace is a marketplace for discovering and gaining access to third-party datasets made available by various organizations.

C. The third-party datasets on Data Marketplace are always free.

D. Except for VPS Snowflake accounts, all Snowflake accounts have access to the Snowflake Data Marketplace.

Performance

THE SNOWPRO CORE EXAM TOPICS COVERED IN THIS CHAPTER INCLUDE THE FOLLOWING:

✓ **Domain 1.0: Snowflake Data Platform Features and Architecture**

- 1.4 Outline Snowflake storage concepts.
  - Types of column metadata clustering
  - Search Optimization Service

✓ **Domain 3.0: Performance Concepts**

- 3.1 Explain the use of the Query Profile.
  - Explain plans
  - Data spilling
  - Use of the data cache
  - Micro-partition pruning
  - Query history
- 3.2. Explain virtual warehouse configurations.
  - Multi-clustering
  - Warehouse sizing
  - Warehouse settings and access
- 3.3 Outline virtual warehouse performance tools.
  - Monitoring warehouse loads
  - Query performance
  - Scaling up compared to scaling out
- 3.4 Optimize query performance.
  - Using materialized views
  - Using specific SELECT commands

Snowflake includes several optimization features, such as the metadata cache, the query result cache, the virtual warehouse cache, and partition pruning, that Snowflake automatically uses to optimize performance. Snowflake also provides additional performance capabilities that can be manually configured to improve performance. These capabilities include scaling up and down a virtual warehouse or autoscaling a virtual warehouse to accommodate increased concurrency. This chapter focuses on the performance optimization features and techniques that you can use to improve query performance and, at times, reduce costs.

Snowflake Performance Considerations

Snowflake generally does not require much query tuning due to its unique architecture and the underlying micro-partitions storage mechanism. However, some performance improvement techniques can be employed to improve performance in Snowflake. These techniques include the following:

- Scaling up the size of a virtual warehouse to provide more processing power for complex queries
- Scaling out a multi-cluster virtual warehouse to provide more capacity for handling many concurrent users and concurrent queries
- Automatic static and dynamic partition pruning that can eliminate unneeded partitions during query execution
- Using clustering keys to redistribute data in micro-partitions to achieve better partition pruning
- Built-in caching mechanisms that work transparently behind the scenes to improve performance
- Using materialized views to precompute results of complex, frequently executing queries

Before you choose a performance technique, you must be able to read a query profile to correctly understand the execution plan of a query and deduce what sort of optimization technique will benefit a query. The query profile can be accessed through the following two methods in the classic Snowflake web user interface:

- After executing a query, click the Query ID link on the Results tab in Worksheets view. Clicking the resulting Query ID will show the profile for the query.
- The History tab shows a list of queries that have been previously executed. Clicking a Query ID opens the profile for that query.

You can use the following methods to access the query profile using the new Snowflake interface:

- After executing a query, click the ellipsis button under the Query Details section and select View Query Profile.
- On the Query History tab under Activity, clicking any query opens the query profile.

The query profile for a sample query is shown in Figure 8.1.

FIGURE 8.1 Query profile

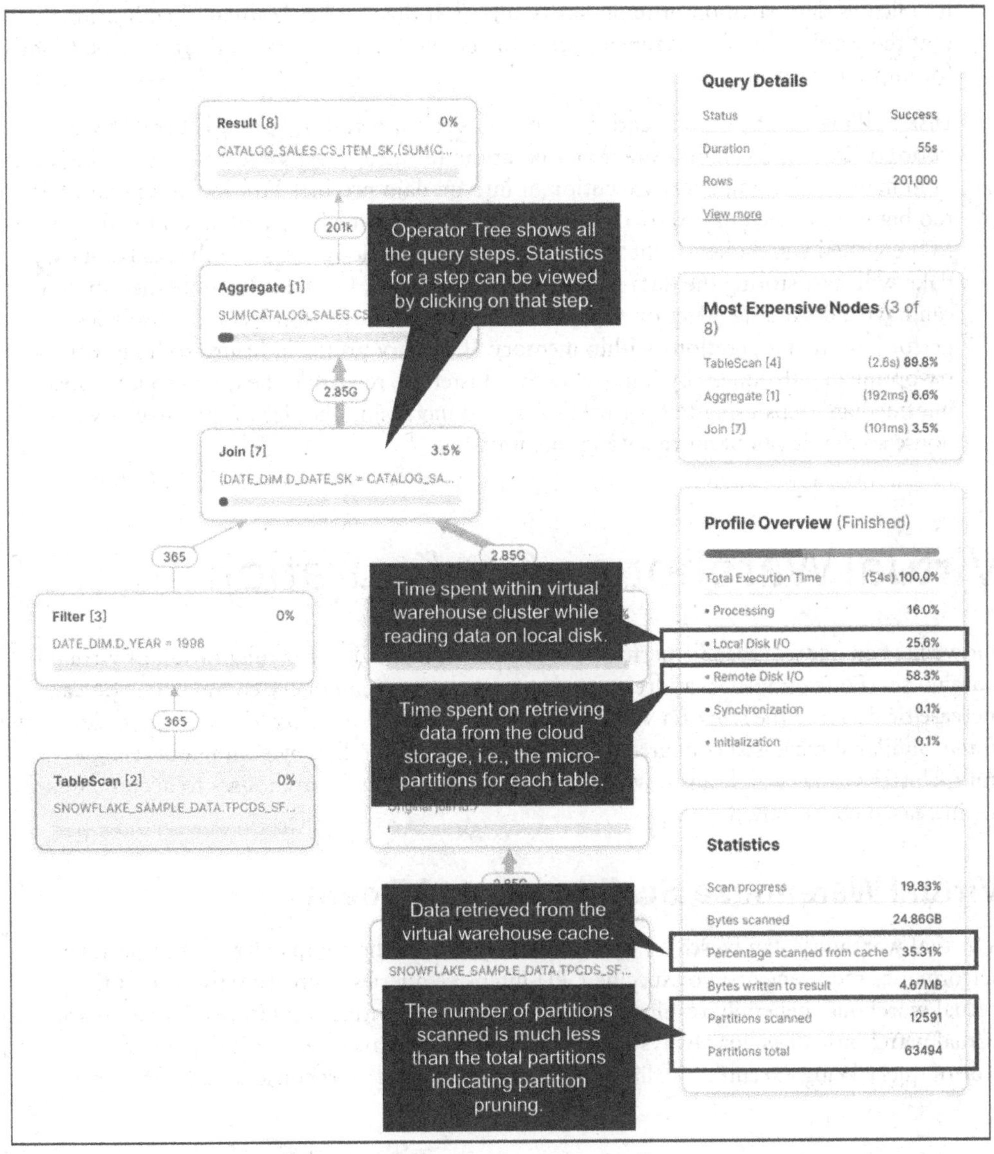

The middle pane, also known as the *operator tree*, shows all the operator nodes and their relationship. The right pane shows the overview of the query profile. If a specific operator node is selected, the right pane will display the details for that specific query node. The right pane shows the execution times and statistics for the complete query or the selected operator node. Some essential statistics and execution times that can help you analyze and optimize queries are as follows:

Partitions Total and Partitions Scanned `Partitions Total` and `Partitions Scanned` provide information on how many partitions are present in the table and how many were scanned by a query. If the number of Partitions Scanned is less than the total, it indicates that partition pruning has occurred. If the number is equal, then it means that the whole table was scanned during query execution; therefore, there may be room for improvement.

Disk Spilling `Bytes spilled to local storage` and `Bytes spilled to remote storage` can indicate if an operation during a query's execution is too big to fit in memory. During query execution, if interim data produced during an operation is too big to fit in memory, Snowflake will start storing some interim data on the disk local to the virtual warehouse. If the local disk is not large enough to store that data, Snowflake will start storing the data in remote cloud storage. Local and remote disk spilling can have a degrading effect on the query execution because disk I/O is typically less performant than operations within memory. If a query profile indicates spilling, you can try optimizing the query by improving the clustering, rewriting the query to introduce intermediate steps using temporary tables, and increasing the size of the virtual warehouse so that it can fit more data in memory.

Virtual Warehouse Configuration

Snowflake can address specific performance concerns through the configuration of virtual warehouses. For example, to address an increase or decrease in query complexity, you can increase or decrease the size of a virtual warehouse, referred to as *scaling up* or *scaling down*. Similarly, increased concurrency of queries can be handled by scaling out using multi-cluster virtual warehouses, which can spin up additional warehouses to accommodate for increased concurrency.

Virtual Warehouse Scaling Up and Down

A virtual warehouse can be scaled up or down relative to the complexity of the queries and performance requirements. For specific CPU-intensive queries, increasing the size of the virtual warehouse generally results in improved query performance. However, scaling up a virtual warehouse does not always improve query performance since it is dependent on the type of query being executed. Scaling up enables the virtual warehouse to expand to meet the increasing task complexity. When a virtual warehouse is scaled up, additional nodes are added to the compute cluster.

When a virtual warehouse is scaled up, charging for the new size does not begin until all the new nodes in the larger virtual warehouse have been provisioned. Only new queries benefit from the larger size; existing queries on the virtual warehouse remain unaffected.

Scaling down a virtual warehouse is often done in response to decreased query complexity, where a smaller virtual warehouse may meet the performance requirements. Continuing to use a larger virtual warehouse when the queries can be completed more efficiently and rapidly on a smaller virtual warehouse wastes resources and incurs additional costs. In such cases, scaling down the virtual warehouse size is viable. Nodes are removed from the compute cluster when a virtual warehouse is scaled down.

When a virtual warehouse is scaled down, nodes are removed from the virtual warehouse only when there is no active query on the virtual warehouse.

Scaling a virtual warehouse up or down is generally a manual activity managed by a system administrator, although it could be automated through Tasks. Following is the syntax for scaling a virtual warehouse up or down. Scaling up and down is achieved by altering the size of the virtual warehouse, a larger size for scaling up and a smaller size for scaling down.

```
ALTER WAREHOUSE <warehouse_name> SET WAREHOUSE_SIZE = XSMALL | SMALL | MEDIUM
| LARGE | XLARGE | XXLARGE | XXXLARGE | X4LARGE | X5LARGE | X6LARGE;
```

Scaling Out Using Multi-cluster Virtual Warehouses

Multi-cluster virtual warehouses allow you to add and delete virtual warehouses in an automated manner. Also referred to as *scaling out* or *autoscaling*, multi-cluster virtual warehouses are often utilized in scenarios where the number of concurrent users exceeds the capacity of a single virtual warehouse. A single virtual warehouse can handle up to eight concurrent queries by default. Additional queries begin queuing when the concurrent workload exceeds the maximum for a given virtual warehouse. This problem is addressed through multi-cluster virtual warehouses, which dynamically add extra clusters based on demand. Finally, the additional clusters are removed as demand decreases. A minimum of Snowflake Enterprise edition is required to use the multi-cluster virtual warehouse capabilities.

Scaling out using multi-cluster virtual warehouses addresses increased concurrency when many concurrent queries are running on the system and cannot be handled by existing virtual warehouses; thus, additional warehouses in the multi-cluster virtual warehouse are started. On the other hand, the scaling up of a virtual warehouse is used to improve performance for complex queries by increasing the size of a virtual warehouse.

The syntax for defining a multi-cluster virtual warehouse is similar to creating a standard virtual warehouse, with a few additional parameters. The following syntax emphasizes relevant parameters for further multi-cluster virtual warehouse discussion. For the complete syntax, refer to the Snowflake documentation.

```
CREATE WAREHOUSE <name>
    WITH WAREHOUSE_SIZE = <size>
    MAX_CLUSTER_COUNT = <num>
    MIN_CLUSTER_COUNT = <num>
    SCALING_POLICY = STANDARD | ECONOMY
    AUTO_SUSPEND = <num> | NULL
    AUTO_RESUME = TRUE | FALSE
    INITIALLY_SUSPENDED = TRUE | FALSE;
```

When creating a multi-cluster virtual warehouse, the key differentiator from a standard virtual warehouse is that you specify a minimum and a maximum cluster count. The maximum cluster count can be any value from 2 to 10 and specifies the maximum number of virtual warehouses that this multi-cluster virtual warehouse can spin up. The minimum cluster count can be any value from 1 up to the maximum cluster count and specifies the initial number of virtual warehouses. The other important configuration for a multi-cluster virtual warehouse is the scaling policy.

In addition to the emphasized properties, multi-cluster virtual warehouses support the standard virtual warehouse properties and actions, including the following:

- Specifying a warehouse size, which applies to each warehouse in the multi-cluster virtual warehouse.
- Changing the warehouse size, which again applies to all warehouses in the multi-cluster virtual warehouse.
- Suspend or automatically suspend a multi-cluster virtual warehouse. Note that a multi-cluster virtual is suspended as a whole. Therefore, it is not possible to suspend an individual warehouse in a multi-cluster virtual warehouse.
- Resume or automatically resume a suspended multi-cluster virtual warehouse.

A multi-cluster virtual warehouse can be set in maximized or autoscaling modes.

Maximized Mode

Maximized mode is enabled by setting the multi-cluster's minimum and maximum warehouse count to the same value. Therefore, as soon as the multi-cluster virtual warehouse is started, all warehouses in the multi-cluster are started up, ensuring that the maximum defined capacity is available at all times. This mode is useful when you have many concurrent users and the query workload does not fluctuate substantially.

Autoscale Mode

Autoscaling mode is enabled by setting different values for the multi-cluster's minimum and maximum warehouse count. As a result, Snowflake starts and stops warehouses dynamically based on the workload requirements. When a multi-cluster virtual warehouse using autoscaling mode is started, the number of active virtual warehouses is equal to the minimum warehouse count. Snowflake spins up additional warehouses based on the demand, up to the maximum warehouse count. As the demand reduces, Snowflake shuts down virtual warehouses until the number is equal to the minimum warehouse count.

Figure 8.2 illustrates autoscaling mode, depicting a multi-cluster virtual warehouse of size Small, with a minimum cluster count of 2 and a maximum cluster count of 4. The active warehouse count is two when the multi-cluster virtual warehouse is initially started. Autoscaling occurs due to increased query demand, and Snowflake adds additional warehouses to meet those query demands. As the demand wanes, warehouses are shut down, bringing the active count back to two.

The autoscaling mode is helpful for scenarios where the number of concurrent queries on the system fluctuates. Therefore, it is not performant and not cost-effective to configure a set number of warehouses.

FIGURE 8.2 Multi-cluster warehouse in autoscaling mode

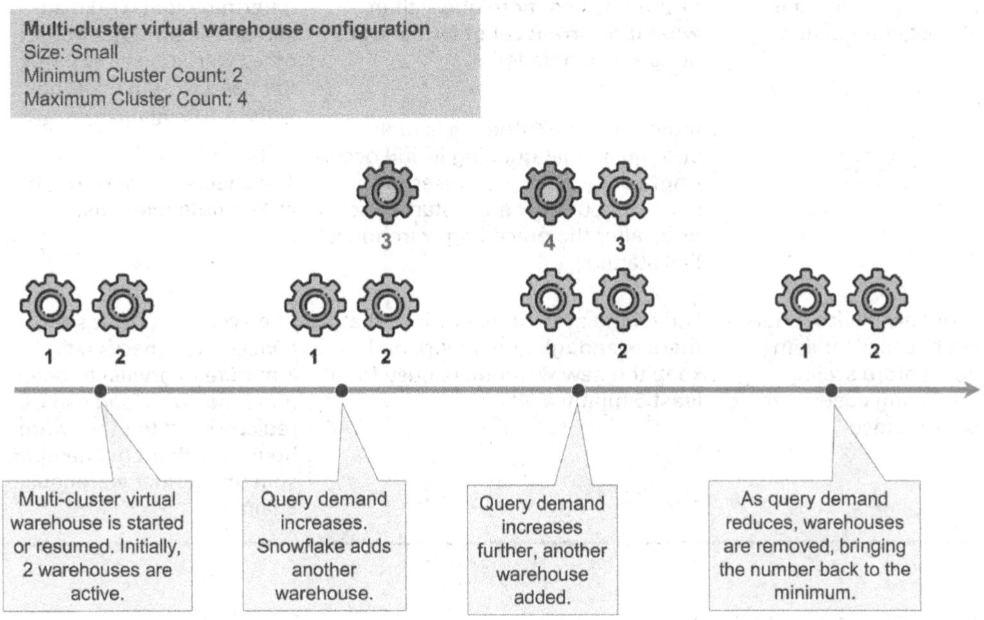

Scaling Policies

Snowflake provides autoscaling policies to control how rapidly a multi-cluster virtual warehouse reacts to increased query demands. The two policies are Standard and Economy. If no scaling policy is specified, then it defaults to Standard.

Standard

With the scaling policy set to Standard, Snowflake spins up additional virtual warehouses as soon as it detects that queries are starting to queue up. The Standard scaling policy aims to prevent or minimize queuing.

Economy

The Economy scaling policy aims to conserve credits over performance and user experience. It doesn't spin up additional virtual warehouses as soon as queuing is detected but instead applies additional criteria to ascertain whether or not to spin up additional virtual warehouses.

Table 8.1 compares the two scaling policies.

TABLE 8.1 Comparison between Standard and Economy scaling policies

Scaling policy	Scales up/additional warehouse started when. . .	Scales down/a warehouse is shut down when. . .
Standard – minimizes queuing by starting additional warehouses almost immediately	The first additional warehouse is started as soon as a query is queued, or there is one more query than what the current set of virtual warehouses can handle. If the number of queries is high enough so that queuing is still occurring, additional warehouses are spun up, but they must start 20 seconds after the preceding warehouse has started.	The system performs 2–3 consecutive checks to determine that workload can be redistributed to other warehouses without the need to spin up another warehouse again. The checks are performed at 1-minute intervals.
Economy – allows queuing to occur for some time before scaling up, saving costs over performance	Only if the system determines that there is enough query workload to keep the new warehouse busy for at least 6 minutes.	The system performs 5–6 consecutive checks (at 1-minute intervals) to determine that workload can be redistributed to other warehouses without the need to spin up another warehouse again.

Monitoring Warehouse Load

A key aspect of performance optimization is monitoring query workload for nonperforming queries, query queuing, unnecessary credit usage, and query utilization spikes. The Snowflake web interface provides a warehouse usage screen that displays running and queued queries for the selected period. Based on the usage, you can quickly identify hotspots that may require further drilling down. If needed, you can query the QUERY_HISTORY view to find and analyze queries that may require optimization.

Based on your analysis, if you identify that queries are queuing, you can move them to a dedicated virtual warehouse or use the multicluster virtual warehouse to scale up when queueing occurs automatically. Similarly, if you see that a query is executing slowly, a larger-sized virtual warehouse can help.

Caching in Snowflake

Snowflake provides a variety of caching mechanisms to improve query performance. It can return the query results immediately through the metadata cache or the query result cache when a new query is submitted for execution. For example, if the query is simply counting the number of rows or trying to find the minimum or maximum value for a column, the results for such queries can be fulfilled through the metadata cache. The metadata cache stores statistics for each table, its micro-partitions, and every column in the micro-partition.

Alternatively, if the query has previously been executed and the underlying data hasn't changed, Snowflake can return the results from the previous execution directly from the query result cache. As a result, queries fulfilled through the metadata cache or the query result cache do not require an active virtual warehouse.

If a query cannot be fulfilled by the metadata cache or the query result cache, it is sent to a virtual warehouse for execution. Each virtual warehouse has its own cache, which it builds over time by copying the required micro-partitions from the cloud storage to its SSD storage. If similar queries are executed on a virtual warehouse, a percentage of data required for those queries may likely be already available in the virtual warehouse cache, thus improving the query performance.

Figure 8.3 illustrates the various types of caches in Snowflake and their placement in the architecture. In the following sections, we discuss each of these caches in detail.

FIGURE 8.3 Types of caches in Snowflake

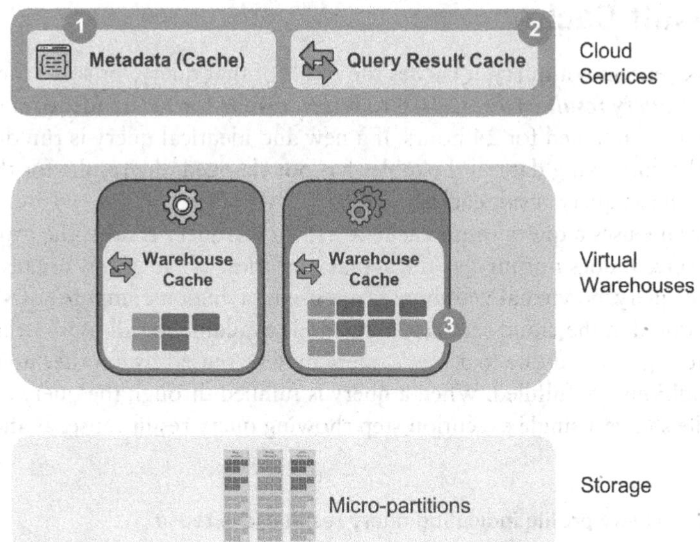

Metadata Cache

For simple queries that count the number of rows or find the minimum or maximum value of a column, Snowflake can return results for such queries using the metadata cache. As described in Chapter 2, "Snowflake Architecture," in the section "The Database Storage Layer: Micro-partitions and Clustering," Snowflake maintains several different kinds of metadata for a given table. It stores the range of column values in its metadata: the maximum and the minimum values for each column in each micro-partition. This metadata is stored in the cloud services layer and is used by Snowflake to optimize query processing. So, COUNT, MIN, and MAX queries can generally be fulfilled through the metadata cache.

When a query result is returned based on metadata results, the query profile produces the output shown in Figure 8.4.

FIGURE 8.4 Query profile indicating metadata-based result

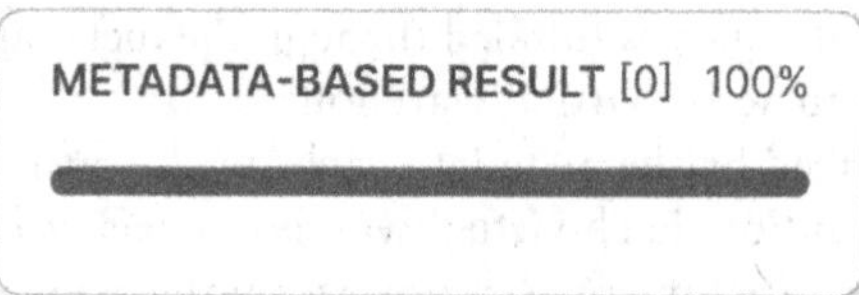

Snowflake can fulfill COUNT, MIN, and MAX queries using the metadata cache and doesn't require an active warehouse for such queries. Please note that the metadata cache cannot provide the MIN and MAX for character columns.

Query Result Cache

When Snowflake executes a query, it caches the result of that query for some time. The cache, called the *query result cache*, is used to return results for future identical queries. The query result cache is retained for 24 hours. If a new and identical query is run during those 24 hours and the underlying data in the tables has not changed, the results for the new query are returned from the query result cache.

When Snowflake uses a query result cache to return the query results, the process is extremely fast since it does not involve the actual execution of the query. Because there is no execution of the query, no virtual warehouses are used, saving on compute costs. The query result cache is stored in the cloud services layer and is available for all users—that is, the query result cache generated due to a user's query may be reused by another user's query as long as the conditions are fulfilled. When a query is fulfilled through the query result cache, the query profile shows a single execution step showing query result reuse, as shown in Figure 8.5.

FIGURE 8.5 Query profile indicating query result cache reuse

QUERY RESULT REUSE [0] 100%
01a43982-0402-066e-006d-d583000a...

As shown in Figure 8.6, the query result cache for a query is initially valid for 24 hours; however, when a new query uses the result cache, the query result cache is again valid for the next 24 hours. This extension of the initial query result cache can continue up to a maximum of 31 days from the time a query result cache was first generated. After 31 days, the result cache for a query is purged nonetheless. Additionally, the result cache is purged if it is not utilized in a 24-hour period.

FIGURE 8.6 Query result cache generation and purge over time

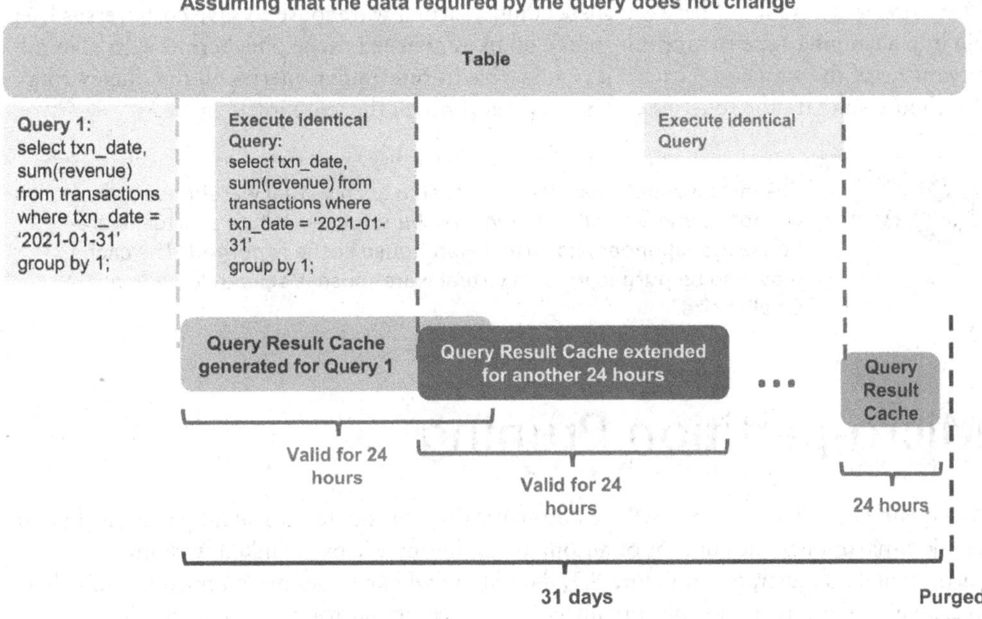

Snowflake generally uses the query result cache if the following conditions are fulfilled:

- A new query matches a previously run one.
- The underlying data contributing to the query results has not changed. Note that data that is not part of the query processing can still change and doesn't impact the query result cache reuse.
- The table(s)' micro-partitions have not changed due to reclustering or consolidation.
- The query does not use user-defined functions or external functions.
- The query does not use functions evaluated at runtime, such as `CURRENT_TIMESTAMP`. However, `CURRENT_DATE` is an exception, and queries using the `CURRENT_DATE` function are eligible for the query result cache reuse.

Virtual Warehouse Cache

Snowflake also uses a local cache stored in SSD disks within a virtual warehouse cluster and incrementally built over time as different queries execute. Snowflake caches the columns and micro-partitions accessed in the virtual warehouse cache for each query executed on the virtual warehouse. For subsequent queries, requests for data for columns and micro-partitions can be fulfilled partially or entirely by the virtual warehouse cache, eliminating or reducing the need to retrieve data from the cloud storage layer, which is a relatively slower operation.

As a virtual warehouse is kept running and new queries are executed, the local cache grows and more queries can make use of the warehouse cache. If a virtual warehouse is suspended, the cache is purged. When the virtual warehouse is resumed, there is initially slower performance due to an empty cache; the cache is rebuilt as queries are executed. Therefore, it is a trade-off between suspending a virtual warehouse to save costs versus keeping it in a running state to take advantage of an established cache. Furthermore, to take full advantage of the warehouse cache, it is advisable to run similar queries on the same virtual warehouse so that more queries can be serviced through the warehouse cache.

The virtual warehouse cache is local to each virtual warehouse and cannot be shared with other virtual warehouses. When a virtual warehouse is suspended, its virtual warehouse cache is purged. The cache may also be purged when a virtual warehouse is scaled down to a smaller size.

Micro-partition Pruning

As explained in Chapter 2, Snowflake automatically stores data into small partitions known as micro-partitions. The concept of automatic clustering is closely linked with micro-partitioning. As illustrated in Figure 8.7, data in Snowflake tables are mapped to individual micro-partitions and are further organized using a columnar format. Micro-partitions are added to a table in the order of how the data arrived in the table. When data is added to a table, additional micro-partitions are created. Because the column values are spread across multiple micro-partitions, Snowflake must keep track for each column of what range of data is stored in which set of partitions. This metadata allows Snowflake to ignore unnecessary micro-partitions when executing queries, improving the overall performance of a query.

Consider the following query executed on the table from Figure 8.7:

```
SELECT * FROM sales_table WHERE Sale_Dt = '01/22';
```

The query retrieves all data for the date 01/22. Snowflake query optimizer knows that the data for 01/22 is present in two micro-partitions; therefore, it does not scan micro-partition 1 and micro-partition 4. This concept is known as *partition pruning*.

However, Snowflake has to scan all micro-partitions for the following query, since product A is spread across all micro-partitions:

```
SELECT * FROM sales_table WHERE Product = 'A';
```

FIGURE 8.7 Table data stored in micro-partitions

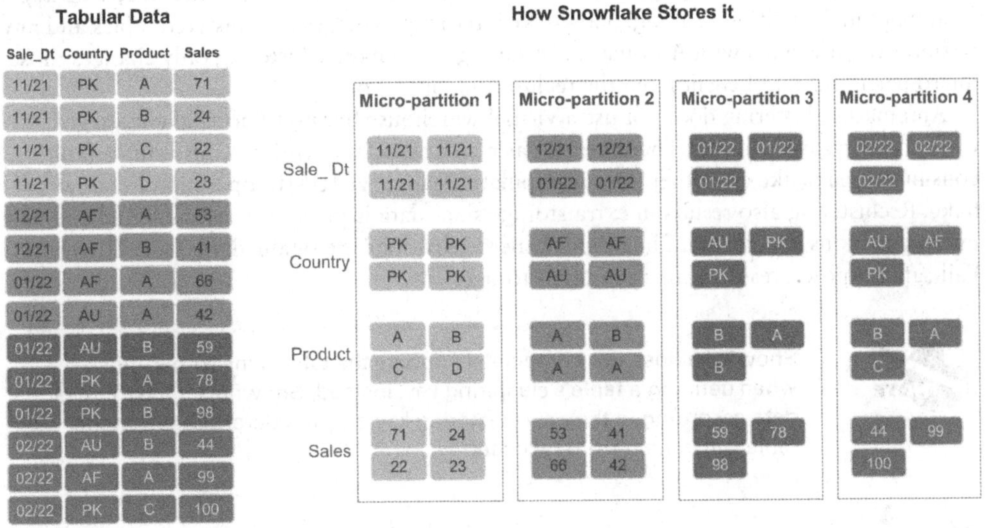

Tabular Data

Sale_Dt	Country	Product	Sales
11/21	PK	A	71
11/21	PK	B	24
11/21	PK	C	22
11/21	PK	D	23
12/21	AF	A	53
12/21	AF	B	41
01/22	AF	A	66
01/22	AU	A	42
01/22	AU	B	59
01/22	PK	A	78
01/22	PK	B	98
02/22	AU	B	44
02/22	AF	A	99
02/22	PK	C	100

How Snowflake Stores it

	Micro-partition 1	Micro-partition 2	Micro-partition 3	Micro-partition 4
Sale_ Dt	11/21 11/21 11/21 11/21	12/21 12/21 01/22 01/22	01/22 01/22 01/22	02/22 02/22 02/22
Country	PK PK PK PK	AF AF AU AU	AU PK PK	AU AF PK
Product	A B C D	A B A A	B A B	B A C
Sales	71 24 22 23	53 41 66 42	59 78 98	44 99 100

Micro-partitions and Data Clustering

Generally, tables in Snowflake are well clustered by default; however, the data may not be stored optimally for very large tables, especially if queries on a large table are mostly predicated on a column or a limited set of columns. Since micro-partitions are created in the order of the arrival of the data, over time the data in micro-partitions may not be optimally stored and may not support optimal partition pruning. For example, the micro-partitions shown in Figure 8.7 do not support optimal partition pruning if most queries are predicated on the Product column. One could assume that this is because the natural order of arrival of data in that table may be based on the date. Since micro-partitions are created in the order of arrival of data, the micro-partitions are naturally clustered on the Sale_Dt column.

If queries are mostly predicated on the Product column, as shown in the following example, queries will perform better if the table is clustered on the Product column.

```
SELECT * FROM sales_table WHERE Product = 'A';
```

A table can be reclustered by defining a clustering key. Figure 8.8 illustrates the same table but clustered on the Product column. Compare the two figures and note how similar products are stored in the same micro-partitions. With the new clustering key, Snowflake needs to scan only two partitions for the preceding query to fulfill the query requirements.

The advantages of clustering a table on a different column may not be evident for tables with a small amount of data, but as the table data and its micro-partitions grow, clustering a table on the right set of columns can provide considerable gains in performance.

What Happens Behind the Scenes

To store new data, micro-partitions are created in the order of arrival of the data. For tables that do not have any clustering keys defined, the data is not redistributed for the life of the table. However, for tables with a clustering key defined, Automatic Clustering, a Snowflake service, manages reclustering as needed, redistributing data according to the clustering key to ensure optimal partition pruning. Snowflake internally manages the clustered tables and any resource requirements with Automatic Clustering. Automatic Clustering only changes those micro-partitions that benefit from the reclustering operation.

Automatic Clustering does not use a virtual warehouse but uses Snowflake-managed CPU, memory, and so forth. Therefore, it has a cost associated with it. Clustering a table consumes credits like any other data manipulation language (DML) operation in Snowflake. Reclustering also results in extra storage since data is physically redistributed and new micro-partitions are created. The original micro-partitions are retained for Time Travel and Fail-safe purposes, resulting in additional storage.

Snowflake does not immediately update the table's micro-partitions when defining a table's clustering key. Instead, Snowflake redistributes data according to the new clustering key only if it determines that the table will benefit from reclustering.

Clustering Keys

The syntax for reclustering a table is shown in the following code snippet:

```
ALTER TABLE <table_name> CLUSTER BY ( col1 [ , <col2> , <expr3> ... ] );
```

As you can see from the syntax, the clustering key for a table can have multiple columns in its definition. Also, a table may be clustered based on expressions rather than exact column names, so it is possible to cluster a table on part of a column value by using the substring function in the clustering definition.

Considering the table in Figure 8.8, a clustering key on the Product column may be created using the following SQL:

```
ALTER TABLE sales_table CLUSTER BY (Product);
```

Or if clustering is desired on more than one column, for example, the Sale_Dt column, the SQL could look like the following code:

```
ALTER TABLE sales_table CLUSTER BY (Sale_Dt, Product);
```

Clustering Depth

Snowflake maintains clustering metadata for a table's micro-partitions. The clustering metadata includes the total number of micro-partitions in the table, micro-partitions that overlap with each other for a given column or a subset of columns, and the overlap depth. The depth, also known as clustering depth, measures the average depth of the overlapping micro-partitions for given columns. A smaller average depth indicates that the table is well clustered for the specified columns. The concept is illustrated in Figure 8.9 and Figure 8.10. Figure 8.9 depicts a well-clustered table for the specified columns. There is no overlap between micro-partitions and the values distributed in individual partitions. The clustering depth, in this case, is 1.

FIGURE 8.8 Table reclustered on the Product column

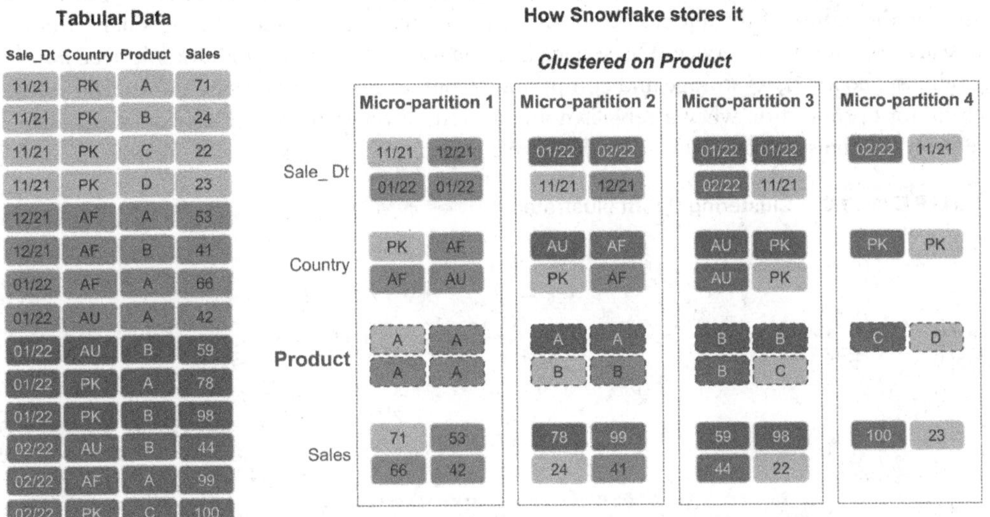

FIGURE 8.9 A well-clustered table

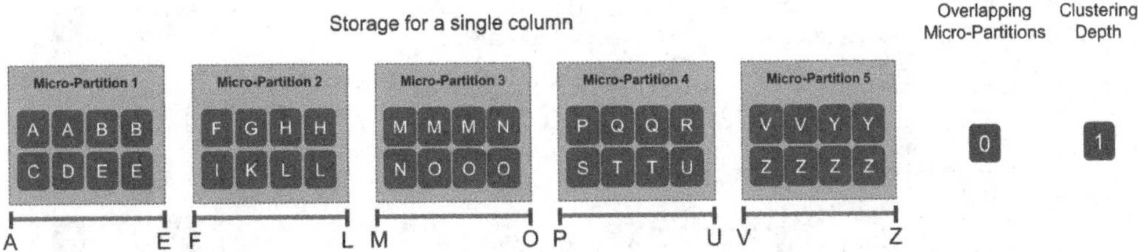

Figure 8.10 illustrates how overlapping micro-partitions impact the clustering depth. The figure contains five different examples. The first example is a simplification of the example in Figure 8.9 and shows a well-clustered table with a clustering depth of 1. The second example shows two overlapping micro-partitions and a clustering depth of 2. The third example also has a clustering depth of 2 but notice that four partitions overlap in two sets, so the clustering depth stays at 2.

The fourth example has three overlapping micro-partitions, so the clustering depth is 3. And finally, the last example overlaps all micro-partitions, resulting in a clustering depth of 5.

The smaller the clustering depth, the more well clustered a table is for given columns; however, note that clustering depth is not a precise indicator of the table's performance. If the queries are performing well, the table is very likely well clustered.

Search Optimization

Search optimization is a background service in Snowflake that can be used to improve performance for point lookup queries. The search optimization service creates and maintains search access paths separately in a persistent data structure. When you alter a table and enable search optimization on the table, the service creates and maintains search access paths based on the nature of the queries being run. A minimum of Enterprise edition is needed for the search optimization service. The service is managed by Snowflake and doesn't need a warehouse; however, its storage and computing resources cost money. Search optimization is helpful for optimization when a table is not clustered, or the table is regularly queried using the WHERE clause on columns other than the clustering key.

FIGURE 8.10 Clustering depth illustrated

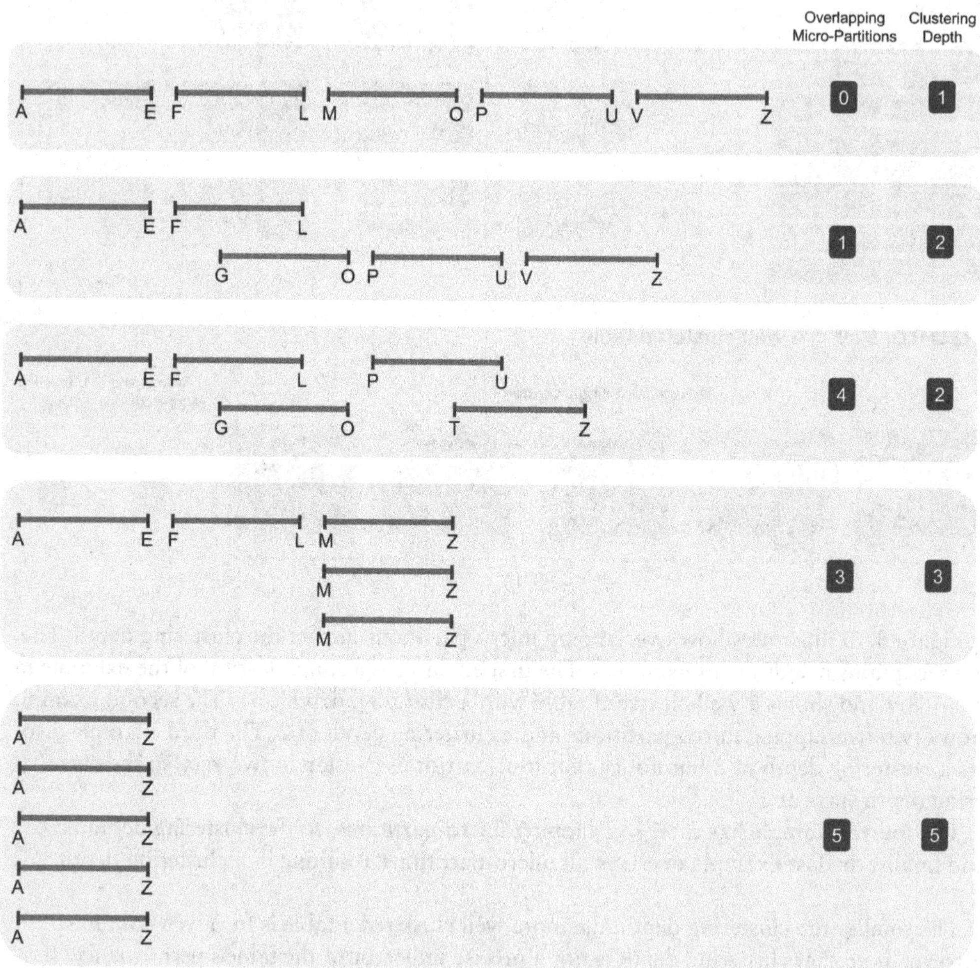

Materialized Views

A materialized view is a type of view that stores precomputed data based on a SELECT query. In materialized views, the query results are precomputed and stored physically to improve the performance of the query. The performance gains from a materialized view can be significant if the query benefiting from materialization is complex or is executed frequently.

Materialized views automatically update when the underlying table is updated, requiring zero maintenance. The update is transparent to the user and is accomplished by a background service managed by Snowflake. Therefore, the data accessed through a materialized view is always in sync with the data in its base table. However, when the base table has just been updated and the materialized view hasn't been synced yet, Snowflake transparently routes the query to the base table, ensuring that consistent results are returned to the user. Figure 8.11 illustrates the functioning of a materialized view and how the optimizer may choose to use a materialized view with faster query execution.

FIGURE 8.11 Materialized View illustrated

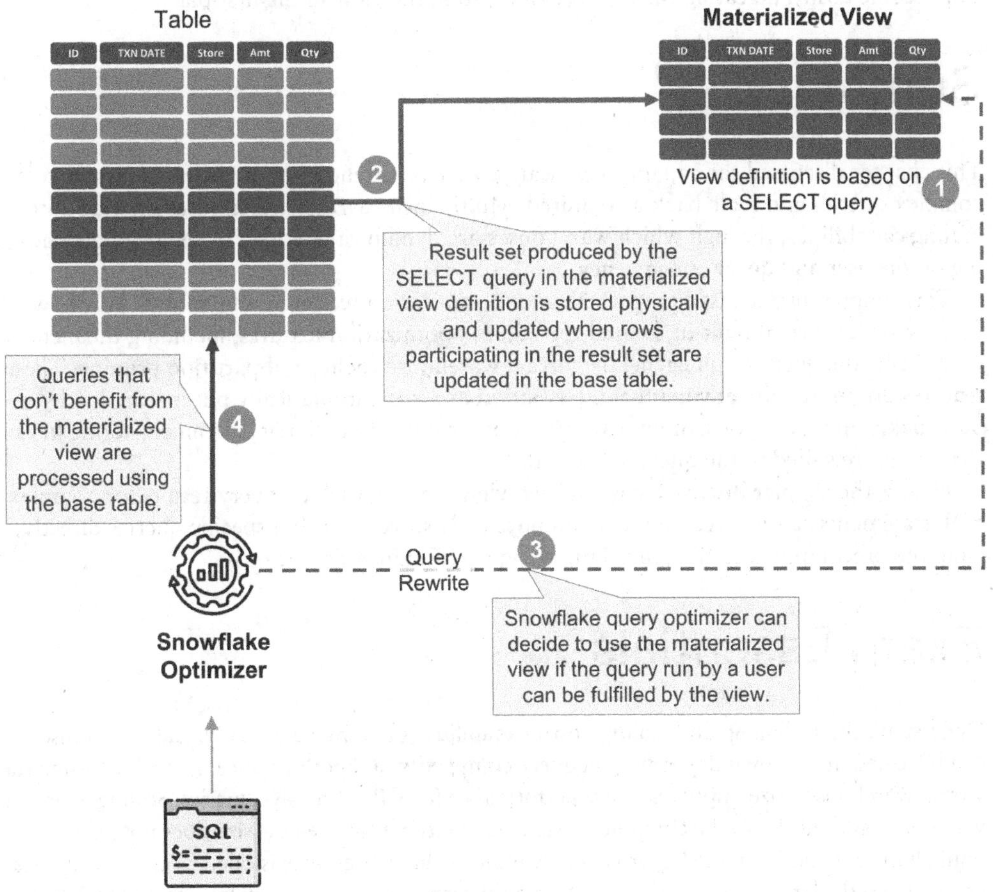

Table
ID | TXN DATE | Store | Amt | Qty
Materialized View
ID | TXN DATE | Store | Amt | Qty
1 View definition is based on a SELECT query
2 Result set produced by the SELECT query in the materialized view definition is stored physically and updated when rows participating in the result set are updated in the base table.
3 Query Rewrite
Snowflake query optimizer can decide to use the materialized view if the query run by a user can be fulfilled by the view.
4 Queries that don't benefit from the materialized view are processed using the base table.
Snowflake Optimizer
SQL

Materialized views are updated transparently by a background service managed by Snowflake. Snowflake charges for the compute used by this background service separately.

A materialized view can be beneficial and can provide performance gains for the following scenario:

- The query or a variation of the query is executed frequently.
- The query (or its variation) is complex and consumes a lot of processing time or resources.
- The result from the query remains consistent and does not change frequently.

A materialized view is helpful for this scenario because a complex set of similar queries frequently executing consumes time and credits to complete for every execution. A materialized view can provide the precomputed results that can fulfill these queries much faster. The materialized view is not the best approach if the base table data used in the query is constantly updated. In such a case, each update results in materialized view maintenance, which can become costly, defeating the purpose of creating the view in the first place.

Summary

This chapter discussed the capability to scale a virtual warehouse to a larger size to process complex queries and scale back as required. Multi-cluster virtual warehouses provide autoscaling capabilities, through which warehouses are dynamically added or removed depending on the user and query concurrency.

This chapter also focused on performance optimization techniques in Snowflake. Snowflake provides several built-in, behind-the-scenes optimization features, including the metadata cache, the query result cache, the virtual warehouse cache, and partition pruning. These features do not require any manual intervention and are automatically put into action by Snowflake. However, you can improve partition pruning by defining custom clustering keys that are more suited to the query workload.

Finally, the chapter discusses materialized views through which query results for complex SQL statements can be precomputed and physically stored to fulfill specific queries directly from the precomputed results, thus improving performance significantly.

Exam Essentials

Understand the scaling up and scaling down capabilities of Snowflake. A virtual warehouse can be scaled up or down depending on query complexity and performance needs. Increasing the virtual warehouse's size improves query performance for CPU-intensive queries. Scaling a virtual warehouse adds nodes to the compute cluster, and charging for the new size does not begin until all the new nodes in the larger virtual warehouse have been provisioned. Only new queries benefit from the larger size; existing queries on the virtual warehouse remain unaffected. When a virtual warehouse is scaled down, nodes are removed only when there is no active query.

Understand the purpose of scaling out. Multi-cluster virtual warehouses allow you to add and delete virtual warehouses in an automated manner. Scaling out using multi-cluster virtual warehouses is used to address increased concurrency when a large number of concurrent queries run on the system and cannot be handled by existing virtual warehouses.

A multi-cluster virtual warehouse can be in autoscale or maximized mode. Maximized mode is enabled by setting the cluster's minimum and maximum warehouse count to the same value. As the multi-cluster virtual warehouse starts, all clusters in the cluster start up. Autoscaling mode is enabled by setting a different value for the cluster's minimum and maximum warehouse count. As a result, Snowflake starts and stops warehouses dynamically based on the workload requirements.

Snowflake provides Standard and Economy autoscaling policies. When the scaling policy is set to Standard, Snowflake creates new virtual warehouses when queries start to queue. The Economy scaling policy prioritizes credit savings over performance.

Define caching. Snowflake keeps metadata in the cloud services layer for each table to optimize query processing. The metadata cache can generally handle COUNT, MIN, and MAX queries without requiring a table scan or a virtual warehouse.

Snowflake also caches the results of queries it executes. The cache is used to return results for future queries. The query result cache stores results for 24 hours, during which if a new identical query is run, the results are returned from the cache, and the cache is renewed. The cache may be renewed up to a maximum of 31 days, after which it is purged. Snowflake uses the query result cache if the underlying data contributing to the query results has not changed and the query matches a previously run query.

Snowflake also uses a local cache built incrementally within a virtual warehouse cluster as queries are run. Snowflake caches the columns and micro-partitions accessed in the virtual warehouse cache for each query. Subsequent queries can use the virtual warehouse cache to fill data requests for columns and micro-partitions, eliminating or reducing the need to use the cloud storage layer.

Describe data clustering in Snowflake. Tables in Snowflake are generally well clustered by default; however, data in large tables may not be stored optimally. Queries may perform better if the table is clustered on the query predicate's columns. Behind the scenes, Automatic Clustering, a Snowflake service, manages reclustering. It only changes micro-partitions that benefit from the reclustering. Snowflake redistributes data according to the new clustering key only if the table benefits from it. Automatic Clustering uses Snowflake-managed resources, which use Snowflake credits, and additional storage may be consumed during a reclustering operation.

Clustering metadata contains the total number of micro-partitions in the table, overlapping micro-partitions for a column or subset of columns, and the overlap depth. The depth, also known as clustering depth, measures the average depth of the overlapping micro-partitions for given columns. A smaller average depth indicates that the table is well clustered for the specified columns.

Understand the purpose of materialized views. A materialized view stores precomputed data from a `SELECT` query to improve query performance. As the underlying table is updated, the data in a materialized view is always kept in sync with data in its base table through a Snowflake-managed background service that performs the update transparent to the user. Snowflake charges for the compute costs for this background service separately. A materialized view can help improve performance when there is a frequently used query or variation, when the query is complex and takes a long time to process, and when the query's result is generally stable and does not change too frequently.

Review Questions

1. Which of the following is true when a virtual warehouse is scaled up to a larger size? (Choose all that apply.)
   - **A.** Charging for the new size does not begin until all the new nodes in the larger virtual warehouse have been provisioned.
   - **B.** Charging for the new size begins immediately.
   - **C.** Any queries that were already running on the virtual warehouse do not benefit from the new size.
   - **D.** Only new queries can take advantage of the increased cluster size.
   - **E.** A virtual warehouse cannot be scaled up if there are any active queries on the virtual warehouse.
2. Which of the following is true when a virtual warehouse is scaled down to a smaller size? (Choose all that apply.)
   - **A.** When a virtual warehouse is scaled down, nodes are withdrawn from the compute cluster.
   - **B.** When a virtual warehouse is scaled down, nodes are removed only when there are no active queries on the nodes that are to be removed.
   - **C.** The decrease in size does not impact any queries that were already running on the virtual warehouse.
3. Scaling up a virtual warehouse to a larger size is suitable for which of the following scenarios?
   - **A.** There are a large number of concurrent users on the system.
   - **B.** There are a large number of concurrent queries on the system.
   - **C.** Complex queries are running on the system and are required to finish faster.
4. Which of the following statements describe scaling out in Snowflake? (Choose all that apply.)
   - **A.** Scaling out is achieved by using multi-cluster virtual warehouses.
   - **B.** Scaling out is achieved by increasing or decreasing a virtual warehouse size.
   - **C.** Scaling out can help reduce query queuing.
5. What is the minimum Snowflake edition that supports multi-cluster virtual warehouses?
   - **A.** Standard
   - **B.** Enterprise
   - **C.** Business Critical
   - **D.** Virtual Private Snowflake
6. Which of the following scaling policies aims to minimize query queuing?
   - **A.** Standard
   - **B.** Economy

7. Consider the following configuration and select the mode of operation for this multi-cluster virtual warehouse.

   Minimum cluster count = 2

   Maximum cluster count = 5

   Size = Large

   A. Maximized

   B. Autoscale

8. Which of the following statements are true regarding a multi-cluster virtual warehouse in autoscale mode?

   A. Additional warehouses are started up when Snowflake detects that queries are starting to queue.

   B. Warehouses are progressively shut down when the query demand reduces.

   C. Multi-cluster virtual warehouses support all the properties and actions as regular virtual warehouses. They can be suspended, resumed, and reconfigured to be of a different size.

   D. Once a multi-cluster virtual warehouse is created, its configuration cannot be changed. It cannot be suspended or resumed.

9. Which of the following conditions must be met for Snowflake to reuse the query result cache for a query? (Choose all that apply.)

   A. The query does not use runtime functions.

   B. The underlying data contributing to the query results has not changed.

   C. A new query matches an old query.

   D. Reclustering or consolidation has not changed the table micro-partitions.

   E. Neither user-defined nor external functions are used in the query.

10. Which of the following are true regarding the query result cache? (Choose all that apply.)

    A. The query result cache is used if an identical query is run within a 24-hour period of the original query (that produced the query result cache).

    B. The maximum number of days for which a query result cache may be retained is 31 days.

    C. The query result cache is stored in virtual warehouse SSD storage.

    D. The query result cache is stored in the cloud services layer.

    E. The query result cache is purged if it is not reused within 24 hours.

11. Which of the following are examples of caches in Snowflake? (Choose all that apply.)

    A. Query result cache

    B. Cloud platform cache

    C. Virtual warehouse cache

    D. Metadata cache

    E. High-speed cache

12. To process SQL queries, a virtual warehouse must generally be running. Which types of queries can produce results without the need for a running virtual warehouse? (Choose all that apply.)
    - **A.** Queries that have previously been run and have produced a result cache
    - **B.** Queries such as count of rows, minimum and maximum for a column
    - **C.** Queries that produce less than 100 MB of a result set
    - **D.** Queries that use only one table
13. Which of the following caches are stored in the cloud services layer? (Choose all that apply.)
    - **A.** Query result cache
    - **B.** Metadata cache
    - **C.** Virtual warehouse cache
    - **D.** Browser cache
    - **E.** SnowSQL cache
14. How does clustering keys improve query performance?
    - **A.** By precalculating query results and physically storing them
    - **B.** By compressing data in columns
    - **C.** By distributing data in micro-partitions such that a more optimized partition pruning can occur during query execution
    - **D.** By distributing the data over multiple compute clusters so that each computer cluster has a subset of data to process
15. Which of the following are true regarding materialized views? (Choose all that apply.)
    - **A.** A materialized view automatically updates when the underlying table's data changes.
    - **B.** Materialized views are used to improve query performance. They precompute query results and store the results physically.
    - **C.** A materialized view can provide precomputed results that can fulfill some queries much faster.
    - **D.** Materialized views are automatically maintained by a Snowflake service running in the background, transparent to the users.
16. Which of the following statements are true regarding clustering depth? (Choose all that apply.)
    - **A.** The clustering depth measures the average depth of the overlapping micro-partitions for given columns.
    - **B.** The smaller the clustering depth, the more well clustered a table is for given columns.
    - **C.** A larger average clustering depth indicates well-clustered data for given columns.
    - **D.** For an unpopulated table, the clustering depth is –999.
17. The query profile for a complex query shows a large amount of data spilled to local and remote storage. What does that indicate?
    - **A.** The query is using the query result cache.
    - **B.** The query is too big to fit into the virtual warehouse memory.
    - **C.** The query is highly performant and is being computed within memory.
    - **D.** The query is using the metadata cache.

Security

THE SNOWPRO CORE EXAM TOPICS COVERED IN THIS CHAPTER INCLUDE THE FOLLOWING:

✓ **Domain 1.0: Snowflake Data Platform Features and Architecture**

- 1.3 Outline Snowflake's catalog and objects.
  - View types

✓ **Domain 2.0: Account Access and Security**

- 2.1 Outline compute principles.
  - Network security and policies
  - Multifactor authentication (MFA)
  - Federated authentication
  - Single sign-on (SSO)
- 2.2 Define the entities and roles that are used in Snowflake.
  - Outline how privileges can be granted and revoked
  - Explain role hierarchy and privilege inheritance
- 2.3 Outline data governance capabilities in Snowflake.
  - Accounts
  - Organizations
  - Databases
  - Secure views

Snowflake provides several features that enable security at various levels in the Snowflake software stack. Security in Snowflake is implemented starting from the data storage layer and applied at other levels such as authentication control, data access control or authorization, and finally, network-level controls to control access into your Snowflake instance. Since Snowflake is hosted exclusively on cloud platforms, those cloud providers' software security and physical data center security provide additional security support. Figure 9.1 illustrates important security features provided by Snowflake at various layers. These features are explained in greater detail in this chapter.

FIGURE 9.1 Security features in Snowflake

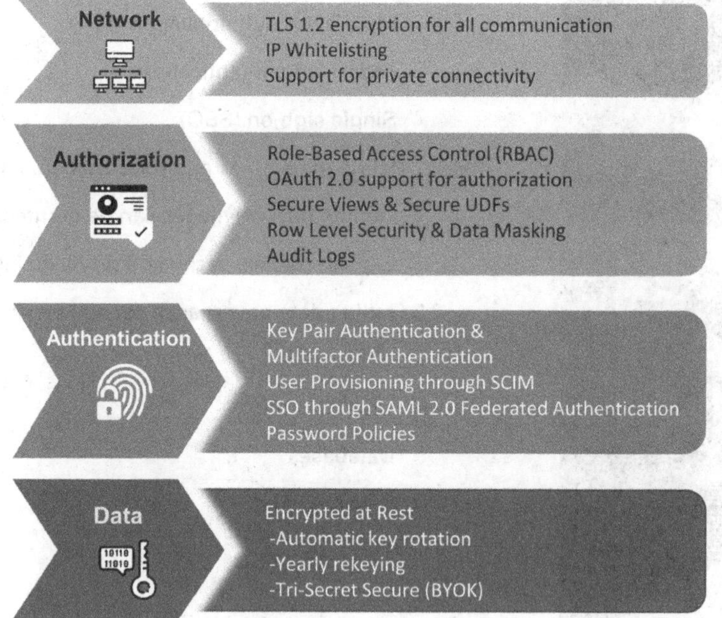

Data Encryption at Rest

All customer data in Snowflake is encrypted by default using AES-256 bit encryption. By default, Snowflake manages the encryption keys without requiring any customer intervention. The Snowflake managed keys are rotated regularly (at 30-day intervals), and a yearly rekeying process re-encrypts data with brand-new keys. The data encryption and key management are entirely transparent.

Key Rotation and Rekeying

Snowflake-managed keys are automatically rotated by Snowflake when they are 30 days old. New keys are created and made active as part of the rotation process, and active keys are retired. Retired keys are used only for decrypting data and are only used during the data access process. Active keys are used for both encrypting and decrypting data.

In addition to the key rotation, Snowflake can re-encrypt data if periodic rekeying is enabled. For example, if a retired encryption key is older than one year, Snowflake creates a new encryption key and re-encrypts all the data that was previously protected by the retired encryption key. Rekeying requires a minimum of Enterprise edition and must be enabled at the account level by the account administrator.

Tri-Secret Secure

Tri-Secret Secure is the name given to the combination of a Snowflake managed key and a customer-managed key, which creates a composite master key to protect your data. The customer-managed key is in the cloud provider that hosts your Snowflake instance. If the customer-managed key in the master key is revoked, Snowflake can no longer decrypt the data. Tri-Secret Secure, therefore, provides an additional level of security above the standard encryption provided by Snowflake. Tri-Secret Secure requires a minimum of Business Critical edition and can be enabled by contacting Snowflake support.

Authentication

In addition to the standard username & password authentication, Snowflake supports a variety of other authentication mechanisms, including multifactor authentication, key pair authentication, and single sign-on. The authentication mechanisms supported by Snowflake are discussed in detail in the following section.

Multifactor Authentication (MFA)

Snowflake supports multifactor authentication (MFA) to provide additional security when users log in. MFA is automatically enabled for all Snowflake accounts, and any Snowflake user can self-enroll into MFA through the Snowflake web interface. Snowflake provides MFA capabilities through the Duo Security service and associated Duo Mobile app installed on a device.

Figure 9.2 shows the multifactor authentication flow in Snowflake. When an authentication request is made for a user with MFA enabled, the request waits for second-factor authentication to be completed. The second factor is generally achieved through the Duo Mobile app installed on the user's mobile device or tablet. There are three ways to provide the second factor of authentication. The first is through the user approving the login request through the Duo Mobile app, also known as the push method. Alternatively, the user can use passcodes generated by the app and paste them into the authentication prompt. Note that it is possible to have passcodes delivered to a user as SMS and app-generated passcodes. Finally, the last method is for the user to receive a call and follow the instructions for completing the authentication.

FIGURE 9.2 MFA flow in Snowflake

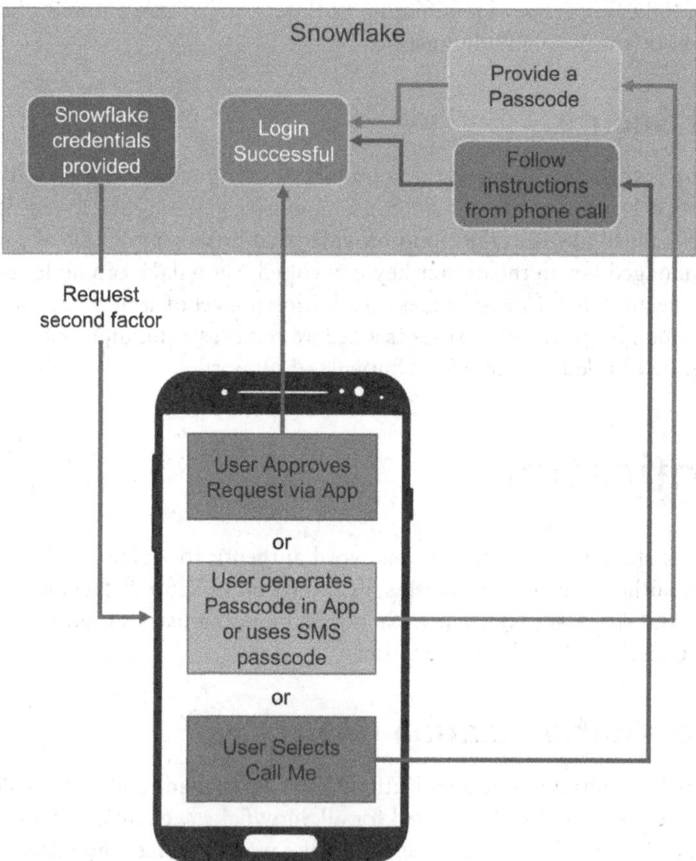

An administrator can disable MFA for a user, in which case the user must re-enroll in MFA to use the MFA capability again. An administrator can also disable MFA for a user temporarily for a defined time so that they can log in. MFA then re-enables after the defined time has passed.

MFA is supported by SnowSQL, Snowflake ODBC, JDBC drivers, and Python Connector. Snowflake defaults to the push method for each connectivity method; a prompt is displayed on the Duo Mobile app for authentication approval. However, it is possible to use the passcodes by specifying the passcode value in the command-line parameters for Snowflake or the connection string for the drivers.

Key Pair Authentication

Key pair authentication is an alternative to the basic username/password authentication method and provides enhanced security. This method, which is supported by Snowflake, consists of private and public keys, where the public key is assigned to a user, and they use the private key for authenticating. A user may be assigned up to two public keys at a time, and the keys can be rotated if required. Key pair authentication is supported by all SnowSQL and all Snowflake drivers and connectors.

SSO via SAML 2.0 Federated Authentication

Snowflake supports federated authentication, enabling users to connect to Snowflake using single sign-on (SSO). With SSO-enabled authentication, users authenticate through an external identity provider (IdP) compatible with the SAML 2.0 standard. After the IdP authenticates the users, they can access Snowflake without logging in. Snowflake supports most SAML 2.0–compliant identity providers, including native support for Okta and ADFS and support for Google G Suite, Microsoft Azure Active Directory, OneLogin, and Ping Identity PingOne.

Password Policies

Snowflake enforces password policies to ensure strong passwords are created for users. Although administrators can create a user with a weak password initially, the recommendation is to force the users to change passwords upon first login. Other than the first-time user creation, Snowflake enforces passwords to be at least eight characters long, containing at least one digit, one uppercase letter, and one lowercase letter. Applying the standard security best practices when choosing a password is also recommended.

User Provisioning Through SCIM

System for Cross-domain Identity Management (SCIM) is an open standard that enables automatic user provisioning and syncing of roles based on information from an identity provider. Snowflake supports SCIM 2.0 and can integrate with Okta and Microsoft Azure AD. Figure 9.3 illustrates user provisioning and role management in Snowflake via SCIM.

FIGURE 9.3 SCIM-based user provisioning

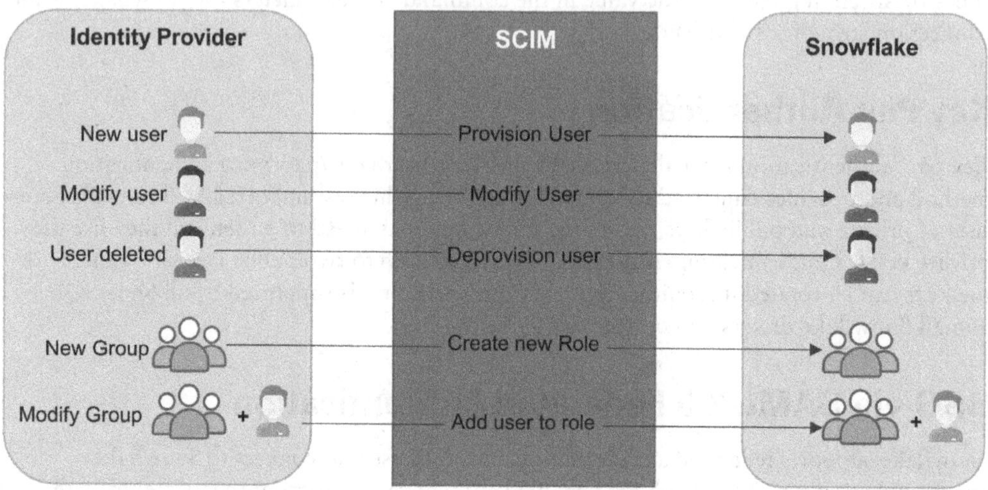

With SCIM in place, when a new user is created in the identity provider, the SCIM provisions the user in Snowflake. Similarly, when a user is removed in an identity management system, SCIM removes the user from Snowflake. SCIM can also sync groups created in an identity provider to roles in Snowflake.

Authorization

Snowflake provides fine-grained access control over objects, including who can access what objects and what operations can be performed on those objects such as read, write, create, or delete. In addition to object-level security, Snowflake provides fine-grained security settings in the form of row-level and column-level security. Snowflake also controls who can define various security configurations and access controls through built-in Snowflake roles and custom privileges.

Access Control in Snowflake

Snowflake's access control is centered around the role-based access control (RBAC) model in which privileges are assigned to roles and roles are assigned to users. All users in a role inherit the privileges assigned to that role. Snowflake also features discretionary access control (DAC), in which the role creating a new object is the owner of that object and can grant access to that object to other roles. Figure 9.4 illustrates various key concepts associated with access control in Snowflake.

FIGURE 9.4 Access control in Snowflake

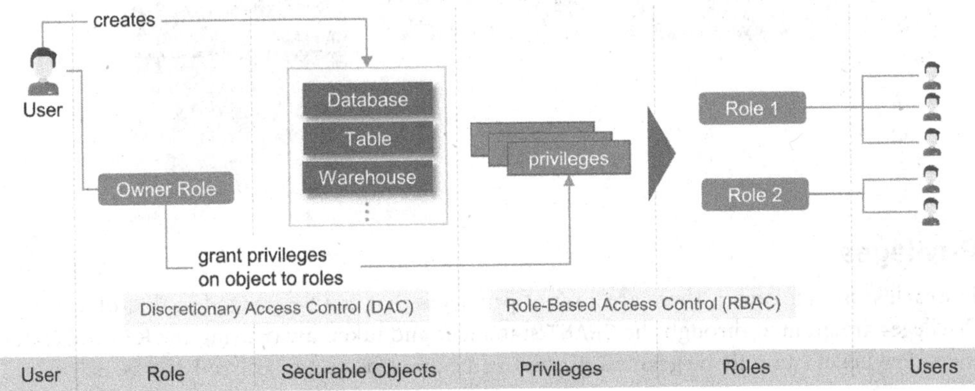

A user can create a new object, such as a database, table, or warehouse. Whichever role the user uses while creating the new object becomes the owning role of the new object—in other words, the role has `OWNER` privilege on the object. Any user who is part of that role has the same privilege on the created object. Ownership of an object can also be transferred to another role if desired. The owning role can perform DAC, which means that they can assign privileges on the created object to other roles. The assignment of privileges to another role is also referred to as RBAC.

Securable Objects

A securable object is any object or entity to which privileges can be granted. If explicit access is not granted to an object, it defaults to denying access. Figure 9.5 shows an example of securable objects in Snowflake. The securable objects may be tables, views, and user-defined functions (UDFs), to name a few, and are contained in a schema, which in turn is contained in a database. Warehouses, resource monitors, users, and roles are examples of securable objects to which certain privileges can be granted.

FIGURE 9.5 Securable objects in Snowflake

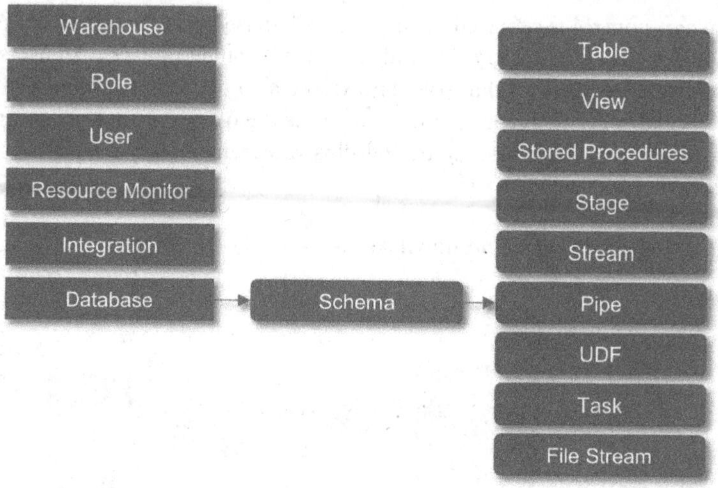

Warehouse
Role
User
Resource Monitor
Integration
Database → Schema → Table, View, Stored Procedures, Stage, Stream, Pipe, UDF, Task, File Stream

Privileges

For each securable object, there are a set of privileges that can be granted to that object. Privileges are granted through the `GRANT` statement and taken away using the `REVOKE` statement. Privileges can only be granted to roles and cannot be granted directly to users.

Users

The concept of *user* refers to a user identity that can be used to log into Snowflake. The user identity may be associated with a human user or it could be a machine account used to run extract, transform, load (ETL) jobs.

Roles

A *role* is an entity to which privileges on other objects can be granted. The roles themselves can then be granted to other users or other roles. You create a role hierarchy when you assign a role to another role. Users can switch between multiple roles and choose their active role for a session. The active role is called the primary role for the session; however, other roles (secondary roles) that the user has access to can be activated in the session. A user can be assigned a default role so that their session role is set to the default role every time they log in.

Built-in Snowflake Roles

There are a small number of predefined system roles in Snowflake that are provided out of the box. However, these roles cannot be dropped, and the privileges assigned to these roles also cannot be dropped. A brief description of each of these system roles follows:

ORGADMIN ORGADMIN is responsible for managing tasks at an organizational level. A user with the ORGADMIN role can create new accounts, list existing accounts, see usage metrics at an organizational level, and enable replication for accounts in that organization.

ACCOUNTADMIN ACCOUNTADMIN is the account administrator role that has full privileges. Because this is the most powerful role, access to this role should be strictly regulated. This role also includes the responsibilities of the other ADMIN roles.

USERADMIN This role gives you the ability to create USERS and ROLES.

SECURITYADMIN In addition to having the privileges provided to the USERADMIN role, this role has the privilege to manage object grants globally.

SYSADMIN This role has the privilege to create and manage most objects in your Snowflake account, like databases, tables, views, virtual warehouses, and so forth.

PUBLIC PUBLIC is the least restrictive role since it is automatically assigned to everyone. If you're not concerned with the security of a particular item, you can easily make it accessible to all Snowflake users by using the PUBLIC role.

Snowflake provides the concept of *Organizations* that enable a business entity to link together all accounts owned by that entity. The organization construct simplifies billing, account management, replication, failover, data sharing, and other administrative tasks. The Organization administrator or ORGADMIN role is in charge of managing operations at an organizational level. For example, an ORGADMIN can create new accounts, view a list of existing accounts, view a combined account usage at an organizational level, and enable replications for specific accounts. An ACCOUNTADMIN role can assign the ORGADMIN role to themselves or another user; therefore, it is recommended that the ORGADMIN role be enabled for only one account in an organization for clarity on who can act as an ORGADMIN.

Role Hierarchy

Roles in Snowflake, including the built-in roles, are organized in a role hierarchy. The hierarchy is formed when a role is granted to another role, which effectively gives all the privileges of the sub-role to the higher role. Figure 9.6 shows the predefined system roles and their hierarchical relationship, demonstrating that the lower roles all roll up to the ACCOUNTADMIN role.

It is also possible to create new roles in Snowflake, which can be granted to users and other roles. All custom roles should be granted directly or indirectly to the SYSADMIN role so that the system administrator can manage all objects in the Snowflake system regardless of which role owns those objects.

FIGURE 9.6 Snowflake roles and role hierarchy

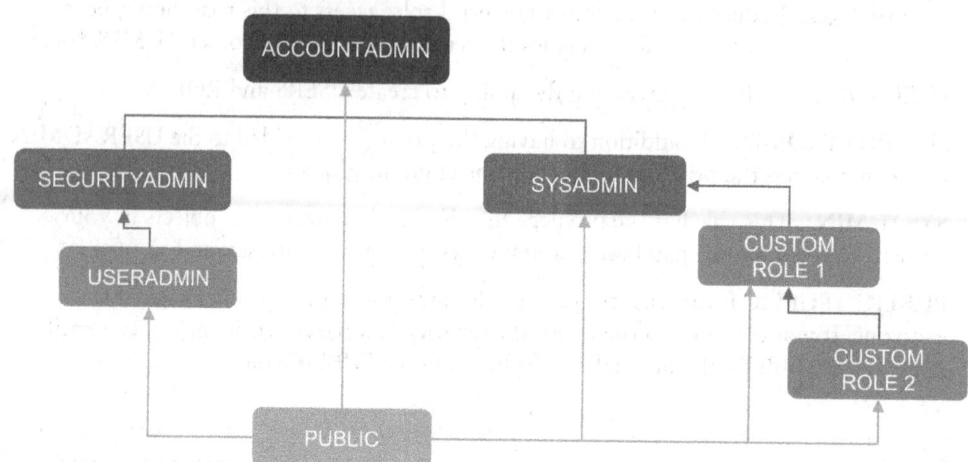

Column-Level Security

Snowflake's column-level security capability allows you to apply a masking policy to a column within a table or view. Snowflake currently supports two methods for column-level security:

Dynamic Data Masking With dynamic data masking in place, queries run on protected columns may return masked text or the actual column data depending on the role under which a query is executed.

External Tokenization The external tokenization method allows Snowflake customers to tokenize data before loading it into Snowflake and detokenize it during query execution. Tokenization is the name given to replacing sensitive data with an undecipherable token. External tokenization provides tokenization capabilities through external functions.

Dynamic data masking and external tokenization are applied by defining masking policies and attaching them to columns.

Masking Policies

Snowflake provides masking policies that can be applied to columns to provide column-level security. When a user executes a query on a table containing columns with masking policies, the masking policy determines at runtime which roles see masked or tokenized data and which roles see the actual data. Masking policies contain conditions and functions that can dynamically transform data. The following example shows a typical masking policy. Notice the `case` statement with conditions that show unmasked data to the PII_USERS privileged roles and masked data to all other roles when evaluated:

```
CREATE MASKING POLICY mask_email_address AS (val STRING) RETURNS STRING ->
  CASE
    WHEN CURRENT_ROLE() IN ('PII_USERS') THEN val
```

```
    ELSE '*****@***.***'
END;
```

Row-Level Security

Snowflake also supports row-level security functionality, through which Snowflake can determine which rows to return to the users when they execute a query. Row-level security is implemented using row access policies that contain conditions and functions that determine the rows to be returned. Row access policies can have a simple definition that allows specific roles to view rows. They can also have a more complex definition using a mapping table to determine the rows to return during query execution.

Secure Views and Secure UDFs

Due to internal query optimizations, data underlying a general (nonsecure) view is required to be available to the user accessing the view. Therefore, a standard view cannot be used to hide part or all of the underlying data from users. Secure views can hide the underlying data by removing the internal optimizations. You can use secure views to create views that provide data security. You create a secure view by specifying the `SECURE` keyword when creating the view. Any view can be converted to and from a secure view by setting the `SECURE` option.

Like secure views, secure UDFs ensure that underlying data is not available to the user executing the UDFs.

User Access Audit Log

Snowflake automatically logs all user access events on the system, including login and query histories. These history logs can be extracted using table functions and views provided in the ACCOUNT_USAGE schema under the Snowflake database and the INFORMATION_SCHEMA schema. The ACCOUNT_USAGE schema can provide 365 days of historical logs, although it has some data latency. The INFORMATION_SCHEMA schema provides real-time information on log data, but with less data retention. Chapter 10, "Account and Resource Management," discusses these schemas, various views, and functions in more detail.

Network

Snowflake provides control over the network through network policies that can allow or deny access, support for private connectivity, and automatically encrypt all communication. These network-related security features are discussed in detail in the following section.

Network Policies

By default, Snowflake allows users to connect from any IP address. However, administrators can configure the system to allow or deny access to specific IP addresses through network policies. A network policy consists of the policy name, a comma-separated list of allowed IP addresses, and a list of blocked IP addresses. If both the allowed IP address list and the blocked IP address list is populated, Snowflake applies the block list first before applying the allowed list. You can provide an exact IP address or an IP address range in the allowed or blocked IP addresses list; however, note that only IPv4 addresses are supported by network policies currently.

Only security administrators—SECURITYADMIN or a higher role or a role with CREATE NETWORK POLICY privilege—can create a network policy.

Network policies can be attached at an account level, in which case the policy applies to the whole account. Network policies can also be attached to individual users, in which case they apply only to that user. If a user-level network policy is applied, the user-level network policy takes precedence over the account-level policy.

Support for Private Connectivity

Your Snowflake instance is accessible over the public Internet by default, with the access protected through various security means such as MFA, HTTPS, and network policies. Snowflake provides support for private connectivity if your organization requires that your Snowflake instance not be accessible over the Internet. Through private connectivity, you can ensure that access to your Snowflake instance is over a private connection and can optionally block all Internet access.

Private connectivity to Snowflake requires a minimum of the Business Critical edition.

Snowflake supports the following private connectivity methods depending on your cloud provider:

- AWS PrivateLink
- Azure Private Link
- Google Cloud Private Service Connect

Encryption for All Communication

Snowflake encrypts all communications end to end. Data is encrypted in transit using TLS 1.2. All connections to Snowflake go through HTTPS, including connectivity to the Snowflake web UI, JDBC, ODBC, Python connector, and other connection methods. These connectivity methods use HTTPS because all access to Snowflake services is through REST APIs invoked over the HTTP protocol.

Compliance with Standards

Snowflake supports a variety of security and financial standards and certifications and currently complies with the following standards and certifications:

SOC 2 Type II The SOC2 Type 2 report, produced by an independent auditor, certifies that Snowflake had adequate security measures throughout the period covered by the report.

SOC 1 Type II The SOC1 Type 2 report, produced by an independent auditor, certifies that Snowflake had adequate financial controls.

PCI DSS The Payment Card Industry Data Security Standard (PCI DSS) is a data security standard for businesses that process credit card transactions. Snowflake is attested PCI DSS-compliant through an independent auditor assessment.

HIPAA The Health Insurance Portability and Accountability Act of 1996 (HIPAA) is a federal law that mandated the development of healthcare standards to safeguard health information. Snowflake is compliant with these standards.

ISO/IEC 27001 The ISO/IEC 27001 is an information security standard applicable to an organization's information security management systems. Snowflake is complaint with this standard.

FedRAMP Moderate FedRAMP (Federal Risk and Authorization Management Program) governs cloud computing security for regulated unclassified information. Snowflake supports the moderate level meant for cloud service providers handling nonpublic government data.

GxP GxP is an abbreviation for Good Practices, where *x* represents different industries. Snowflake is compliant with GxP, enabling life sciences businesses to assure data integrity and develop GxP-compliant solutions using a secure, certified cloud data platform.

ITAR According to the International Traffic in Arms Regulations (ITAR), foreign nationals are banned from physically or intellectually entering an ITAR environment. A third-party assessment validated that Snowflake's Microsoft Azure Government (MAG) and Amazon Web Services (AWS) GovCloud deployments are ITAR-compliant.

IRAP – Protected The Australian Signals Directorate (ASD) oversees the Infosec Registered Assessors Program (IRAP). Following the Australian Government Information Security Manual (ISM) guidelines, IRAP offers a security framework and assessment methodology for Australian government departments and their clients. Snowflake is assessed at an IRAP-protected level.

Summary

This chapter described the security capabilities provided by Snowflake. Snowflake includes several security capabilities that provide security at various levels of the Snowflake software stack. Snowflake security is implemented starting with the data storage layer and progressing to further levels such as authentication control, data access control or authorization, and network-level controls to govern access into your Snowflake instance. The chapter also covered the various financial and security standards supported by Snowflake.

Exam Essentials

Describe data encryption at rest. All customer data in Snowflake is encrypted by default using AES-256 bit encryption. The Snowflake managed keys are rotated regularly (at 30-day intervals), and a yearly rekeying process re-encrypts data with brand-new keys. For example, if an encryption key is retired after a year, Snowflake generates a new encryption key and re-encrypts any data secured by the retired encryption key, a process known as rekeying. Rekeying requires Enterprise edition or above. Tri-Secret Secure (requiring a minimum of the Business Critical edition) protects your data by combining a Snowflake managed key and a customer-managed key.

Describe authentication in Snowflake. Snowflake supports key pair authentication using private and public keys, with the user receiving the public key and using it to authenticate. Snowflake also supports federated authentication, allowing single sign-on (SSO). Users authenticate via an external identity provider (IdP) that supports SAML 2.0. Snowflake supports SCIM, an open standard that enables automatic user provisioning and role syncing based on information from an identity provider. Snowflake supports SCIM 2.0 and can integrate with Okta and Microsoft Azure AD. Snowflake also enforces password standards to ensure users have strong passwords.

Define multifactor authentication. Snowflake supports multifactor authentication (MFA) and enables it by default for all Snowflake accounts. Users can self-enroll by using the Snowflake web interface. Snowflake delivers MFA via the Duo Security service and Duo Mobile app. An administrator can disable MFA for a user who must re-enroll in MFA. An administrator can also temporarily disable MFA for a user to allow them to log in. SnowSQL, Snowflake ODBC, JDBC, and Python Connector support MFA.

Describe authorization in Snowflake. Securable objects are objects or entities to which privileges can be granted. For each securable object, there are a set of privileges that can be granted to that object. Privileges are granted through the `GRANT` statement and taken away using the `REVOKE` statement. A role is an entity to which privileges on other objects can be granted. The roles themselves can then be granted to other users or other roles. A role hierarchy is formed when a role is assigned to another role.

Explain access control in Snowflake. Snowflake's access control is built on the RBAC concept, where privileges are granted to roles and roles to users. Snowflake also supports discretionary access control (DAC), where the role generating an object owns it and can provide access to other roles. Ownership of an object can also be transferred to another role if desired.

Describe the built-in roles in Snowflake. Snowflake comes with a small set of preconfigured system roles. ACCOUNTADMIN is the account administrator role that has full privileges. USERADMIN gives you the ability to create USERS and ROLES. SECURITYADMIN has the privileges to manage object grants globally and inherits USERADMIN privileges. SYSADMIN has the privilege to create and manage most objects in your Snowflake account. PUBLIC is the least restrictive role since it is automatically assigned to everyone. Snowflake's roles are organized in a role hierarchy. When a role is granted to another role, the higher role gains all the privileges of the lower role.

Describe column-level and row-level security in Snowflake. Snowflake's column-level security feature lets you mask a column within a table or view. Masking policies are attached to columns to apply dynamic data masking or external tokenization. External tokenization uses external functions to tokenize. Snowflake also provides row-level security, which allows it to determine which rows to return to users when they run queries. Row-level security policies contain conditions and functions that determine which rows should be returned.

Explain network security in Snowflake. Administrators can set network policies to enable or prevent access to specified IPv4 addresses. In a network policy, there are three parts: name, authorized IP addresses, and blocked IP addresses. If both the authorized and blocked lists are populated, Snowflake applies the blocked list first. Snowflake supports private connectivity to ensure that access to your Snowflake instance is private rather than the public Internet. Snowflake's private connectivity requires the Business Critical edition. Snowflake encrypts all communications end to end. Data is encrypted in transit using TLS 1.2.

Know the standards that Snowflake supports. Snowflake supports the following security and financial standards: SOC 1 Type II, SOC 2 Type II, PCI DSS, HIPAA, ISO/IEC 27001, FedRAMP Moderate, GxP, ITAR, and IRAP – Protected.

Review Questions

1. Snowflake supports which of the following security features? (Select all that apply.)
   A. AES 256 encryption of data at rest
   B. MD5 encryption of data at rest
   C. Tri-Secret Secure encryption
   D. Key rotation
2. What is the minimum Snowflake edition that supports Tri-Secret Secure encryption?
   A. Standard
   B. Enterprise
   C. Business Critical
   D. Virtual Private Snowflake
3. Which of the following statements are true regarding Snowflake's multifactor authentication (MFA)? (Select all that apply.)
   A. MFA is provided only in the Business Critical and above editions.
   B. MFA is only supported by the Snowflake web interface and SnowSQL.
   C. MFA is enabled for all users by default; however, users need to enroll themselves into MFA manually.
   D. An administrator can disable MFA for a user.
4. Snowflake supports which of the following authentication mechanisms? (Select all that apply.)
   A. Key pair authentication
   B. Multifactor authentication
   C. SAML 2.0 federated authentication
   D. Google Authentication
5. Which of the following is true regarding key pair authentication in Snowflake? (Select all that apply.)
   A. A user can be assigned up to two public keys.
   B. Key pair authentication requires providing your Snowflake username and password when prompted.
   C. The keys can be rotated if desired.
   D. Key pair authentication is available only for the VPS edition.

6. Which of the following statements are true regarding federated authentication in Snowflake? (Select all that apply.)
   A. Snowflake supports most SAML 2.0 identity providers.
   B. Once authenticated by an external identity provider, a user does not need to provide a Snowflake username.
   C. Users need to provide a Snowflake username and password after being authenticated by an external identity provider.
   D. Snowflake has native support for Okta and ADFS.
7. Which of the following is supported by Snowflake for autoprovisioning of users and groups?
   A. MFA
   B. SCIM
   C. FedRAMP
   D. ITAR
8. Which of the following are built-in roles provided by Snowflake? (Select all that apply.)
   A. SECURITYADMIN
   B. ACCOUNTADMIN
   C. PUBLIC
   D. USERADMIN
   E. LOADADMIN
9. Which of the following access control methods are supported by Snowflake? (Select all that apply.)
   A. Attribute-based access control (ABAC)
   B. Role-based access control (RBAC)
   C. Discretionary access control (DAC)
   D. Redundant access control (RAC)
10. Which of the following statements are true regarding access control in Snowflake? (Select all that apply.)
    A. Securable objects are objects or entities to which privileges can be granted.
    B. Roles cannot be granted to other roles.
    C. Privileges are granted through the `GRANT` statement and taken away using the `REVOKE` statement.
    D. Roles can be granted to other users or other roles.

11. Which of the following are methods to implement column-level security in Snowflake? (Select two.)
    A. User policies
    B. Dynamic data masking
    C. Row-level policies
    D. External tokenization
12. If an IP address is in both the block list and the allowed list in a network policy, what is Snowflake's behavior when enforcing the network policy?
    A. The network policy is invalid as both the allowed and blocked lists cannot be populated.
    B. Snowflake applies the blocked list first, ensuring that the IP address is blocked from connecting, even if it is also defined in the allow list.
    C. Snowflake applies the allowed list first, ensuring the IP address is allowed to connect, even if it is defined in the block list too.
    D. The IP address is ignored.
13. What minimum Snowflake version is required for private connectivity to Snowflake?
    A. Standard
    B. Enterprise
    C. Business Critical
    D. Virtual Private Snowflake
14. True or False: Snowflake encrypts all communication automatically using TLS 1.2, including communication for the Snowflake web UI, SnowSQL, and all the connectors and drivers.
    A. True
    B. False
15. Snowflake supports which of the following standards?
    A. FedRAMP
    B. BASEL II
    C. IRAP – Protected
    D. HIPAA
    E. PCI DSS

Account and Resource Management

THE SNOWPRO CORE EXAM TOPICS COVERED IN THIS CHAPTER INCLUDE THE FOLLOWING:

✓ **Domain 1.0: Snowflake Data Platform Features and Architecture**

- 1.4 Outline Snowflake storage concepts.
  - Data storage monitoring

✓ **Domain 2.0: Account Access and Security**

- 2.3 Outline data governance capabilities in Snowflake.
  - Information schemas
  - Access history and read support

✓ **Domain 3.0: Performance Concepts**

- 3.3 Outline virtual warehouse performance tools.
  - Resource monitors

Snowflake provides prebuilt views and table functions that enable users to keep track of their Snowflake credit and storage usage. In addition to this tracking, Snowflake provides resource monitors through which you can track credit usage and take actions such as suspending virtual warehouses and notifying administrators when credit usage crosses defined thresholds. This chapter describes these views in detail, explains how to use resource monitors, and provides several hands-on exercises to reinforce learning. Finally, the chapter discusses Snowflake release management processes.

Resource Monitors

In Snowflake, resource monitors help you manage costs and avoid unexpected credit usage by virtual warehouses and other compute services. Resource monitors allow credit usage to be controlled by monitoring it against a defined upper limit, notifying administrators when a specific percentage of the limit is reached, and even suspending virtual warehouses if required.

Resource monitors can monitor a single virtual warehouse, a group of virtual warehouses, or a complete Snowflake account against a defined credit quota. Based on the percentage of the credit quota used, you can choose to notify administrators and optionally choose to suspend virtual warehouses so that no further compute use occurs.

As shown in Figure 10.1, you can create multiple resource monitors to monitor and manage credit usage at different levels and against different thresholds. You can create a resource monitor at an *account level*, which involves tracking the credit usage at the account level, including all virtual warehouses' credit usage. You can also configure the resource monitor to suspend user compute resources when the credit consumption at the account level reaches a certain threshold.

Resource monitors can only suspend user-managed virtual warehouses. A resource monitor at an account level does not control the credit usage by serverless features such as Snowpipe, Automatic Reclustering, or Materialized View maintenance. An account-level resource monitor also does not control the cloud services costs.

FIGURE 10.1 Monitoring at virtual warehouse and account levels

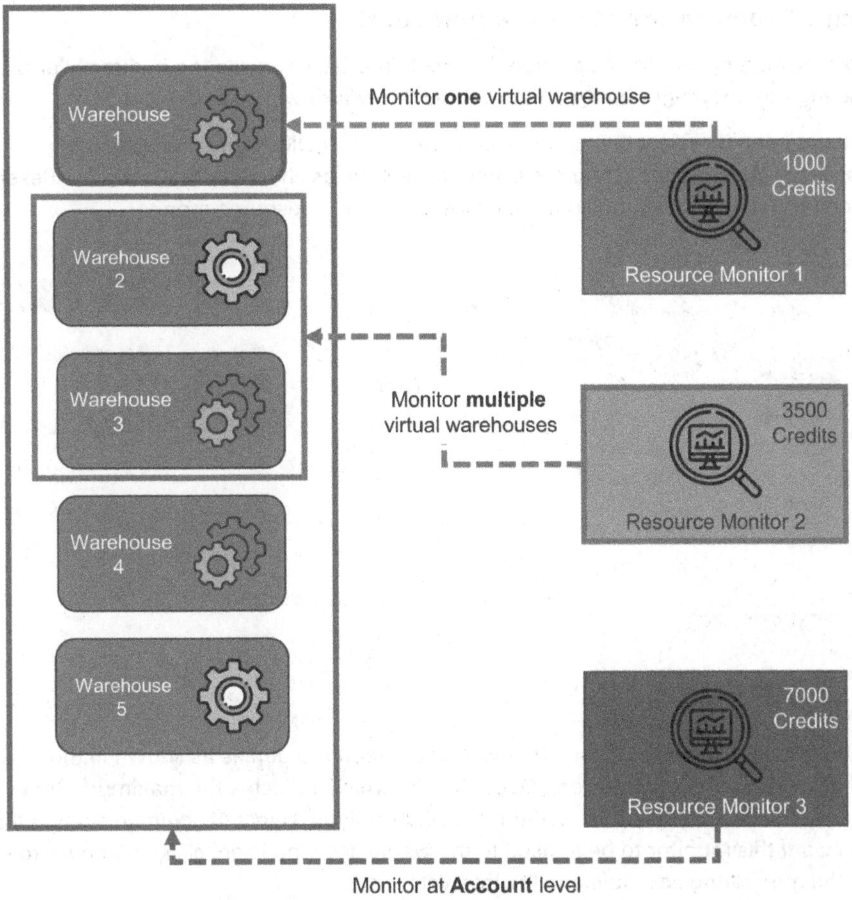

You can also create resource monitors to track a single virtual warehouse's usage. When the credit usage for that virtual warehouse reaches the specified threshold, the resource monitor can notify administrators and suspend further executions on that virtual warehouse. Resource monitors can also be configured so that they track multiple virtual warehouses.

If a resource monitor monitors a virtual warehouse, another resource monitor cannot monitor the same virtual warehouse.

Exercise 10.1 demonstrates the concept of creating a resource monitor at an account level using the new Snowflake web interface. A resource monitor configured at an account level monitors credit usage by all of the virtual warehouses in that account.

EXERCISE 10.1

Setting a Credit Quota at an Account Level

1. Start by logging into the new Snowflake web interface. You can log in directly or by clicking the Snowsight button in the classic Snowflake web interface.
2. After logging in, select the current role as ACCOUNTADMIN and then select the Resource Monitors tab under the Compute section, as shown here. Click the + Resource Monitor button to start the creation process for a new resource monitor.

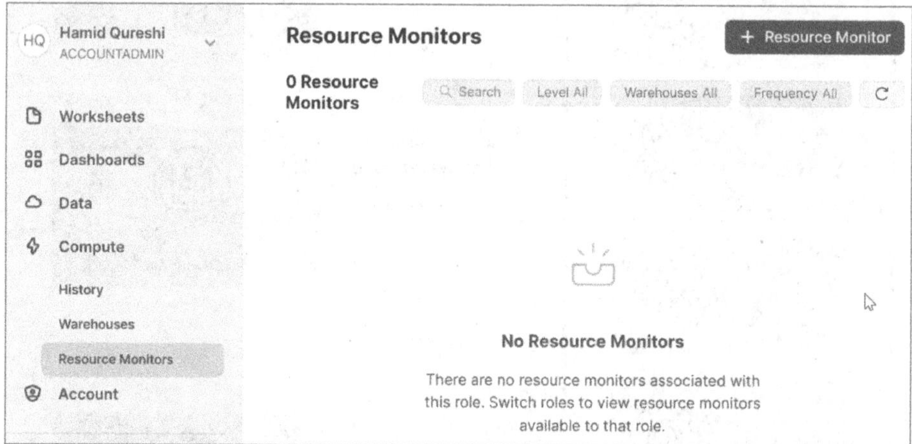

3. In the New Resource Monitor window, add the required details as shown in the following screenshot. Set Credit Quota to 100, which indicates the maximum Snowflake credits allowed by this monitor. For Monitor Type, select Account, indicating that you want this monitor to be applied to the whole account. Then, click Customize to set up the monitoring schedule and the interval.

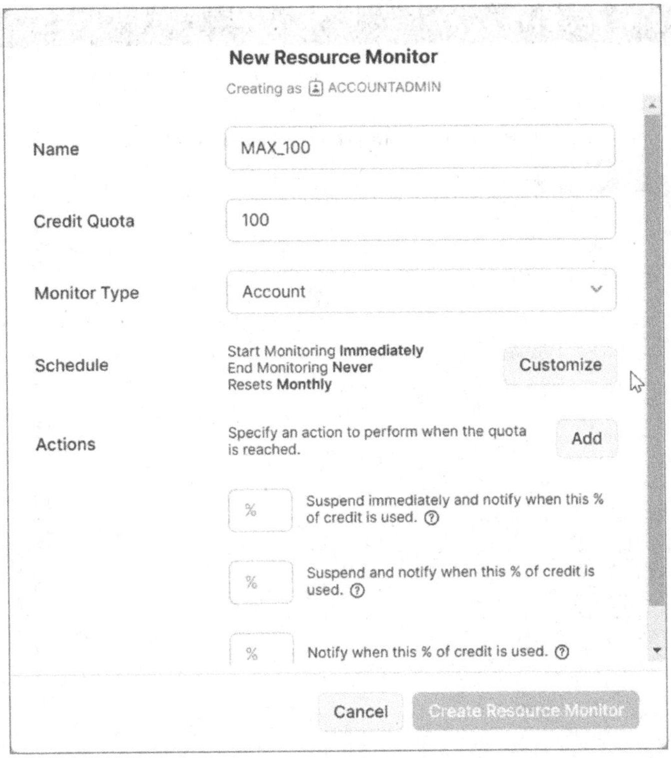

4. In the Customize Resource Monitor Schedule window, specify when you want the resource monitor to become active. In our example, we have configured the resource monitor to start immediately, but you can configure it to start monitoring at a specific date. You also need to specify the reset interval, which indicates the duration after which the resource monitor resets and starts monitoring from zero. In our example, we have set Resets to Monthly, which means the monitor will allow usage of 100 Snowflake credits from the date it is set up to the same date in the next month. Once you have configured the options, click Apply.

EXERCISE 10.1 *(continued)*

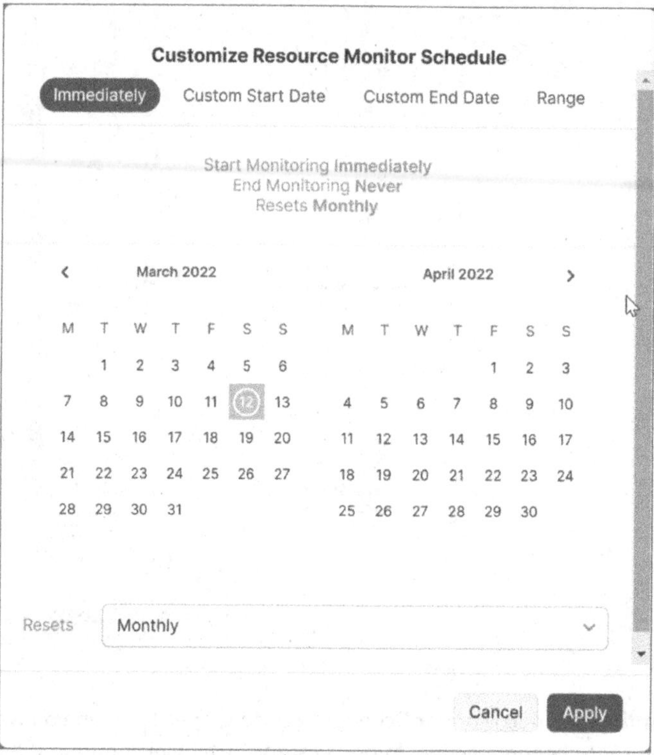

5. The final step is to specify the actions that the resource monitor should take depending on the percentage of the allocated credit quota used. In our example, we configured the resource monitor to notify account administrators when 50 percent of the credit is used; to suspend all virtual warehouses and notify administrators when 75 percent of the credit is used; and to immediately suspend all virtual warehouses and notify administrators when 95 percent of the credit is used. Once you have performed your desired configuration, click Create Resource Monitor.

New Resource Monitor
Creating as ACCOUNTADMIN
Name MAX_100
Credit Quota 100
Monitor Type Account
Schedule Start Monitoring **Immediately** End Monitoring **Never** Resets **Monthly** Customize
Actions Specify an action to perform when the quota is reached. Add
95 Suspend immediately and notify when this % of credit is used.
75 Suspend and notify when this % of credit is used.
50 Notify when this % of credit is used.
Cancel Create Resource Monitor

You configured an account-level resource monitor using the Snowflake web interface in this exercise. Note that account administrators can receive notifications via email or the web interface. However, the notifications are not enabled by default. Each account administrator must enable and configure notification settings through preferences in the web interface to receive notifications.

When a resource monitor suspends a virtual warehouse, the suspend process allows existing queries to finish. In contrast, when set to Suspend Immediately, the monitor suspends the virtual warehouse right away, stopping all running queries.

Exercise 10.2 demonstrates creating a resource monitor for a virtual warehouse by using SQL. For example, a resource monitor configured at a virtual warehouse level monitors the credit usage for only that virtual warehouse.

EXERCISE 10.2

Setting a Credit Quota at a Warehouse Level

1. While logged into the Snowflake web interface, switch to the Worksheets view. In a new worksheet, change your role to ACCOUNTADMIN using the following SQL:

```
USE ROLE ACCOUNTADMIN;
```

2. Next, you'll create a new resource monitor that allows a maximum of 10 Snowflake credits of usage. The monitor resets at a weekly interval, so the virtual warehouse assigned to this virtual warehouse is allowed a maximum of 10 Snowflake credits every week. You'll also configure the resource monitor to start immediately, to notify administrators when 50 percent of allocated credits are used, and to suspend immediately when 95 percent of credits are used. To do all this, run the following SQL:

```
CREATE RESOURCE MONITOR "VW_10" WITH CREDIT_QUOTA = 10, frequency = 'WEEKLY',
start_timestamp = 'IMMEDIATELY', end_timestamp = null
 TRIGGERS
 ON 95 PERCENT DO SUSPEND_IMMEDIATE
 ON 50 PERCENT DO NOTIFY;
```

You should see a success message.

3. Next, you'll assign this resource monitor to the COMPUTE_WH virtual warehouse. To do so, run the following SQL:

```
ALTER WAREHOUSE "COMPUTE_WH" SET RESOURCE_MONITOR = "VW_10";
```

You should see a success message, indicating that the resource monitor was successfully allocated.

4. At this stage, you can validate that the resource monitor has been created and configured, by navigating to the Resource Monitors tab under the Compute section.

5. Finally, you can configure additional roles such as SYSADMIN to view and alter the configuration of your resource monitor. To do that, run the following SQL to provide the necessary permissions:

```
GRANT MONITOR, MODIFY  ON RESOURCE MONITOR "VW_10" TO ROLE SYSADMIN;
```

In this exercise, you configured a resource monitor for monitoring credit usage of a virtual warehouse using SQL. Because only account administrators can create new resource monitors, you switched to the ACCOUNTADMIN role before starting the creation process. However, once a resource monitor is created, the account administrator can provide privileges to other roles to see and modify the resource monitor.

System Usage and Billing

Snowflake provides two methods for viewing metadata and usage information. First, it provides metadata and usage information through the INFORMATION_SCHEMA schema, automatically created for every database in Snowflake. Second, Snowflake provides usage information through a shared database called Snowflake, which is a system-defined, read-only shared database automatically imported into every Snowflake account. The Snowflake database contains several schemas, as shown highlighted in Figure 10.2, each containing views that, among other information, provide storage and compute usage details.

FIGURE 10.2 Schemas within the Snowflake database

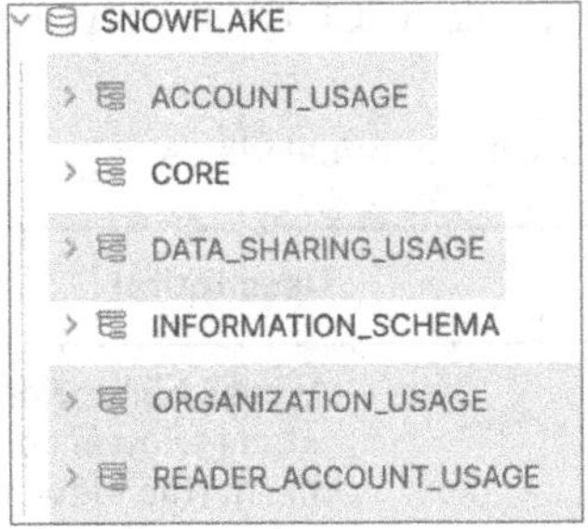

A brief description of the key schemas is as follows. Schemas that are important from an exam perspective are described in further detail.

- The ACCOUNT_USAGE schema provides usage metrics and metadata information at an account level. This schema is covered in more detail in the next section.
- The READER_ACCOUNT_USAGE schema provides usage metrics and metadata information for all reader accounts that have been created for your accounts. The views in this schema are a small subset of the ACCOUNT_USAGE schema views.
- The ORGANIZATION_USAGE schema contains views that provide historical usage information for all of the accounts in your organization.
- The DATA_SHARING_USAGE schema contains views that provide information about listings that have been published in the Snowflake Marketplace or Data Exchange. The views provide information such as listing access, clicks, and the number of queries run by other organizations on the shared data.

The ACCOUNT_USAGE Schema

The ACCOUNT_USAGE schema provides usage metrics and metadata information at an account level, exposed through a set of views. The views may either provide object metadata or provide historical usage information. More information about the ACCOUNT_USAGE schema can be found here:

`https://docs.snowflake.com/en/sql-reference/account-usage.html`

The historical information views generally end in the HISTORY postfix and provide historical data about a specific aspect of your system, such as a history of queries executed or of login attempts. The data in these views is not real time and generally updates with a lag of 45 minutes to 3 hours for different views. The data in these views is retained for up to 365 days—that is, the last 365 days of history is available at any given point. Table 10.1 shows all of the historical views in the ACCOUNT_USAGE schema.

TABLE 10.1 ACCOUNT_USAGE historical views

View	Description
ACCESS_HISTORY	Access history of Snowflake objects such as tables, views, columns, etc., as a query accesses them. This view requires the Enterprise edition or higher. The view provides query information, the username, and three JSON arrays. The JSON arrays contain information on objects that were directly accessed; objects that were indirectly accessed, such as via a view; and objects modified as part of the query.
AUTOMATIC_CLUSTERING_HISTORY	This view contains automatic reclustering history for Snowflake tables, showing the number of rows and bytes reclustered and credits used for reclustering.
COPY_HISTORY	This view contains data loading history for both the `COPY INTO` command and Snowpipe data loading.
DATABASE_STORAGE_USAGE_HISTORY	This view contains the daily average storage used for databases in your account. The storage includes data used (in bytes) by tables, Time Travel, and Fail-safe.
DATA_TRANSFER_HISTORY	This view contains information on data transferred from Snowflake tables into a different cloud provider or a different region.

View	Description
LOAD_HISTORY	This view shows the data loading history for only the `COPY INTO` command and does not contain Snowpipe history. The view provides a good deal of information on the files loaded, rows processed, errors encountered, the row number of the first error encountered, and table information in which the data was loaded.
LOGIN_HISTORY	This view contains successful and unsuccessful login attempts. It contains the conventional login/password login attempts as well as SSO, OAuth, and multifactor authentication attempts. In addition, the view provides error codes for unsuccessful attempts.
MATERIALIZED_VIEW_REFRESH_HISTORY	This view contains the refresh history of materialized views, refresh times, and credits used to refresh the view.
METERING_DAILY_HISTORY	This view contains daily compute credit usage and cloud services usage broken down by service type. It also includes the cloud services discount. In addition, the view provides information at the date and service type level, where the service may be warehouse, reader account warehouse, automatic clustering, materialized view maintenance, Snowpipe usage, and replication.
METERING_HISTORY	This view is similar to METERING_DAILY_HISTORY and contains compute credit usage and cloud services usage broken by service type but for every hour. This view also contains the service names, rows, bytes, and files populated for different service types.
PIPE_USAGE_HISTORY	This view contains the history of data loaded and credits used for data loaded using Snowpipe.
QUERY_HISTORY	The view contains the history of query execution against various dimensions such as user, warehouse, session, and query type. The view provides a rich view of query attributes such as rows scanned, rows written, time information, and query status.

TABLE 10.1 ACCOUNT_USAGE historical views *(continued)*

View	Description
REPLICATION_USAGE_HISTORY	This view contains historical information on database replication. It contains the database name, bytes transferred, and credit used for each replicated database.
SEARCH_OPTIMIZATION_HISTORY	This view contains information on credit usage by search optimization service for each table with search optimization enabled.
SERVERLESS_TASK_HISTORY	This view contains the history of serverless task executions, including task name, credits used, and execution time.
SESSIONS	This view contains information on each session, including authentication method, username, and client information.
STAGE_STORAGE_USAGE_HISTORY	This view contains average storage usage in bytes for all Snowflake internal stages (including named internal stages, table stages, and user stages).
STORAGE_USAGE	This view contains daily storage usage in bytes for the complete account, including tables and stages. Shows tables storage usage, stage storage usage, and Fail-safe storage separately.
TASK_HISTORY	This view contains the history of standard (not serverless) task executions, including SQL, execution times, and execution status.
WAREHOUSE_EVENTS_HISTORY	This view contains the history of warehouse events, including creation, deletion, suspension, and resumption of a warehouse and spinning up and down of warehouses in a multi-cluster virtual warehouse.
WAREHOUSE_LOAD_HISTORY	This view can be used to analyze the workload on a virtual warehouse for a specified date range. This view provides information on the number of queries executed, average queued queries, and more for each warehouse.
WAREHOUSE_METERING_HISTORY	This view contains hourly credit usage for every warehouse in an account. It shows the credits used and the cloud service usage for each warehouse.

Data in any view in the ACCOUNT_USAGE schema is not real time and is available with some latency. The latency may range from 45 minutes to 3 hours, depending on the view.

The INFORMATION_SCHEMA Schema

INFORMATION_SCHEMA is a special schema created automatically for every database created in Snowflake. It serves as a data dictionary, providing metadata information on the objects created in that database and views that provide information on account-level objects such as roles, databases, and warehouses. The schema provides several table functions that can be used to return account-level storage, compute usage, login history, and query history.

Some information provided by the INFORMATION_SCHEMA overlaps with the ACCOUNT_USAGE schema. However, there are some critical differences in data retention and recency between the two schemas. Table 10.2 captures the key differences.

TABLE 10.2 Differences between INFORMATION_SCHEMA and ACCOUNT_USAGE

Difference	ACCOUNT_USAGE	INFORMATION_SCHEMA
Data Latency	Latency varies from 45 minutes to 3 hours, depending on the view. The latency is a result of data being extracted and consolidated from the Snowflake internal metadata store.	No data latency. Information is available immediately.
Historical Data Retention	1 year.	Shorter retention period, ranging from 7 days to 6 months depending on the view.
Dropped Objects included	Yes—a DELETED column indicates if the information relates to a dropped object. It also includes an ID column to differentiate between objects with the same names, which may have been dropped and re-created.	No.

For more details on INFORMATION_SCHEMA and the kind of information that it can provide, visit the following URL:

`https://docs.snowflake.com/en/sql-reference/info-schema.html`

Exercise 10.3 demonstrates some of the views from the ACCOUNT_USAGE schema and a table function from the INFORMATION_SCHEMA, which can be used to view credit usage information for your account.

EXERCISE 10.3

Viewing Credit Usage

1. Let's look at the first method to see the credit usage using the ACCOUNT_USAGE schema in the Snowflake database. Since by default this database is accessible to ACCOUNTADMIN only, first switch to the ACCOUNTADMIN role and then run a query on the WAREHOUSE_METERING_HISTORY table to extract the credit usage:

```
USE ROLE ACCOUNTADMIN;

SELECT WAREHOUSE_NAME,
       SUM(CREDITS_USED) AS TOTAL_CREDIT_USED,
       SUM(CREDITS_USED_COMPUTE) AS TOTAL_WAREHOUSE_CREDIT_USED,
       SUM(CREDITS_USED_CLOUD_SERVICES) AS TOTAL_CREDITS_USED_CLOUD_SERVICES

FROM SNOWFLAKE.ACCOUNT_USAGE.WAREHOUSE_METERING_HISTORY
GROUP BY 1;
```

2. The results of the preceding query are captured in the following screenshot. You have results for two warehouses. The cloud services is not a user-managed virtual warehouse but is shown in this view for completeness. The other is the virtual warehouse called COMPUTE_WH (created by default in a new Snowflake trial instance). Also, note that it is possible to view the total credit usage at the virtual warehouse level as well as associated cloud services credit usage.

	WAREHOUSE_NAME	TOTAL_CREDIT_USED	TOTAL_WAREHOUSE_CREDIT_USED	...	TOTAL_CREDITS_USED_CLOUD_SERVICES
1	CLOUD_SERVICES_ONLY	0.000519444	0		0.000519444
2	COMPUTE_WH	9.268539722	9.238888891		0.029650831

3. You can also use the METERING_DAILY_HISTORY view to see daily credit usage for each service type using the following SQL. This view does not show the information at a virtual warehouse level but rather at the service type level. You can see more details regarding this view here:

   https://docs.snowflake.com/en/sql-reference/account-usage/metering_daily_history.html

```
USE ROLE ACCOUNTADMIN;

SELECT USAGE_DATE,
       SERVICE_TYPE,
       SUM(CREDITS_USED_COMPUTE) AS CREDITS_USED_COMPUTE,
       SUM(CREDITS_USED_CLOUD_SERVICES) AS CREDITS_USED_CLOUD_SERVICES,
       SUM(CREDITS_USED) AS TOTAL_CREDITS_USED,
```

```
        SUM(CREDITS_ADJUSTMENT_CLOUD_SERVICES)
        AS CREDITS_ADJUSTMENT_CLOUD_SERVICES,
        SUM(CREDITS_BILLED) AS CREDITS_BILLED

FROM SNOWFLAKE.ACCOUNT_USAGE.METERING_DAILY_HISTORY
GROUP BY 1,2
ORDER BY USAGE_DATE DESC;
```

4. The results of step 3 are shown in the following screenshot. Notice that the only service type showing is WAREHOUSE_METERING, indicating virtual warehouse usage. This view returns usage information for other services such as auto clustering, materialized view, and other compute-consuming services in real-world scenarios.

	USAGE_DATE	SERVICE_TYPE	CREDITS_USED_COMPUTE	CREDITS_USED_CLOUD_SERVICES	TOTAL_CREDITS_USED	CREDITS_ADJUSTMENT_CLOUD_SERVICES	CREDITS_BILLE
1	2022-03-13	WAREHOUSE_METERING	0.183055556	0.000870833	0.183926389	-0.000870833	0.183055556
2	2022-03-12	WAREHOUSE_METERING	0.102777777	0.000109167	0.102886944	-0.000109167	0.102777777
3	2022-03-11	WAREHOUSE_METERING	0	0.000065556	0.000065556	0	0.000065556
4	2022-03-10	WAREHOUSE_METERING	0	0.000055556	0.000055556	0	0.000055556
5	2022-03-07	WAREHOUSE_METERING	0.100555556	0.000558333	0.101113889	-0.000558333	0.100555556
6	2022-03-02	WAREHOUSE_METERING	0.147222222	0.001070556	0.148292778	-0.001070556	0.147222222
7	2022-03-01	WAREHOUSE_METERING	0.470833333	0.002389722	0.473223055	-0.002389722	0.470833333
8	2022-02-24	WAREHOUSE_METERING	0.100833334	0.000345278	0.101178612	-0.000345278	0.100833334
9	2022-02-09	WAREHOUSE_METERING	0.056666667	0.001569722	0.058236389	-0.001569722	0.056666667
10	2022-02-08	WAREHOUSE_METERING	0.016666667	0.000416111	0.017082778	-0.000416111	0.016666667
11	2022-01-05	WAREHOUSE_METERING	0	0.000014444	0.000014444	0	0.000014444
12	2021-12-22	WAREHOUSE_METERING	0.060833333	0.000265278	0.061098611	-0.000265278	0.060833333
13	2021-12-21	WAREHOUSE_METERING	0.058055556	0	0.058055556	0	0.058055556

5. So far, we have used the ACCOUNT_USAGE schema to view historical credit usage information. It is also possible to see the credit usage through the INFORMATION_SCHEMA, which provides real-time information, although with less history. To do so, use the WAREHOUSE_METERING_HISTORY table function in INFORMATION_SCHEMA. Since this schema is available in every database, you can use any database. Replace the *<database_name>* placeholder with an actual database name.

```
USE ROLE ACCOUNTADMIN;

USE DATABASE <database_name>;

SELECT *
FROM TABLE(INFORMATION_SCHEMA.WAREHOUSE_METERING_HISTORY(DATEADD('DAYS',-10,
CURRENT_DATE())));
```

6. The results of the query are shown in the following screenshot. Notice that the credit usage is shown hour by hour. Also, you can see another virtual warehouse called MNT_WH. We created this virtual warehouse before executing this exercise. You can see that the historical account usage view did not show this virtual warehouse due to ACCOUNT_USAGE data latency; however, it is shown through the INFORMATION_SCHEMA views.

EXERCISE 10.3 *(continued)*

	START_TIME	END_TIME	WAREHOUSE_NAME	CREDITS_USED	CREDITS_USED_COMPUTE	CREDITS_USED_CLOUD_SERVICES
1	2022-03-12 17:00:00.000 -0800	2022-03-12 18:00:00.000 -0800	MNT_WH	0.019166667	0.019166667	0
2	2022-03-02 03:00:00.000 -0800	2022-03-02 04:00:00.000 -0800	COMPUTE_WH	0.148292778	0.147222222	0.001070556
3	2022-03-07 00:00:00.000 -0800	2022-03-07 01:00:00.000 -0800	COMPUTE_WH	0.101113889	0.100555556	0.000558333
4	2022-03-10 13:00:00.000 -0800	2022-03-10 14:00:00.000 -0800	COMPUTE_WH	0.000055556	0	0.000055556
5	2022-03-11 14:00:00.000 -0800	2022-03-11 15:00:00.000 -0800	COMPUTE_WH	0.000065556	0	0.000065556
6	2022-03-11 18:00:00.000 -0800	2022-03-11 19:00:00.000 -0800	COMPUTE_WH	0.050884444	0.050833333	0.000051111
7	2022-03-11 19:00:00.000 -0800	2022-03-11 20:00:00.000 -0800	COMPUTE_WH	0.000058056	0	0.000058056
8	2022-03-11 21:00:00.000 -0800	2022-03-11 22:00:00.000 -0800	COMPUTE_WH	0.051944444	0.051944444	0
9	2022-03-12 16:00:00.000 -0800	2022-03-12 17:00:00.000 -0800	COMPUTE_WH	0.027135	0.026666667	0.000468333
10	2022-03-12 17:00:00.000 -0800	2022-03-12 18:00:00.000 -0800	COMPUTE_WH	0.087349166	0.067222222	0.000126944

Exercise 10.4 demonstrates how to view storage used by databases and tables in your account.

EXERCISE 10.4

Viewing Storage Usage

1. To view the storage used by databases, you can use the DATABASE_STORAGE_USAGE_HISTORY view in the ACCOUNT_USAGE schema. This view provides daily storage usage for every database in the system.

```
USE ROLE ACCOUNTADMIN;

SELECT  USAGE_DATE,
        DATABASE_ID,
        DATABASE_NAME,
        DELETED,
        AVERAGE_DATABASE_BYTES /1024 / 1024 AS AVERAGE_DATABASE_MB,
        AVERAGE_FAILSAFE_BYTES / 1024 / 1024 AS AVERAGE_FAILSAFE_MB

FROM SNOWFLAKE.ACCOUNT_USAGE.DATABASE_STORAGE_USAGE_HISTORY
WHERE DATABASE_NAME = 'DEMO_DATA_LOADING'
ORDER BY USAGE_DATE DESC;
```

The query returns the following results for each day:

	USAGE_DATE	DATABASE_ID	DATABASE_NAME	DELETED	AVERAGE_DATABASE_MB	AVERAGE_FAILSAFE_MB
1	2022-03-12	31	DEMO_DATA_LOADING	null	0.0078125	0
2	2022-03-11	31	DEMO_DATA_LOADING	null	0.0078125	0
3	2022-03-10	31	DEMO_DATA_LOADING	null	0.0078125	0
4	2022-03-09	31	DEMO_DATA_LOADING	null	0.0078125	0
5	2022-03-08	31	DEMO_DATA_LOADING	null	0.0078125	0

2. To view the tables' storage, you can use the TABLE_STORAGE_METRICS view in the ACCOUNT_USAGE schema, which provides storage usage at a table level.

```
USE ROLE ACCOUNTADMIN;

SELECT TABLE_CATALOG AS DATABASE_NAME,
       TABLE_SCHEMA,
       TABLE_NAME,
       ACTIVE_BYTES / 1024 / 1024 AS ACTIVE_BYTES_MB,
       TIME_TRAVEL_BYTES / 1024 / 1024 AS TIME_TRAVEL_BYTES_MB,
       FAILSAFE_BYTES / 1024 / 1024 AS FAILSAFE_BYTES_MB

FROM   SNOWFLAKE.ACCOUNT_USAGE.TABLE_STORAGE_METRICS
WHERE TABLE_CATALOG = 'DEMO_DATA_LOADING';
```

The query returns the results shown in the following screenshot. Note that the results contain storage used by the tables and the Fail-safe and Time Travel storage usage.

	DATABASE_NAME	TABLE_SCHEMA	TABLE_NAME	ACTIVE_BYTES_MB	TIME_TRAVEL_BYTES_MB	FAILSAFE_BYTES_MB
1	DEMO_DATA_LOADING	PUBLIC	VEHICLE	0.0078125	0	0

3. The TABLE_STORAGE_METRICS view is also available in INFORMATION_SCHEMA, providing information similar to that from the preceding step. However, this view provides real-time information compared to the ACCOUNT_USAGE view, which has 45 minutes to 3 hours of data latency. Since this schema is available in every database, you can use any database. Replace the *<database_name>* placeholder with an actual database name.

```
USE ROLE ACCOUNTADMIN;

USE DATABASE <database_name>;

SELECT TABLE_CATALOG AS DATABASE_NAME,
       TABLE_SCHEMA,
       TABLE_NAME,
       ACTIVE_BYTES / 1024 / 1024 AS ACTIVE_BYTES_MB,
       TIME_TRAVEL_BYTES / 1024 / 1024 AS TIME_TRAVEL_BYTES_MB,
       FAILSAFE_BYTES / 1024 / 1024 AS FAILSAFE_BYTES_MB

FROM   INFORMATION_SCHEMA.TABLE_STORAGE_METRICS
WHERE TABLE_CATALOG IN ('DEMO_DATA_LOADING','TEST_CLONING');
```

Snowflake Releases

Snowflake deploys new software releases every week. The updates occur transparently behind the scenes, thus avoiding downtime and disruptions. The automatic releases deploy bug fixes, enhancements, and new features, ensuring that the customer is always running on the latest release of the software.

Snowflake deploys two planned or scheduled releases every week. The releases may be categorized as follows:

- Patch releases contain only fixes to an issue.
- Full releases may have new features, feature enhancements, or fixes.

Snowflake also deploys a behavior change release once per month, which contains changes to existing behaviors and may impact existing customers. The behavior change release happens over two months. The behavior change is not enabled during the first month unless the customer opts in. It is automatically enabled in the second month, but a customer can opt out.

Phased Release Process for Full Releases

Snowflake does not deploy a full release to all Snowflake accounts simultaneously; instead, existing customer accounts are updated to the new release in a phased manner.

- **Day 1 (early access):** Deployed for those Enterprise edition (or higher) accounts who have opted for early access
- **Day 1 or 2 (regular access):** Deployed for all Snowflake accounts using the Standard edition
- **Day 2 (final):** Deployed for remaining Enterprise edition (or higher) accounts

The minimum time between an early access deployment and a final deployment is 24 hours. This phased manner of deployment ensures that Snowflake can detect and react to any software issues found during early access.

You can designate an Enterprise edition (or higher) account for early access to full releases by contacting Snowflake support.

Summary

This chapter described resource monitors and how they can control credit usage at a virtual warehouse and an account level. The chapter also covered views and table functions in ACCOUNT_USAGE and INFORMATION_SCHEMA schemas, demonstrating how to view storage and credit usage. Finally, the chapter described the Snowflake release processes and how accounts can opt in for early access.

Exam Essentials

Be able to describe resource monitors. Resource monitors can track a single virtual warehouse, a group of virtual warehouses, or an entire Snowflake account. Resource monitors can notify and optionally suspend virtual warehouses based on credit quota utilization percentage. Only user-managed virtual warehouses can be suspended by resource monitors. Serverless capabilities such as Snowpipe, Automatic Reclustering, Materialized View, and cloud services charges cannot be managed by a resource monitor.

Be familiar with the ACCOUNT_USAGE and INFORMATION_SCHEMA schemas. Snowflake is a shared database that provides usage information. It is a read-only, system-defined common database automatically imported into all Snowflake accounts containing several schemas. The ACCOUNT_USAGE schema exposes account-level use metrics and metadata through views that provide historical usage information.

A special schema, INFORMATION_SCHEMA, which is available in every database, acts as a data dictionary, providing metadata for database objects and views for account-level items like roles, databases, and warehouses. For example, account-level storage, compute consumption, login history, and query history are some of the table functions in INFORMATION_SCHEMA.

The INFORMATION SCHEMA data overlaps with the ACCOUNT_USAGE schema but with some key differences. For example, the data latency in ACCOUNT_USAGE varies from 45 minutes to 3 hours, depending on the view, whereas data in the INFORMATION_SCHEMA is real time. Similarly, the ACCOUNT_USAGE schema has 365 days of data retention, whereas INFORMATION_SCHEMA has data retention ranging from 7 days to 6 months. INFORMATION_SCHEMA does not contain information on deleted objects, whereas the ACCOUNT_USAGE schema shows the deleted objects.

Understand the Snowflake release process. Every week, Snowflake releases new updates. The updates are transparent and cause no downtime or interruptions. Snowflake does not roll out a full release to all accounts at once; instead, accounts are updated gradually. For accounts opted in to early access, the changes are deployed on day 1. Enterprise and above editions not opted in to early access get the changes on day 2. Standard edition Snowflake accounts may get the updates on day 1 or 2.

Review Questions

1. When configuring a resource monitor, which of the following are actions that can be configured? (Choose all that apply.)

   A. Notify

   B. Suspend and Notify

   C. Suspend Immediately and Notify

   D. Stop

2. Which of the following statements are true regarding resource monitors? (Choose all that apply.)

   A. Resource monitors cannot be deleted once they have been created.

   B. If a resource monitor monitors a virtual warehouse, another resource monitor cannot monitor the same virtual warehouse.

   C. Resource monitors can be configured to track multiple virtual warehouses.

   D. A resource monitor can be created at an account level, which means that the monitor tracks the credit usage at the whole account level, including all virtual warehouses' credit usage.

   E. Only account administrators can create new resource monitors.

3. True or False: Resource monitors can be used to control credit usage for serverless services such as cloud services, Snowpipe, or Auto Clustering.

   A. True

   B. False

4. Which of the following privileges must be granted to other roles by the account administrator for other roles to see and modify resource monitors? (Choose all that apply.)

   A. READ

   B. MODIFY

   C. MONITOR

   D. WRITE

5. Which of the following are valid methods through which account administrators can receive notifications generated by resource monitors? (Choose all that apply.)

   A. SQS notification

   B. Snowflake web interface

   C. Email

   D. SMS notification

6. Which of the following can you use to view the last 365 days of the history of warehouse credit usage?
   A. The WAREHOUSE_METERING_HISTORY view in the ACCOUNT_USAGE schema
   B. The TABLE_STORAGE_METRICS view in the ACCOUNT_USAGE schema
   C. The WAREHOUSE_METERING_HISTORY table function in the INFORMATION_SCHEMA schema
   D. The TABLE_STORAGE_METRICS view in the INFORMATION_SCHEMA schema

7. Which of the following statements are true regarding the ACCOUNT_USAGE schema? (Choose all that apply.)
   A. ACCOUNT_USAGE views can only have 7 days of history.
   B. The data in ACCOUNT_USAGE views is real time.
   C. The data in ACCOUNT_USAGE views can have a latency of 45 minutes up to 3 hours.
   D. ACCOUNT_USAGE views can have 365 days of history.

8. Which of the following statements are true regarding the INFORMATION_SCHEMA schema? (Choose all that apply.)
   A. Data in INFORMATION_SCHMEA has a latency of 3 hours.
   B. Every database in Snowflake has an INFORMATION_SCHEMA schema.
   C. Data in INFORMATION_SCHEMA is real time.
   D. History retention of data in INFORMATION_SCHEMA varies from 7 days to 6 months.
   E. INFORMATION_SCHEMA is a special schema found only under the Snowflake database.

9. True or False: INFORMATION_SCHEMA provides several table functions that can be used to return account-level storage, compute usage, login history, and query history.
   A. True
   B. False

10. You want to write a SQL query that shows successful and failed login attempts made in the last 10 minutes. Which of the following should you use?
    A. ACCOUNT_USAGE.LOGIN_HISTORY view.
    B. ACCOUNT_USAGE.ACCESS_HISTORY view.
    C. The table function LOGIN_HISTORY in INFORMATION_SCHEMA.
    D. It is not possible to view login attempts.

11. Snowflake releases new features or bug fixes at what frequency?
    A. Daily
    B. Weekly
    C. Monthly
    D. Yearly

12. When Snowflake releases new features or bug fixes, which accounts get the new software ahead of all other accounts?

    A. Standard edition accounts

    B. All Enterprise edition and above accounts

    C. Business-critical accounts

    D. Enterprise edition accounts that have opted for early access

Appendix

Answers to the Review Questions

Chapter 1: Introduction and Overview

1. A, B, E. Snowflake provides four editions. Each edition builds on the features and capabilities of the previous edition. The four editions are:
   - Standard
   - Enterprise
   - Business Critical
   - Virtual Private Snowflake (VPS)
2. B. The Enterprise edition provides all the capabilities of the Standard edition but adds 90 days of Time Travel, multi-cluster virtual warehouses, materialized views, dynamic data masking, and external data tokenization.
3. B. The Standard edition of Snowflake provides only one day of Time Travel capability. Starting with the Enterprise edition, 90 days of Time Travel is available.
4. B. The Enterprise edition provides all the capabilities of the Standard edition but adds dynamic data masking, 90 days of Time Travel, multi-cluster virtual warehouses, materialized views, and external data tokenization.
5. A. Data sharing capabilities are available starting with the Standard edition.
6. A, C, D. Snowflake is supported on three public cloud platforms:
   - Amazon Web Services
   - Microsoft Azure
   - Google Cloud Platform
7. A. Data replication is available in the Standard edition.
8. B. Search optimization is available starting with the Enterprise edition.

Chapter 2: Snowflake Architecture

1. C. Snowflake uses a hybrid architecture approach in which the data is stored on a shared-data storage layer but multiple compute clusters can simultaneously perform processing on that data. The architecture is often referred to as multi-cluster, shared-data architecture. Another important aspect of this architecture is that the data is independent of the compute.
2. B. The cloud object storage is virtually unlimited—you can keep adding data to it, and it is guaranteed that there will always be disk space available to write. Since Snowflake uses cloud object storage to store data, the capacity of a Snowflake solution is virtually unlimited. There is no limitation on the amount of data you can store in a Snowflake-based solution, and there is no on-premises version of Snowflake, as it is a cloud-only solution.

3. A, C, D. Virtual warehouses refer to compute clusters in Snowflake and are used to process queries and load data into Snowflake. One or many virtual warehouses can be created and started at the same time. When not required, they can be suspended to save costs, and they can be resumed if there are queries or load jobs to be processed. They can be deleted altogether if needed. A virtual warehouse can also be resized to a smaller or larger size, regardless of whether they are running or suspended. It is worth noting that any queries already running on a virtual warehouse are not impacted by the change in size while the virtual warehouse is being resized.

4. B. When a virtual warehouse is resumed, a minimum of one minute's worth of Snowflake credits is consumed, even if the virtual warehouse is suspended before the one minute in the resumed state is reached. Once the first minute is passed, the virtual warehouse reverts to per-second billing; for example, if a virtual warehouse were suspended after 1 minute, 45 seconds, 1 minute, 45 seconds' worth of Snowflake credits would be charged. But if it was suspended after 35 seconds, a minimum of one minute would apply.

5. C. The architecture for Snowflake is often referred to as multi-cluster, shared-data architecture. This term refers to Snowflake's capability to create many virtual warehouses of the desired configuration providing massively parallel processing capability to Snowflake while still accessing a single shared data.

6. A. Snowflake credit usage is directly proportional to the size of the virtual warehouse. The larger the virtual warehouse size, the higher the number of nodes in the virtual warehouse. Therefore, a larger virtual warehouse costs more in terms of Snowflake credits used.

7. A. The number of micro-partitions in a table increases as the size of a table increases. For a very large table, the number of micro-partitions can run into millions or hundreds of millions.

8. B. Virtual warehouses, which are the compute clusters in Snowflake, do not share any memory or CPU resources. Each virtual warehouse has its dedicated memory and CPU resources that are not shared with any other virtual warehouse.

9. A, B, C. Snowflake stores the following for each micro-partition in its metadata:

    - Range of values, including Max, Min, and Count
    - Number of distinct values
    - Other optimization metadata

10. A. The columns are compressed in a micro-partition, and Snowflake determines the compression method automatically depending on the column's characteristics.

11. C. The compute clusters in Snowflake are referred to as virtual warehouses. The virtual warehouses are entirely independent of the storage. You can have as many or as few of them running simultaneously; however, each virtual warehouse accesses the same shared data.

12. A. A virtual warehouse may be suspended when it is not being used to save costs and resumed when required. A suspended virtual warehouse does not consume any credits and therefore does not cost the customer.

13. A. When a virtual warehouse is provisioned or resumed, a minimum of one minute's worth of Snowflake credit is immediately consumed, even if the virtual warehouse is suspended before the one minute is reached. Once the first minute is passed, the virtual warehouse reverts to per-second billing.

14. B. When a virtual warehouse is scaled down, nodes are removed from the virtual warehouse only when they are no longer running a query.

15. A. A virtual warehouse can be resized at any time, whether it is in a suspended state or running queries. When a virtual warehouse is resized while in a suspended state, there are no nodes to decommission or provision; therefore, the updated size takes effect only when the virtual warehouse is resumed. Snowflake adds or removes new nodes per the new size when a running virtual warehouse is resized. The removal of nodes takes place when all active queries on those nodes have finished.

16. A. When a request is made for a virtual warehouse to suspend, it does not enter a suspended state until all active queries using that virtual warehouse have been completed.

17. C. The correct answer is 50 MB to 500 MB of uncompressed data per micro-partition.

18. A. Like the underlying cloud storage, Snowflake partitions are immutable—they cannot be changed once created. Therefore, any updates to existing data or loading new data into a table results in new micro-partitions.

19. B. Snowflake automatically clusters the data as it is inserted into a table. Snowflake automatically clusters the data even if a specific clustering key is not defined.

20. A, B, D. Snowflake architecture has three distinct layers:

    - Database storage—Inexpensive cloud storage on AWS, Azure, or Google Cloud
    - Query processing—Primarily composed of virtual warehouses
    - Cloud services—The brain of the whole system

21. B. Within each micro-partition, Snowflake stores each column in a columnar storage format. Each column in a micro-partition is compressed individually. Snowflake determines the best and most efficient compression algorithm for each column in each partition. Storing data in a columnar format enables Snowflake to optimize the queries by retrieving only the referenced columns.

22. B. Multi-cluster virtual warehouse capability is available starting with the Enterprise edition of Snowflake, but the Standard edition does not have this capability.

Chapter 3: Interfaces and Connectivity

1. A, B. Snowflake provides a variety of connectors and drivers. Only the Go driver and the JDBC driver are valid examples of programs downloaded through the Snowflake web UI in the given list. There is no connector for Snowpipe and no drivers for OAuth or Kerberos.

2. A, D, E. Each worksheet has its own context under which the query in that worksheet executes. These include the Role, the Virtual Warehouse, the Database, and the Schema. Each worksheet can have a different context.

3. C. The top navigation bar has a button called Warehouses, which a user with the correct privileges can use to create and manage compute clusters, also known as virtual warehouses. Warehouses can also be resumed and suspended from this page.

4. B. You can open several worksheets in the Snowflake web UI simultaneously. Each worksheet has its own context under which the query in that worksheet executes. These include the Role, the Virtual Warehouse, the Database, and the Schema. Each worksheet can have a different context.

5. A, B, C. Worksheets, Warehouses, and Databases are examples of buttons on the top navigation bar. Here is the complete list of buttons available on the top navigation bar:

   - Databases
   - Shares
   - Data Marketplace
   - Worksheets
   - History
   - Account
   - Snowsight
   - Partner Connect
   - Help
   - Notifications

6. B. The Account page is one of the essential administrative pages in the classic Snowflake web interface. Depending on the role selected on the top-right side of the screen, a user may or may not see the Account page in the navigation bar. By default, the Account page is visible only to the built-in ACCOUNTADMIN and SECURITYADMIN roles.

7. B, C. On this page, users with the correct privileges can create and manage virtual warehouses. Warehouses can also be resumed and suspended from this page. Virtual warehouses are computing clusters in Snowflake and can be created, dropped, suspended, and resumed as needed.

8. A. A logged-in user can access user preferences at the top-right corner of the navigation bar. Through the preferences, users can set up multifactor authentication (MFA).

9. B. Snowflake provides a variety of connectors and drivers for various languages and frameworks. For Java-based programs, it would be appropriate to use the JDBC driver.

10. B, C. ODBC and JDBC are the prevalent methods of connecting tools to databases. Snowflake provides drivers for both JDBC- and ODBC-based connectivity. Depending on what your business intelligence tool supports, you can use the ODBC or JDBC drivers to connect to Snowflake.

11. A. Matillion is a data integration partner. To see a list of all Snowflake partners and their categorization, visit

    `https://docs.snowflake.com/en/user-guide/ecosystem-all.html`

12. B. An external UDF can access third-party API services outside of Snowflake. An external function does not contain code but calls code stored and executed outside Snowflake.

13. A. Snowflake Scripting is an extension to SQL, which allows procedural logic typically found in programming languages. Snowflake Scripting supports variables, if-else constructs, looping mechanisms, cursors, result set management, and exception handling.

Chapter 4: Loading Data

1. B. Snowflake provides an alternative approach called external tables to query data in external cloud storage. External tables can be queried like regular tables. They can be connected to other tables and have views developed on them.

2. A. Snowflake supports the loading of continuous data through a serverless service called Snowpipe. Snowpipe allows you to load data in micro-batches. It is typically utilized when a steady stream of small data must be loaded, such as transactions or events.

3. A, B, D. External tables can be queried the same way a standard table is queried. They can be joined to other tables, and views can be created on an external table. External tables are read-only since they point to an external storage location; therefore, DML or update operations cannot be performed on an external table.

4. B, C. Snowpipe is serverless and is managed, scaled up, and scaled down automatically without requiring any intervention from the user. Costs for Snowpipe are charged separately from virtual warehouse costs.

5. A, C. Snowpipe does not rely on virtual warehouses for processing because it is serverless and has its own compute power. Snowflake takes care of the Snowpipe's computational capacity and scaling up and down automatically. A Snowpipe's cost is billed separately from the costs of a virtual warehouse.

6. A, B, D. The `COPY` command requires a virtual warehouse to execute. Snowpipe is serverless and has its own compute capacity, which means that Snowpipe doesn't depend on virtual warehouses for processing.

7. A, B. Stages help load and unload data in Snowflake. To process data into a Snowflake table, it must first be available in a Snowflake stage. Once the data is staged, it may be copied into a table using the `COPY` command. Broadly, the two types of stages in Snowflake are external stages and internal stages.

8. A, B, D, E. Snowflake provides built-in support for handling a variety of semi-structured data formats, among them JSON, Avro, ORC, Parquet, and XML.

9. D, E. Snowflake supports the following file formats for unloading data:

    - Delimited text files—CSV, TSV

- JSON—NDJSON only
- Parquet

The following file formats cannot be used to export data but can be used to load data:

- Avro
- ORC
- XML

10. B. The `VARIANT` data type can store any data type and can store up to 16 MB of uncompressed data for each row.
11. A. The load metadata includes information such as the name of each file loaded into that table and the time stamp for the file's most recent load. Snowflake uses this load metadata to ensure that it does not reprocess a file that has already been loaded. After 64 days, the load metadata expires.
12. A, B. Data from tables and views can be extracted to Snowflake's internal and external stages through the `COPY` command. The `GET` command can be used to download data from an internal stage to your PC. Data extracted to external stages is often accessible via cloud storage access techniques, such as directly accessing the S3 bucket that the external stage referenced.
13. A, B, C, D. Data from tables and views can be extracted to Snowflake's internal and external stages through the `COPY` command. Once the data is in an internal stage, it can be downloaded to your computer using the `GET` command. Data must be uploaded to internal stages through the `PUT` command using SnowSQL. `REMOVE` can be used to delete files from Snowflake's internal stages and external stages. The `GET` and `PUT` commands cannot be run from the Worksheets view but are generally run from a client utility such as SnowSQL.
14. A, B, C. The `COPY` command doesn't support joins, filtering, or aggregations. Snowflake allows you to apply basic transformations to data while loading it into a table. The `COPY` command supports changing the order of columns, omitting one or more columns altogether, and casting data into specific data types during the ingestion process. The `COPY` command also supports truncating data that exceeds the target column width.
15. A, B. Snowpipe can load data from external or internal stages. You must trigger a Snowpipe through the REST API when using internal stages with Snowpipe.
16. B. All data files loaded to a Snowflake internal stage are encrypted automatically using 256-bit encryption. They are encrypted by the client program, like SnowSQL, before being uploaded to a Snowflake stage.
17. A. For optimal loading performance through the `COPY` command, it is recommended to have the file size approximately 100–250 MB after compression. This applies both to regular loads and for data loaded through Snowpipe.
18. A, C. Snowflake unloads data to multiple files, where the maximum size of each file is 16 MB by default. The maximum size can be changed using the MAX_FILE_SIZE parameter, allowing up to 5 GB per file. The default behavior of unloading data to multiple files can be changed by setting the SINGLE parameter to true, resulting in data exported to a single file.

Chapter 5: Data Pipelines

1. C. The history of user-managed tasks' execution can be found by using the `task_history()` table function. This function returns the last 7 days of the history of executed task and the scheduled executions within the next 8 days.

2. B. Only roles with the `EXECUTE TASK` privilege can resume a task.

3. B, C. Snowflake tasks can be scheduled using CRON expressions or a more straightforward approach by providing the number of minutes after which the task will execute.

4. A. Newly created tasks are created in a suspended state and must be set to resume for them to start executing according to the defined schedule. Only roles with the `EXECUTE TASK` privilege can resume a task.

5. A, B, D. Numerous Snowflake tasks can be linked together in a tree-like structure with a single root node and multiple child nodes. The task tree starts with a root node and has one or more child tasks. There can only be one parent task per task; however, one parent task can have several child tasks. All tasks in a tree of tasks must have the same task owner—that is, the `OWNER` privilege on all tasks in the tree must be held by the same role.

6. A, B, C. The serverless tasks let you leverage Snowflake-managed compute resources for task execution. Snowflake may scale the computational resources up or down as needed, depending on the workload demands of each task. To offset the administration costs of serverless operations, Snowflake applies a 1.5 multiplier to the Snowflake credit computation.

7. B. Snowflake's streams feature helps you keep track of data modifications to a table. Any data changes made to a table, including inserts, updates, and deletes, can be tracked using a stream. Change data capture (CDC) is a method that allows users and processes to determine what has changed in a table since the last time they consumed it.

8. A, B, C. A stream can track any data changes made to a table's data, including inserts, updates, and deletes.

9. A, C, D. Streams can be queried in the same way that tables are, allowing users to read and process data from a stream in the same way they can read and process data from a table. Think of streams as bookmarks that encapsulate changes and advances to point to future changes as they occur after you have consumed the most recent updates.

Chapter 6: Continuous Data Protection

1. A, B, C, D. All Snowflake editions provide Time Travel capability. The Standard edition provides only one day of Time Travel, and from the Enterprise edition upward, 90 days of Time Travel is provided.

2. A. Enterprise is the minimum Snowflake edition that provides 90 days of Time Travel.

3. A. True. Snowflake charges for data storage for Time Travel and Fail-safe storage purposes. Costs for storage are incurred because historical micro-partitions are kept to enable Time Travel and Fail-safe functioning.

4. C. The Standard edition provides only one day of Time Travel.

5. C. Temporary tables are limited to one day of Time Travel and do not include a Fail-safe period.

6. B, C. For those who want to avoid the costs associated with Time Travel and Fail-safe storage, Snowflake supports two table types: temporary tables and transient tables. Both table types do not support Fail-safe storage. Additionally, temporary and transient tables allow only one day of Time Travel, which helps to keep costs down.

7. B. Only Snowflake support can recover data that is in Fail-safe mode. For example, Snowflake support can leverage the Fail-safe storage to restore data in severe cases when data has been lost or destroyed due to unanticipated failures.

8. C. Transient tables are limited to one day of Time Travel and do not include a Fail-safe period.

9. B. Enterprise edition allows 90 days of Time Travel for permanent tables. Business Critical and Virtual Private Snowflake also allow 90 days of Time Travel. The Standard edition only has up to one day of Time Travel for permanent tables.

10. B. Fail-safe cannot be turned off for an account, a database, or a table. Instead, it is an ever-present Snowflake feature. Transient and temporary tables are the only types of tables in Snowflake that do not have Fail-safe protection by default.

11. A. Fail-safe storage can only be accessed by Snowflake support. Unlike with data in Time Travel, a Snowflake customer cannot access data in Fail-safe storage.

12. A, B, C. Databases, schemas, and tables can be undropped. When databases or schemas are undropped, their child objects, such as views and tables, are also undropped.

Chapter 7: Cloning and Data Sharing

1. B, C, D. Snowflake's cloning capability allows users to duplicate a table, schema, or database without physically transferring the data. Cloning doesn't require extra storage because data isn't copied. Because cloning does not duplicate data physically, the operation is substantially faster as compared to physically copying data.

2. A. No micro-partitions are copied during zero-copy cloning; the cloned table is pointed to the existing micro-partitions via metadata. The cloned table shares the source table's micro-partitions. This is a metadata-only operation; thus, no data movement or additional storage is required.

3. A, B, C. All of these are examples of objects that can be cloned. Zero-copy cloning can be performed for a table or even at a schema or a database level. When a complete database is cloned, child objects in that database (including children schema) are made available in the clone. When a schema is cloned, its child objects are cloned and made available in the cloned schema. Certain objects cannot be cloned, such as external tables.

4. B. Zero-copy clones of a table point to the same micro-partitions as the source table. However, after a table is cloned, the two tables exist independently—updates, inserts, and deletes can be performed to either table, and they do not impact each other.

5. B, D. When you clone a database, all of its child schemas and the objects contained within those schemas are also cloned. When a database or schema is cloned, only the privileges on the child objects are copied. However, a cloned object does not inherit any of the privileges from the source object.

6. A, C. Cloning internal named stages is not possible. Snowpipes that reference an internal named stage are not cloned when a database or schema is cloned.

7. A, C, D. Snowflake's data sharing offerings include Direct Sharing, Snowflake Data Marketplace, and Data Exchange.

8. B. After a share has been granted to a consumer and the consumer has created a read-only database on the share, all new objects added to the share by the provider automatically become accessible to the consumer.

9. B. The consumer account is responsible for paying for the compute resources used to conduct queries on the data shared with them. The only exception is reader accounts, which are created by a data provider and billed to the provider.

10. A. The provider account is responsible for the compute cost on reader accounts. Data providers create and own reader accounts, and therefore, the management and costs associated with reader accounts are billed to the creating/provider account.

11. A. It is possible to add multiple consumer accounts to a single share, simultaneously sharing the data with several consumers. There is no limitation regarding the Snowflake edition or the cloud provider.

12. A, D. A share can be created only by the ACCOUNTADMIN role or roles that have been explicitly granted the `CREATE SHARE` privilege.

13. A, D. As a consumer account, a read-only database on the share can be created only by the ACCOUNTADMIN role or roles that have been explicitly granted the `IMPORT SHARE` privilege.

14. A, B, C, D. All of this is true. Data Exchange is a private data sharing hub where you can share data with a small number of people. The Data Exchange owner invites members and specifies whether they can share, consume, or do both. Data sharing allows businesses to share data with trustworthy partners, providers, and customers.

15. A, B, D. Snowflake Data Marketplace is a marketplace for discovering and gaining access to third-party datasets made available by diverse organizations. These third-party datasets are frequently supplied for a fee but can be offered free. Snowflake accounts can also publish and monetize datasets on the Marketplace.

Chapter 8: Performance

1. A, C, D. When a virtual warehouse is scaled up, billing for the larger virtual warehouse does not begin until all the additional nodes in the larger virtual warehouse have been provisioned. Only new queries benefit from the increased size; existing queries in the virtual warehouse are unaffected. A virtual warehouse can be scaled up at any time whether or not queries are running on that virtual warehouse.

2. A, B, C. All of these are true when a virtual warehouse is scaled down. Nodes are removed from the compute cluster when a virtual warehouse is scaled down. Nodes are removed only when there are no active queries on the virtual warehouse.

3. C. A virtual warehouse may be scaled up or down based on the complexity of the queries and the required performance. In general, increasing the size of the virtual warehouse improves query speed for particular CPU-intensive queries. However, scaling up does not help with a large number of users or a large number of queries. A multi-cluster virtual warehouse (scaling out) is used to cater to an increased number of users and queries.

4. A, C. A single virtual warehouse may handle up to eight concurrent requests by default. When the concurrent workload for a specific virtual warehouse exceeds the limit, additional queries are queued. This issue is solved by multi-cluster virtual warehouses, which add new clusters dynamically based on demand. This is also known as scaling out or autoscaling.

5. B. A minimum of Snowflake Enterprise edition is required to use the multi-cluster virtual warehouse capabilities.

6. A. The Standard scaling policy minimizes queuing by starting additional warehouses as soon as it detects query queuing. The Economy scaling policy allows queuing to occur for some time before scaling out, saving costs over performance.

7. B. Set the cluster's minimum and maximum warehouse count to different values to allow autoscaling. Snowflake thus starts and stops warehouses dependent on the workload. Set the cluster's minimum and maximum warehouse counts to the same value to enable maximized mode. So all warehouses in the cluster are started when the multi-cluster virtual warehouse starts.

8. A, B, C. When a multi-cluster virtual warehouse using autoscaling mode is started, the number of active virtual warehouses is equal to the minimum warehouse count. Snowflake spins up additional warehouses based on the demand, up to the maximum warehouse count. As the demand reduces, Snowflake shuts down virtual warehouses until the number is equal

to the minimum warehouse count. Multi-cluster virtual warehouses support the standard virtual warehouse properties and actions, including specifying and changing warehouse size, suspending or automatically suspending, resuming, or automatically resuming a suspended multi-cluster virtual warehouse.

9. A, B, C, D, E. All of these are true. If the following conditions are met, Snowflake uses the query result cache: A new query matches an old query, and the underlying data contributing to the query results has not changed. Due to clustering or consolidation, the table micro-partitions have not changed. The query does not use user-defined or external functions or runtime functions. However, queries using the `CURRENT_DATE` function are eligible for query result caching.

10. A, B, D, E. The query result cache is valid for 24 hours. During those 24 hours, if a new query matching the previous query is run, the results are returned from the query result cache. The query result cache is stored in the cloud services layer and can be used to return query results for any user. A query's result cache is initially valid for 24 hours, but it is valid for another 24 hours when a new query uses it. This extension can last up to 31 days, after which it is purged. The query result cache is purged after 24 hours if not used.

11. A, C, D. The Snowflake caching system improves query performance. If the query simply counts rows or finds the minimum or maximum value for a column, the metadata cache can provide the results. The metadata cache keeps statistics for each table, micro-partition, and column.

    If the query has already been run and the data hasn't changed, Snowflake can return the results from the query result cache.

    Each virtual warehouse also has its own cache, built by copying micro-partitions from cloud storage to SSD storage over time. Similar queries executed on a virtual warehouse may already have some data in the cache, improving query performance.

12. A, B. When Snowflake executes a query, it caches the result of that query for a period of time. The query result cache returns results for future identical queries without reexecuting the query and an active virtual warehouse. Snowflake can also fulfill COUNT, MIN, and MAX queries using the metadata cache and doesn't require an active warehouse for such queries.

13. A, B. The query result cache and the metadata cache are stored in the cloud services layer. The virtual warehouse cache is stored in a virtual warehouse SSD storage and is purged when a virtual warehouse is shut down. A browser cache and SnowSQL cache are not examples of valid caching mechanisms in Snowflake.

14. C. For tables with a clustering key, Snowflake redistributes data in micro-partitions according to the clustering key. The redistribution of data into new micro-partitions ensures optimal partition pruning.

15. A, B, C, D. All of these are true statements. To improve query performance, materialized views precompute and store query results physically. The performance gains can be significant if the query benefiting from materialization is complex or executed frequently.

    As the underlying table is updated, the materialized view automatically updates. Snowflake manages a background service that performs the update invisibly to the user. Therefore, data in a materialized view is always in sync with data in its base table.

16. A, B. The clustering depth measures the average depth of the overlapping micro-partitions for given columns. A smaller average depth indicates that the table is better clustered for the specified columns.

17. B. Local and remote spillage in the query profile indicates a large query that cannot fit into the memory. Snowflake stores interim data on the virtual warehouse's disk if it's too large to fit in memory during query execution. If the local drive isn't large enough, Snowflake will use cloud storage. Local and remote disk spilling can slow query execution since disk I/O is slower than in-memory operations.

Chapter 9: Security

1. A, C, D. By default, Snowflake encrypts all customer data using AES-256 bit encryption. Snowflake rotates Snowflake-managed keys automatically after 30 days. Tri-Secret Secure is the term used to describe the combination of a Snowflake managed key and a customer-managed key that creates a composite master key that protects your data.

2. C. Tri-Secret Secure requires a minimum of the Business Critical edition and can be enabled by contacting Snowflake support.

3. C, D. MFA is enabled by default for all Snowflake accounts, and any Snowflake user can enroll themselves in MFA via the Snowflake web interface. A user's MFA enrollment can be disabled by an administrator, in which case the user must re-enroll in MFA to take advantage of the MFA capabilities. SnowSQL, Snowflake ODBC, JDBC, and Python Connector all support MFA. MFA is available for all editions of Snowflake.

4. A, B, C. Key pair authentication, which Snowflake supports, is a more secure alternative to the standard username/password authentication mechanism. Snowflake also offers multi-factor authentication to add an extra layer of security to the login process. Snowflake supports federated authentication, enabling users to log in using single sign-on (SSO). Users authenticate via SSO-enabled authentication via an external identity provider (IdP) that adheres to the SAML 2.0 standard.

5. A, C. Snowflake supports key pair authentication as an alternative to conventional username/password login for added protection. This approach uses private and public keys, with the user having a public key and using it to authenticate. A user can have up to two public keys at a time, which can be rotated. All SnowSQL and Snowflake drivers and connectors enable key pair authentication.

6. A, B, D. Snowflake supports federated authentication, allowing single sign-on (SSO). Users authenticate via an external identity provider (IdP) that supports SAML 2.0. Users can access Snowflake without logging in after IdP authentication. For example, Snowflake supports most SAML 2.0–compliant identity providers such as Okta and ADFS natively, as well as OneLogin and Ping Identity PingOne.

7. B. SCIM is an open standard that enables automatic user provisioning and role syncing based on information from an identity provider. With SCIM in place, when a new user is created in the identity provider the SCIM provisions the user in Snowflake. SCIM can also sync groups created in an identity provider to roles in Snowflake.

8. A, B, C, D. Snowflake has the following built-in roles: ACCOUNTADMIN is the full-privilege account administrator role. USERADMIN lets you create USERS and ROLES. SECURITYADMIN inherits USERADMIN rights and can control global object grants. SYSADMIN can build and manage most Snowflake objects. PUBLIC is the most permissive role, since it is assigned to everyone.

9. B, C. Snowflake's access control is built on the RBAC concept, where privileges are granted to roles and roles to users. A role's privileges are inherited by all users in it. Snowflake also supports discretionary access control (DAC), where the role creating an object owns it and can grant access to other roles.

10. A, C, D. Securable objects are objects or entities to which privileges can be granted. A set of privileges can be granted to each securable object. The `GRANT` statement grants privileges while the `REVOKE` statement revokes them. Privileges can only be granted to roles and cannot be granted directly to users. A role is an entity to which privileges on other objects can be granted. The roles themselves can then be granted to other users or other roles.

11. B, D. Snowflake provides masking policies that can be applied to columns to provide column-level security. Column-level security is provided using dynamic data masking or through external tokenization.

12. B. Administrators can set network policies to enable or prevent access to specified IP v4 addresses. In a network policy, there are three parts: name, authorized IP addresses, and blocked IP addresses. If both the authorized and blocked lists are populated, Snowflake applies the blocked list first.

13. C. Through private connectivity, you can ensure that access to your Snowflake instance is over a private connection and can optionally block all Internet access. Private connectivity to Snowflake requires a minimum of the Business Critical edition.

14. A. Snowflake encrypts all data in transit using TLS 1.2. Encryption applies to all Snowflake connections, including the Snowflake web UI, JDBC, ODBC, and the Python Connector.

15. A, C, D, E. Snowflake supports the following security and financial standards: SOC 1 Type II, SOC 2 Type II, PCI DSS, HIPAA , ISO/IEC 27001, FedRAMP Moderate, GxP, ITAR, and IRAP – Protected.

Chapter 10: Account and Resource Management

1. A, B, C. You may notify, suspend and notify, or suspend immediately and notify virtual warehouses based on the percentage of usage of the credit quota. When a resource monitor suspends a virtual warehouse, existing queries are allowed to complete. On the other hand, suspending immediately stops the virtual warehouse immediately, terminating any queries.

2. B, C, D, E. Resource monitors may be created at the account level, which means they track credit utilization across the entire account, encompassing credit usage across all virtual warehouses. A resource monitor can track multiple virtual warehouses, but a virtual warehouse

monitored by one resource monitor cannot be monitored by another resource monitor. Finally, only account administrators can create new resource monitors, though they can provide additional roles, privileges to view and modify resource monitors.

3. B. Resource monitors can only suspend user-managed virtual warehouses. Snowpipe, Automatic Reclustering, and Materialized View maintenance are serverless capabilities that resource monitors cannot track or control. A resource monitor does not control cloud service charges.

4. B, C. Only account administrators can create new resource monitors; however, once a resource monitor is created, the account administrator can provide MONITOR and MODIFY privileges to other roles to see and modify the resource monitor.

5. B, C. Account administrators can receive notifications via email or the web interface. However, the notifications are not enabled by default. Therefore, each account administrator must enable and configure notification settings through preferences in the web interface to receive notifications.

6. A. INFORMATION_SCHEMA views are real time but do not have 365 days of retention. The ACCOUNT_USAGE schema, on the other hand, has 365 days of history but is not real-time account usage. WAREHOUSE_METERING_HISTORY is the correct view for this scenario.

7. C, D. The data in ACCOUNT_USAGE views is not real time, and latency varies from 45 minutes to 3 hours. The data in these views is kept for 365 days; thus, the last 365 days are always available.

8. B, C, D. INFORMATION_SCHEMA is a special schema created automatically for every database created in Snowflake. This schema acts as a data dictionary, providing metadata for database objects and views for account-level items like roles, databases, and warehouses. Account-level storage, compute consumption, login history, and query history are available table functions in INFORMATION_SCHEMA. The data in this schema is real time, and the historical data retention period in this schema ranges from 7 days to 6 months, depending on the view.

9. A. INFORMATION_SCHEMA is a special schema created automatically for every database created in Snowflake. Account-level storage, compute consumption, login history, and query history are available table functions in this schema.

10. C. Since the requirement is to see data from the last 10 minutes, the ACCOUNT_USAGE schema cannot be used due to the latency associated with the ACCOUNT_USAGE schema. Therefore, the table function LOGIN_HISTORY in INFORMATION_SCHEMA provides the required real-time information.

11. B. Every week, Snowflake releases new software. The updates are transparent and cause no downtime or interruptions. So that the consumer is constantly running the newest software release, automated releases deliver bug fixes, improvements, and new features.

12. D. Snowflake does not roll out a full release to all accounts at once; instead, accounts are updated gradually. Accounts with Enterprise edition (or above) with early access get the new software first. Standard editions may get the updates on day 1 or 2 of a software release. Enterprise editions and above that have not opted for early access get the update on day 2.

Index

A

B

C

D

E

F

G

H

I

J

K

L

M

N

O

P

Q

R

T

U

V

W

X

Z

Comprehensive Online Learning Environment

Register on Sybex.com to gain access to the comprehensive online interactive learning environment and test bank to help you study for your Snowflake SnowPro Core certification.

The online test bank includes:

- **Assessment Test** to help you focus your study to specific objectives
- **Chapter Tests** to reinforce what you learned
- **Practice Exams** to test your knowledge of the material
- **Digital Flashcards** to reinforce your learning and provide last-minute test prep before the exam
- **Searchable Glossary** gives you instant access to the key terms you ll need to know for the exam

Go to www.wiley.com/go/sybextestprep to register and gain access to this comprehensive study tool package.